You can take the lad out
but……

*<u>You grow into what you believe about
yourself</u>*

<u>Belief is everything</u>

Copyright.

Graham Stanier has asserted his right to be identified as the author of this work under the Copyright,Designs and Patents Act 1988.

Acknowledgments:

To my family, friends, and to
Terry Cavender for all his and their
support and assistance with this book

Contents

Preface

Chapter 1   -   She's gone!

Chapter 2   -   The Debtors List.

Chapter 3   -   Terminated by Tripe.

Chapter 4   -   Things are going to change around here lads.

Chapter 5   -   Just pull over!

Chapter 6   -   Childhood holidays - Blackpool.

Chapter 7   -   Bogies.

Chapter 8   -   A letter to my 15 years-old self.

Chapter 9   -   Leaving school.

Chapter 10   -   The Army.

Chapter 11   -   The opportunity.

Chapter 12   -   Beyond the blue horizon.

Chapter 13   -   Travelling.

Chapter 14   -   Was his sister there as well?

Chapter 15   -   That was our Ern.

Chapter 16   -   The time after the funeral.

Chapter 17   -   The floodgates open

Chapter 18   -   Saudi Arabia — Sun, Sand and
                   Siddique

Chapter 19   -   Things begin to fall into place and
                   'The Reset'

Chapter 20 -   The woman with the flame-red
                   hair - and The man in Army
                   uniform

Chapter 21   -   Introduction to 'The Jeremy Kyle
                   Show'.

Chapter 22   -   Room mates.

Chapter 23   -   The show.

Chapter 24 -   The 'other' show.

Chapter 25 -   Some gather more than they
                   need/Others get less than they
                   deserve.

Chapter 26 -   Aftercare Service.

Chapter 27   -   Secrets revealed after death.

Chapter 28   -   Missing five years.

Chapter 29   -   Social Reports on Dorothy

You can take the lad out of Rochdale but ......

'Preface'

Behind every person there's a story, a reason why they are the way they are. Before you delve into the pages of this book, I want to take a moment to explain that the idea behind it is not just for me to be able to fire off a few dates and statistics, then polish it all up to make it look very tidy and bordering on the academic — concluding the whole thing with a "Thank you and goodnight," that would be far too clinical and impersonal for me. Like every other story, it has a beginning, a middle and an end, but if you'd bear with me, I'd like to take a few moments to give you a broader overview of what my life's been all about so far, a kind of taster before the arrival of the main course.

I'm the enormously proud son of a man you have more than likely never heard of — and that's my Dad, Ernest 'Ernie' Stanier. He was, like many others, a hard-working Rochdale man who earned an honest crust from being, among other things, an Asbestos factory worker and who also moonlighted in the evenings, working as a Barman to provide enough money to keep our little tight-knit family unit together. My Dad was a thoroughly decent man who was as honest and hardworking as the day was long.
Infinitely kind and endlessly patient, he was the glue that bound our family together.

Sadly, like many parents of that era, he is now no longer with us so it's a privilege for me to be able to place his story on record. He is someone of whom, I'm not ashamed to say, I'm immensely proud and I still think about him with love and affection every single day. Dad wanted his sons to make him proud too and always did his utmost to impress upon us his standards of common decency, honesty, and kindness, qualities that I hope are still with me to this day.

My Mother, Dorothy, was a totally different kettle of fish, having an extraordinarily complex and totally opposite personality to Dad. She left the family circle very early on in our lives, deserting us and causing great resentment, but more importantly, breaking our hearts by unexpectedly and inexplicably vanishing into the ether one day, and in doing so changing our lives forever. I was just three years old when that happened, my brother Warran five, and we heard nothing further about her, or from her, until she reappeared decades later, in rather dramatic circumstances.

Despite my Mother's abandonment, our lives in the small, one-up-one-down, back-to-back terraced house at 227 Rooley Moor Road, Rochdale continued. It wasn't a palace by any stretch of the imagination. But it was our home and it was where we felt loved, safe, and secure, not least because of Dad, 'Our Ernie.'

We Stanier's were no different to the other working-class residents of Rooley Moor Road. Like us, they also 'enjoyed' such luxuries as tin baths, damp living conditions, open fires, and lines of external, gloomy communal lavatories wherein lurked unimaginable and unspeakable horrors waiting to assail the vivid imaginations of young, impressionable children with no other alternative other than to use the facilities. But then things were never easy for anyone back in the day.

From early on in our lives, my brother and I didn't have a Mother to provide us with those all-important cuddles, encouragement, advice, guidance, and cooked meals. Simple but essential things that would have helped ease us through our key early developmental years. We were a one-parent family - much less socially acceptable then than nowadays — and because Dad went out to work every day to earn an honest crust, Warran and I were left pretty much to our own devices throughout each day. It was dangerous ground, with the ever-present threat of us being reported and taken into care by the Social Services. Luckily, we were a good little team and tried our best not to let Dad down by getting caught up in too much mischief, even though, being just two normal lads, 'things' inevitably happened!

We quite easily managed to get into various bits of bother. Nothing particularly criminal, just trivial things like setting the house on fire! As I grew older, it became obvious that I needed something to challenge me. That, coupled with a determination to succeed, made me realise that if I tried hard enough, whatever I did achieve would make my father and other family members proud, which was particularly important to me. It did seem, though, that everything was a challenge in those days — particularly for those who, like me, came from a working-class background and who didn't have any formal educational qualifications to help them open all of the right doors.

I'm still convinced that some of the burning anger lurking in a corner of my heart as a child was as a result of some of the injustices I suffered back then. You never forget those things. Fortunately, my anger was channeled in the right direction, which I passionately believe helped to shape the person I am today. Yes, I am different from anyone else and thankfully we're all that little bit different from each other. What we all have in common, hopefully, is that we share many of the same aims and objectives in life: healthy ambition, a need for job satisfaction and financial security, good physical and mental health and last but not least, happiness and the ability to love and accept ourselves. In my own life it was clear to me that I needed to go that extra mile and determinedly demonstrate that I had the ability to succeed, should the opportunity present itself.

I wanted to tell my story, not because it is anything particularly special, but because I feel that by doing so - with no stone left unturned — others who might be starting out their lives in similar circumstances to mine will be able to see that it's possible to overcome hurdles and difficulties and turn things around - and in doing so, to achieve incredible things. To do that, though, you also need the opportunities and a great support network. I was fortunate in that I had my Dad and my family to help and advise me along the way.

It's been a long, hard and, at times, frustrating journey, with occasional periods of good fortune, the good times offsetting the bad. A key part of my life has been, and continues to be, my husband, Steve.
Steve possesses those rare human qualities of honesty, truth, integrity, compassion and understanding. Without his and my Father's love, support and calming influences over the years, my life might easily have taken off in a completely different direction. Steve is my soulmate and I owe both him and my Father everything.

Having outlined the background, I hope my story will be an interesting, entertaining, illuminating, and enjoyable read. It was definitely cathartic for me. Over the years, there has been a lot of love and laughter amongst the tears in what has been the rich and colourful tapestry of my life - so far. While on many occasions I've felt like a frightened little boy whistling in the dark, fortunately the love, laughter, and friendship in my life has helped to kick those unwanted tears and fears into the long grass.

******

CHAPTER ONE

'She's gone!'

As the saying goes, "I was born at an early age," on the 18th of November 1952 in Rochdale, a gritty Lancashire mill town whose main claim to fame at that time was that it was the birthplace of the Co-operative Society (Co-op). Our 'divvi' (dividend) number was 10972 - it's a number I'll never forget.

Our house, which I shared with my parents and older brother, Warran, couldn't be described any other way than as being dingy, with very little in the way of privacy, comfort, or warmth. It had only two rooms; one upstairs, used as a bedroom for all of us, and a living area downstairs, with a makeshift kitchen under the stairs. There was no bathroom, no central heating, and no hot water. No, I tell a lie, there was running water — it ran down the walls! Cooking had to be done either on the open fire or on a small stove situated in the 'kitchen.' There was also an old 'Belfast' style sink under the stairs to do laundry or to wash up in. We had curtains hung at the windows and at the back of the door, not particularly for decoration but to act as very necessary draft excluders.

Hot water was obtained simply by boiling multiple pans of water on the open fire or small cooker - or both. On Sundays, (bath night), my parents went through the lengthy and laborious process of filling a tin bath with hot water so that we could have the luxury of bathing in front of the fire. If it weren't a Sunday, then it would be a strip-wash in front of the fire, using a bowl full of hot water.

The house itself was very sparsely furnished. In the bedroom, there were just two double-beds, and a single cupboard for storing our clothes. If we needed to go to the lavatory, they were situated in rows at the rear of the houses, communal style, each family being allocated a specific lavatory for their use. Inside, there was always a plentiful supply of newspaper, (in lieu of toilet paper), usually damp and torn into strips with which to do the necessary.

Life was a struggle and it was grindingly spartan, with one example of 'needs must' being that we only had one light bulb! We had a choice though - the light bulb could either be used upstairs or downstairs, with Dad being responsible for transporting the precious object to wherever it was required. So, not exactly the Ritz Hotel, but 227 was our home. Luxury in those days was making sure that everyone was adequately fed and watered - and had a roof over their heads.

Naturally, a source of regular income was a necessity and the 'Turner Brothers Asbestos Factory' was one of the main employers for local people. Its siren call to summon employees to work sounded something akin to a ship's foghorn and could be heard for miles around.

Each morning, at 7.30 am, the horn would sound and those unfortunates who hadn't clocked on by the time the horn ceased blaring would be docked 15 minutes' pay, (and before you ask - 'clocking on' for someone else was a sackable offence). Then at lunchtime and home-time, the same horn would once again bellow out its soulless message.

Our house was adjacent to the factory entrance. As a child, I well remember seeing workers leaving the factory covered with 'the frost', (aka Asbestos dust). Scarily, we children were also allowed to enter the factory premises at any time to see our parents, and effectively experience what the future held for us. The noise was deafening as you walked around the weaving and spinning sheds, watching everyone 'mee-mawing' (lip-reading and gesticulating) with each other because (1) The noise rendered it impossible to hear anything and, (2) The deadly dust was everywhere.

Each day would usually start uneventfully, with our Mother dropping off Warran and I at Meanwood School in Rochdale, just a short walk from our house. On one unforgettable day, however, our routine would be totally disrupted and, unbeknown to us, a massive drama was about to unfold.

That day, suddenly and quite unexpectedly, my Mother physically removed herself from our lives. She just upped and went, leaving me and my elder brother in innocent oblivion, abandoned at school. Before we knew it, at the end of that school day, our Mother having not turned up to collect us and the school had been given no reason for her failure to do so, we were being transported in fits of tears by Police car to the nearest Police Station, located directly underneath Rochdale Town Hall.

Tucked away in a corner of a room and surrounded by strangers - Social Services and Police, who were busy chatting amongst themselves - my brother and I just sat there confused and afraid, if not terrified. We cried inconsolably as a woman in a green tweed suit, who turned out to be a social worker, did her utmost to try to calm us down. She did her best to reassure us but all we wanted was for our Mum and Dad to come fetch us, and no one was giving us any reassuring answers regarding either of them - or the reason for their absence.

We sat there for what seemed like hours and, despite our constant appeals, there was no news of either parent. It was our worst nightmare. We felt alone, vulnerable, lost and abandoned and had no idea of what was going on in this scary world of adult strangers, sat alone in a Police Station. Everyone kept asking us questions about Mum and Dad, and with their every question the fear factor kept rising. It felt as if our safe little world was crashing down around our ears.

My chest ached from sobbing, but by that time no one could get near to comfort me, other than Warran, who never left my side. Even then at his tender age, he was always my protector, telling everyone that approached me to, "get away from him!" He was the one whose hand I normally held when my parents were not around and he was the one I had to listen to in their absence, but even he was afraid and crying on this occasion. The hours just ticked by and, despite many attempts, consoling us was an impossible task. Those moments are still indelibly etched into my memory to this day.

As long as I live, I'll never ever forget the moment I heard my Father's voice from beyond the large, closed oak door and the relief that the sound of his familiar voice brought to my entire being.

At first, it was just a muffled sound, but I knew instinctively that it was him. Suddenly I could clearly make out his voice and at that precise moment my brother and I made a dash for the door at breakneck speed; the woman in the green tweed suit had no chance of stopping us. It felt like we were breaking free from prison and all of a sudden there he was, our Dad, covered from head to toe in Asbestos frost! We clung to him like limpets and all we could both do was cry and cry and cry with relief. I can remember him holding us so tight, and from that point onwards I knew that we were safe again. That feeling of safety wasn't some sort of deep thought process, it was something that was emotionally embedded in my psyche and my Dad triggered that in me.

One by one, more familiar voices could be heard as various members of the Stanier family started to turn up at the police station. It suddenly seemed that my Aunts, Uncles, and Cousins were everywhere and all the adults were engaged in discussions with the Policemen and Social Services. The children, as always, were dismissed by Granddad Stanier (boots covered in mud from his job as a grave digger) to a distance where adult conversations could not be overheard - "This is not for your ears - go and play!"

After we regrouped there was just silence, apart from my brother asking plaintively, "where's Mum?" To which the collective response came, "She's gone!" In no time we were out of the Police Station and heading home on the bus without her. We knew that we were returning to our basic home, but it was our basic home. Even without Mum, our Dad still lived there and we knew, instinctively, that we'd be safe and secure with him still there to look after us.

As for my Mother, she simply disappeared from our lives on that ill-fated day; it was as if she'd been spirited away. It was made quite clear to us children that she was never to be mentioned again. It was as if she'd never existed but, in reality, she had and would continue to do so in my memory. The Mafia-style family Omertà (code of silence) about her was extraordinary. However, it was something that I would come to accept, without question, through the passage of time. Even though I was an inquisitive child, I knew that I should never broach the subject of Mum's disappearance with my Father, nor anyone else on his side of the family. That part of my past had effectively been shut down forever. It became a definite 'no-go' area. Another regrettable consequence was the immediate removal of contact with my maternal Grandparents, Aunts, Uncles and Cousins. They simply vanished into the ether, much as my Mother had on that fateful day when I was just three years old.

The day my Mother made the life-changing choice to pack her bags and abandon us at the school gates was, in the eyes of my family, an unforgivable act of extreme selfishness. Her actions had, in essence, ended her relationship with her sons. The family group and ethos could and would heal us, but she would never be afforded the opportunity to come back into our lives and hurt us ever again. Having said that, as far as I'm aware, she never made any real attempt to do so. Memories of her would bubble to the surface from time to time, but her continued absence coupled with the family's refusal to speak of, let alone acknowledge, her existence, meant she would eventually fade from my mind. I would no longer remember the colour of her hair, her voice or even her facial features.

From that point onwards, there were plenty of extended Stanier family meetings to discuss our welfare and upbringing. These were usually held on Sundays when we visited Grandma and Granddad Stanier, or our Uncles and Aunts – George and Connie, Frank and Connie, George and Gladys, John, and Mickey. All adult meetings were held in private and never within earshot of Warran, myself or our cousins. We learned absolutely nothing about what was being discussed or decided. If by chance you happened to walk in while a meeting was taking place, you'd be told,

"Oy - go and play out! This is not for your ears!" - usually bellowed by Grandad Albert Stanier.

He was without doubt the 'Don' of our family, who always sat at the head of the table for family meetings and meals. He set down all the family rules which had to be followed without question. His motto, "What's said in a Stanier house, stays in the Stanier house!" had to be obeyed to the letter. Unsurprisingly, I was later to learn that it was 'Don Albert' who had ruled my Mother out of our lives forever.

Family Sunday lunches were happy occasions and all the cousins would play outside until called in for the meal. If it was raining, we just played upstairs in the bedrooms. On most occasions, the dining tables wasn't big enough for everyone to be seated around, in which case the living room door would be taken off its hinges and laid on top of the existing small table in order to accommodate everybody. Nobody ever wanted the door handle place and as there were never enough chairs, it was a race to be 'first-come, first-served.'

All the children were expected to stand at the table to eat their dinner. The adults either shared a chair or had their own. I loved being with my brother and cousins and I loved our big extended family - and yes, I would always cry when it was time to leave them. I shed floods of tears at the drop of a hat in those days - and maybe that hasn't changed much either!

Dad and my family tried valiantly to fill the void created by my Mother's departure and although over the years I conditioned myself to accept her absence from my life, it would always be a difficult experience, particularly when listening to friends talking about theirs. The worst thing for me was not having sufficient background knowledge so

17

that I could at least try and explain why my Mother was not in my life. My family felt different to all the other families and there were times when I felt embarrassed and ashamed by not having a Mother figure around.

Equally, there were also times when I worried about her welfare or when I would just ponder 'Why?' and W'here is she?' The one thing I knew for sure though was that she was alive because if she hadn't have been, someone would have willingly told me.

For many years after it would be just 'Dad and his lads.' It was difficult both for him and for us because a broken marriage was a cause for stigma back in the 1950's. A Dad raising two lads by himself was uncommon and, in practical terms, an almost impossible task. But Dad did his absolute best to create a world of stability and happiness for us within a world of harsh realities.

From the day my Mother left us — and despite the family's help and support — life was always going to be tough for Dad. Along with everything else, he was having to care for two growing children as a single parent in poor quality housing. On top of that, he would have to work a six-day week and put in as many hours as he could to keep money coming in just to make ends meet. Money was short for everyone in the family. We had 'not a pot to piss in, nor a window to chuck it out of!'

As well as working a 48-hour week at the Asbestos factory, Dad also had a part-time Barman job in the evenings at the local pub, 'The Woolpack.' For many years, Sunday would be his one and only day off. On top of everything else, there was the constant threat of Social Services catching up with us. Dad's biggest fear, and ours, was that we could be taken away from him and placed into foster care should the authorities think that he wasn't coping. I suspect that many of the Stanier family meetings were set up to ensure that this would never be the case. We could be without a Mother but not money, because money kept the 'wolves away from the door' and protected everything. But his sons were also his everything, as he was ours.

Dad was crystal clear with us from the start, emphasising the risks involved with talking to anyone outside the Stanier family and neighbourhood circle. There existed real 'Stranger Danger.' That person could be a Social Worker or someone who might report us to Social Services should we say the wrong things. The thought of our Dad vanishing, just like our Mother, was unbearable and that fear ran very deep in our minds. In our own way, though, we always felt that we were fine because we had Dad and that's all we needed. He was our rock and we were never short of his love and he always ensured our safety and welfare as best he could.

He was ultimately responsible for our care and he was the best carer — at no time did we ever doubt his love for us. For years we had the same daily routine, both during the week and at weekends. This was especially important for us if we were to survive and avoid the scrutiny of social services. During the week, Dad would be up at 5.30 am and by 6.30 am would have us washed, dressed, and hurriedly walking up the steep hill to our child minder, Mrs. Dawson, who lived about a mile away.

Mrs. Dawson, or Mrs. D as she was affectionately known, was a really bubbly woman who simply oozed love — an archetypal 'Northern Mum.' She was a godsend and we simply adored her. She took immense pride in caring for

19

us, giving us the 'once over' each morning to make sure we were ready for school before we left her house. She would darn our socks, replace missing buttons, put patches on rips and tears and shove newspaper in our shoes when they had holes. She knitted us balaclavas, bobble hats, gloves and scarves and was a genuine, truly kind, and gentle soul.

But despite her love and kindness towards me over several years, I would still struggle daily each time my Father left me with her. Unfortunately, I was that dreaded child who would cry and howl as he left for work. It must have been deeply distressing and exhausting for everyone concerned and extremely difficult for my Father to extricate himself from the situation and go off to work, conscious that he would be docked 15 minutes pay if he arrived late.

He discovered the best way to deal with the dramas was to give me something that belonged to him, (usually a hanky), and ask me to keep it safe until he got home that evening. If he didn't have a hanky it was not unknown for him to cut a button off his coat — which Mrs. D would invariably have to sew back on again later that evening.

I'd keep his hanky in my pocket all day at school, checking it periodically to feel safe in the knowledge that he would come back to collect it, along with us, later that evening. Over time, my separation anxiety improved, with only the occasional relapse.

My habit would be to sit in the window at Mrs. D's, watching him walk off down the road to work (hanky in hand) and then sit in the exact same spot, waiting for him to come back in the evening. As soon as I saw him it was pure excitement. Mrs. D always let us run out of the house to meet and greet him. My big brother and I would then wrap ourselves around him like cling-film before he gave us both a kiss. He always said the same thing: "Hello, my big lad! Hello, my little lad! Have you both been good boys for your Dad?"

Finally, we'd make our way home together and by 7 pm, Dad would have us washed and changed into our pyjamas, ready to carry us to 'The Woolpack' about five or six doors away for his evening shift as a Barman. Dad would settle us down in the landlord's private lounge before working until about 10.30 pm or 11 pm, depending on the day of the week.

My time at 'The Woolpack' was both amazing and memorable. I loved being cocooned in the lounge, watching all the activities, and hearing all the banter before drifting off to sleep. It was also a very lucrative time for the three of us. On Friday and Saturday evenings, (never on school days), when Dad was putting the towels on the beer taps, signifying to all and sundry that the bar was closed, he would wake us early and ask us to go and say goodnight to the men in the Tap Room. Invariably they would give us 'pocket money.' We'd then repeat the performance in the Snug for the women. It was rich pickings.

Once home, we'd pool all our takings, including Dad's tips, and drop the coins into a massive empty whisky bottle on the hearth, which Dad had christened the 'Blackpool Bottle.' That money was to be used to pay for our memorable day trips to the seaside during 'Wakes Week,' where we met up with all the Stanier cousins. At 5.30 am the following morning, 'Groundhog Day' would start all over again.

My Dad worked 18-hour days, six days a week, just to make enough money to feed, clothe and keep a roof over our heads. In his own words - and we heard it often - "My lads are my lads and no one's ever taking them from me, and I mean, no one!" Or, "Over my dead body will someone take my lads away from me!"

******

CHAPTER TWO

'The Debtors List'

"We didn't have everything but we had everything we needed'

The daily routine continued, unabated, for many years and following the move to our council house at 544 Rooley Moor Road, was still set in tablets of stone.

Dad left 'The Woolpack' but was now a Barman at 'The Black Dog' which, conveniently, was opposite our new house. We no longer had to accompany him to the pub in the evenings, as neighbours and family were now able to watch over us while he worked. Our lives were changing for the better, materially speaking at least. We had moved on from the private rented 'basic dwelling' of my birth and into a council house on the Spotland (Brotherod) Estate, Rochdale. Our new three-bedroomed accommodation was 'just as good as a football-pools win' for us. Ah, the joys of social housing.

Our new home was luxurious by comparison and it was certainly warmer, but without central heating. We had a coal fire in the living room to keep us warm which had a back boiler tank, giving us running hot water for the very first time. No more boiling pans and zinc baths for us!

The rest of the house, however, could be freezing cold in winter and we seldom left the living room, if we could possibly help it. In the kitchen, heat was generated by the gas oven and on cold mornings the oven door would be left open with the dial turned up full to warm the room and our clothes while we dressed. On the coldest days I would often arrive in the kitchen wearing pyjamas, a hat or balaclava and wrapped up snuggly in the candlewick bedspread from the bed. Dad would protest: "Nay, bloody hell fire lad, it's not that cold in here." But it was... it really, really was!

If we needed additional heat, we could also use the paraffin heater, but only if we had any 'Esso Blue,' as the domestic fuel was commonly known. Many is the time we were out of that. The paraffin heater was intended for use mainly as the fallback for emergencies.

By far the biggest upside to our new life was having an actual bathroom and indoor toilet, all to ourselves. We now had toilet paper instead of the damp newspaper squares. I wasn't too excited about the new 'San Izal' toilet paper though, because wiping your backside with this disinfected, slightly abrasive, and almost see-through paper was a life skill you needed to acquire very quickly. Full concentration was required throughout the whole cleansing process as any lapses could result in your hand leaving your backside quicker than the land speed record, causing multiple abrasions during its journey. It was not fit for purpose for many - but if you needed tracing paper for school it was perfect. I'm not entirely convinced it was that much of step up from the damp newspaper strips, but there you go — that's progress for you!

In summer, keeping warm wasn't so much of a problem, but without the coal fire being lit there was no longer an abundant supply of hot water. While we had an electric immersion heater that could provide hot running water at the mere flick of a switch, the house rule was that it was only to be used in the direst of emergencies as it 'ate up the electricity.' I swear that my Dad broke into a cold

24

sweat every time that immersion heater got mentioned. He would pace the floor manically for a full 20-minutes once it had been switched on, and on the stroke of the twentieth minute he would loudly proclaim: "Right, switch it off! I'm not made of bloody money!" When it was confirmed that it was indeed off, calm would once again be restored, as he mopped his furrowed brow.

Should Dad ever get distracted during his 20-minute pacing routine and the heater run a couple of minutes over its allotted time, pandemonium would break out. He seemed to believe that if it didn't get turned off immediately it would somehow have built up sufficient pressure and steam to achieve locomotion all by itself, like some modern day version of Stephenson's Rocket. "Switch...it...off before it blasts through the bastard roof!" he'd yell. That immersion heater stressed my Dad out big time. However, despite the cold and lack of heating in winter, we still felt blessed and incredibly fortunate to have moved into our council house.

Dad now had his own bedroom, while Warran and I shared one and a single bed for many years. Every morning we would step out of our bed onto the bare linoleum flooring - none of your fancy bedroom carpets or mats for the likes of us. If you've ever experienced having to get out of a cozy, warm bed and stepping on to a cold linoleum floor on a winter's morning in a room where condensation has frozen to the inside of the single glazed windowpane, the memory of it stays with you for the rest of your life. You certainly didn't linger long, let me assure you of that!

We didn't have the luxury of a fridge or a freezer. Instead, there was a concrete slab in the pantry that was forever cold and which had to do the job. Cheese, milk, and other dairy products were stored on it. But to be honest, those sorts of things didn't stay on the pantry shelf long, before being consumed.

Above the kitchen table, fixed to the ceiling, was a 'Laundry Maiden,' a washing line that could be loaded with wet washing and then hoisted up to dry. Many a meal was eaten with Dad's seemingly huge Y-fronts dangling ominously just a few feet above our heads.

Once settled on the council estate we built new friendships and began to experience the joys of outdoor life, with the freedom to roam until it got dark. The estate was well-maintained, with most residents taking pride in their homes and gardens. You learned pretty quickly never to step on a neighbour's freshly 'donkey-stoned' step. If you did, all hell could break loose.

Most women 'donkey-stoned' their front doorsteps with a scouring stone every couple of weeks, not only because it provided decoration to an otherwise dull grey step, but it was also an outward sign of them being house-proud. So if it got marked by anyone calling at their home and before its due date, then the very least you could expect was a mouthful.

Everyone on our estate seemed happy with their lot and many had stable jobs in the factories. There were large green areas and public gardens all around which were well tended, as were the council's recreational facilities.

Despite these being nearby, we mostly played football, cricket, and hopscotch in the street, which was relatively safe with fewer privately owned cars around. There was hardly any traffic on the street, other than an occasional police car, bus, dustbin truck, coal lorry and, of course, the rag-and-bone man with his horse and cart and from whom we could get donkey stone. In the evening it would be the black pea man, hardware van, pop van and the ever-welcome chimes announcing the arrival of the ice cream van. There were acres of nearby fields and expansive areas of wood and moorland we could roam all around to explore and enjoy nature.

Our estate seemed to operate as a collective and it genuinely felt like we were all in it together and making the most of every opportunity that came our way. We had a safe, secure, and protective upbringing living on the estate. There was immense value attached to the family ethos and everyone there definitely had a hand in raising us.

Talking of hands, all adults, by mutual consent, seemed to have permission to give any errant child a clout if they were caught doing something wrong - and justice would be administered swiftly. If you escaped the punishment at that time you were told in no uncertain terms, "Just wait 'till I see your Dad!"

Everyone took a clout from a neighbour at some time or other and there was no point 'skriking' because crying only meant you would be labelled a 'mard-arse' and nobody wanted to be one of those! If someone did cry, they'd only be told to "Carry on crying, 'cos you'll piss less!" Seldom was anyone brave enough to tell an adult to "Shut your gob!" That particular offence carried a two-clout penalty, with the second much harder than the first. Everyone knew each other and all about their business. It felt like we were all one big family. All of the mothers helped each other out and kept a watchful eye on each other's kids if needed, which was invaluable, especially as many of the women were housewives working shifts or full-time in the factories.

We had a garden and pets for the first time. Oh, the smell of fresh flowers and newly mown grass and the opportunity to have a menagerie of animals, despite Dad's protests every time we brought one home!

"Great... another bloody mouth to feed," he'd say. He had told me that I couldn't have a dog, but he never mentioned any other animals. So, over a short period of time my brother and I accumulated a cat called Ginger, a budgie called Micky, a tortoise called Sammy and a rabbit called Dinky. We loved them all, but Sammy was my favourite. I would feed him fresh tomatoes, dandelion leaves, and lettuce every day throughout summer. In winter, feeding wasn't a problem because he would hibernate in a cardboard box on top of my chest of drawers. As Spring advanced, I would listen intently and wait for the scratching noise on the sides of the box, letting me know that he was awake and that we could hang out together again.

Still relatively 'brassic' (boracic lint - skint) but not poverty-stricken, we all shared what we had. Clothing, food and - should someone run short of them - sugar, tea, milk, bread, or cigarettes, those too. The items could be borrowed or loaned, on the understanding that they had to be returned on Thursdays when everyone got paid. It finally felt like we were just like other ordinary families and, at last, Dad seemed to have some spare money for treats such as swimming and Saturday morning cinema. School trips to Chester Zoo and other exotic locations, on the other hand, were free and the excitement we all felt on such days was palpable. Not just about the location and the coach journey either but more the contents of our packed lunches.

By and large they were happy days on the estate, and I will always have fond memories of my time living there. The feeling of belonging will remain with me forever and I'm still in contact with friends from that estate to this day. We were just one big tribe working together through the hard times, and laughing together through the good times, even though it sometimes felt like it was us against the rest of the world. My Dad, plus the community in which I lived and grew up in, taught me very important lessons in life, the most important being that people's lives mattered and that by working together and supporting each other we could improve our lives. There was no place for selfishness on our estate and any child that strayed down that path would be lambasted and told to "stop being selfish... NOW!"

Children knew the estate like the backs of their hands and just wandered around without a care in the world, often being reminded by parents to enjoy our childhood while we could because we were in for a 'bloody rude awakening' once we started work. That said, playing near the bungalows at the centre of the estate was strictly forbidden. This was sacred ground where the retired folk lived and the rule was expected to be observed at all times - and it was. Some of the boundaries set by our parents were set in tablets of stone. We had to be polite and respectful when in that area. Run errands, carry shopping, give up our seats on buses to allow seniors to sit down - and most importantly, no cheek and no back chat. Sometimes we tried to quietly sneak past the bungalows like an elite SAS squad trying to avoid the call of "Hello, love, could you run an errand for me love?" Because if they called, they had to be obeyed and, unlike a lot of elderly people today, they never seemed lonely.

The perfectly manicured grass area outside the bungalows would have been the ideal spot for a game of football, or a convenient place for meeting up, but it was just not going to happen. Jumpers for goal posts had to be laid down on the road or a playing field for a game of football. Never, ever, anywhere near the bungalows. We played football most evenings as we waited for parents to arrive home from work and always with the same rules: the owner of the ball got to be captain and had first pick of his team. The last one to be picked would end up being the goalkeeper. Which effectively meant they were crap at football but not entirely excluded from the game. Goal scores went well into double digits most evenings and the final whistle blew when we were all called in for our tea. A chorus of voices could be heard summoning children indoors all around the estate at tea-time.

Failure to respond to the first call upped the stakes to: "I can see you, get in here now and don't forget your jumper!" If all else failed, the final call that got everyone running for home would be: "Get in now or you won't be back out playing later!" Especially if that final call was followed by "Mark my words!" or "Believe you me!" Those two phrases terrified us because it meant that they would follow through with their threat to ground us.

In my case, I needed not to forget my hat as well as my jumper. That hat was as precious to me as the hallowed ground outside the bungalows was sacred and it had been since the day my Auntie Connie first bought it. I treasured my ear flap hat, even if my Father wasn't quite so keen. The fact that I wore it most days throughout the year was his biggest bugbear. Apparently, wearing a Winter hat in Spring, Summer and Autumn just made me look like "A bloody simpleton." He issued threats of it being thrown "on't back o' fire," should he get his hands on it. He tried everything, from gentle persuasion to bribery, to get me to stop wearing it, but nothing worked. Finally - after much discussion and to secure its longevity - I agreed to accept his ruling that the hat must never be worn at meal-times and never when visiting family. I say never... well, hardly ever! Occasionally, before family visits, I'd put my foot down and insist on wearing it, until the last minute when I'd accept money to leave it at home.

The hat agreement was always honoured throughout the Winter but by Springtime our agreement would predictably fly straight out the window again. "Are you bloody puddled lad? Sun's cracking flags outside and you're wearing an ear flap hat. Aren't you roasting in that thing?" I was indeed!

In fact, some days in the Summer it felt like my head was radiating more heat than a nuclear power station, purely because Dad had resorted to hat snatching and I was having to wear it with the ear flaps down and tied under my chin. I suspect Dad knew he was fighting a losing battle though and he eventually gave up on the hat snatching. But the list of occasions when it couldn't be worn - and how it had to be worn - was extended: never with ear flaps down or tied under the chin in Summer, never at mealtimes or when visiting family and never to school or to bed.

Over the years the hat wearing restrictions grew ever lengthier until one fateful day when it blew off my head and landed in the Irish Sea. We were on a ferry en route to the Isle of Man – and obviously the loss of my treasured hat was entirely my Father's fault. Had he not imposed a 'no chin strap in Summer' rule, then it would never have ended up at the bottom of Davy Jones' locker. He, and everyone else on board that day, were made all too aware of the fact I had just suffered the most devastating of losses. They all feigned concern and made feeble attempts to console me just to shut me up, whilst Dad kept making repeated promises of a replacement just as soon as we docked.

The hat replacement promise was unfulfilled that holiday as I wasn't especially taken by those on offer on the Isle of Man. Nor was I particularly struck by the selection in

31

Blackpool or Fleetwood on subsequent visits. I definitely knew I would look puddled wandering around the estate in all weathers, wearing a   cowboy hat with *'Kiss Me Quick'* on the front, or a Fez either, for that matter. The gang, most definitely, would not have approved.

We were just one big happy gang without territorial boundaries. We wandered near and far, Winter, Summer, weekdays, or weekends on that estate. If we couldn't be seen we could be heard shouting, screaming, or laughing and that kept our parents happy. That and the fact we weren't indoors annoying them or getting under their feet. If we did disrupt their routine with constant visits home then you could guarantee, without fail, to receive the following threat from them, "I'm warning you now, if you keep coming in and out of this house you'll be stopping in for good!" Once issued, the warning had to be obeyed because parental threats of being grounded would always be followed through.

Only when we were too quiet would they become concerned.Peace on the estate provoked fear in the adults, and they'd be right to be worried, because we'd usually be plotting something and it wasn't for the adults or the Community Copper, Police Constable George, to know what. They'd get to know soon enough via the neighbourhood bush telegraph - our version of social media.

If parents were on the lookout for trouble brewing, they'd stand at their front doors with arms folded, scanning our every move. Either that, or the curtains would twitch as they peered nervously from behind them. This was our version of CCTV. Should a child peel off from the group, we'd be approached with the stock question, "Where's so and so gone?" with the stock reply being, "Don't know, not

32

seen them." They knew that we were lying and vigilance would reign across the whole estate, with stark warnings of dire consequences from parents. "I know you're all up to something and woe betide you if I'm right!"
Nevertheless, their threats never deterred us.

They couldn't watch us all day though and while younger siblings were occasionally ordered to follow us, it was all to no avail. As we left the area, in the distance you could hear our names being called by parents, followed by orders to "Get in this house now!" or "I know you can hear me - and let me tell you there's going to be murder in this house when you get home!" But we were in a world of our own and as the voices became ever more distant, we headed off on another adventure in the Big Dell, Little Dell, Lane Head, Wam Dam or Heaps Dye Works, roamed through the lanes to Norden, or simply walked across miles of fields and woodland with no planned end point in sight. Laughing, playing, and calling each other by our designated nicknames. The innocence of youth - well, nearly!

We all had nicknames chosen by our peers and these gave us a sense of belonging within the group. It might be an abridged version of our actual name or something that rhymed with it. For others, it described or exaggerated their appearance. They were harmless in intention and used as terms of affection but today I'm sure they would be viewed otherwise. If you were even slightly overweight you'd inevitably end up with 'Fats' and you would forever be known by that name even if you lost a ton of weight. Similarly, short people were given 'Titch,''Midge,'
or 'Mouse,'' while the taller ones among us were
designated 'Lanky,'or'Streak.' Anyone with red hair would be 'Ginge,' or 'Red,' while outgoing types were 'Loopy.'

If your last name was White, chances were that you'd be known as 'Chalky' for the rest of your life. I was never Ginge or Red, even though my brother and I were the brightest gingers in the neighbourhood. That nickname was afforded to my brother and I had to settle for 'Mouse.'

The nickname combinations were endless and some parents were fine with it and happily joined in. But not all - some quickly corrected you should you address their child by their designated nickname. "His name is Peter, thank you, and don't use that name ever again!" We always did. We were just copying the adult's banter because it was everywhere. Playful and teasing remarks in good humour between adults was commonplace and we were raised on it. It could also be forthright and always on point when it came down to observational humour. It was certainly character-building and as children we learned the skill of banter from very early on. More importantly, we also learned to build emotional resilience and how to respond - quickly, smartly, and sharply, as if to emphasise the point that, "You can mess with me, but I'm coming right back at you!"

Early dark nights were never in the neighbours' interest because mischievous activities like 'gate swapping,' 'knock-a-door-run,' and 'ghost in the drainpipe,' were common pastimes for bored kids. All garden gate numbers on the estate correlated with house door numbers and, while they were heavy, they were also easy to lift off their double hinges. Under the cloak of darkness, we would set about swapping high-numbered gates with low-numbered ones. Then, the following day/evening, we would just sit watching gleefully as neighbours and parents gathered in search of their missing gates.
Cursing and swearing, they would ask the inevitable

question of all the children sat watching: "Have you got anything to do with this?" And then make no bones about what action would be taken once the perpetrators were discovered. We would sit happily for hours watching them search and then carry their gates backwards and forward until they were all found and restored to their rightful places. Occasionally, we had the brass neck to charge a small fee for searching and retrieving those gates that were proving more difficult to locate. To avert any suspicion, all the kids involved would remove their own gates, but only swap with their next-door neighbours. The search for missing gates could easily go on for days, if not weeks, and was always the topic of the day until they were all found. Then, after a while, the whole game would begin again.

Summers always seemed longer back then and it felt like the sun shone on us most days, with the heat 'cracking the flags.' We spent many happy hours playing out, but conversely the winters were harsh, with some of the biggest snow drifts I've ever seen. It always seemed like cold winter days lasted from December through to March, during which time we would make the biggest, most treacherous ice slides known to man. Unless, of course, eagle-eyed parents spotted them and scattered ashes from the fireplace or sprinkled salt on them to make them melt. They would then disappear in minutes but undaunted, we would slip off to a new location to create another equally treacherous one and keep it a secret as long as we could.

Each Summer we would wait, with bated breath, for the farmer across the little dell to complete his harvest. That was known as 'Swailing Time,' a local term for stubble burning when the straw stumps left behind after crops were harvested were deliberately set on fire. However, we usually got there before the farmer did, setting the field alight and watching it blaze for hours. Then we would walk home with faces like pandas, denying outright that we'd had anything to do with the incident. Our local copper, PC George, was a regular visitor to most houses on the estate during the 'Swailing' season, but he was never quite vigilant enough to prevent our antics.

On the evenings Dad was working at the pub, we would always have to report to him at the designated time and, after checking that we were still in one piece, he would send us home to get washed and ready for bed. We always had to be in bed and asleep by the time he got home, because we had school in the morning. We would linger for a while longer and mither him for a bag of crisps (the ones with a small blue paper bag of salt inside) and, despite his first response always being "No!" we still got them, because we knew how to get round him. Often, we were still awake in bed by the time he got home but pretended to be asleep anyway. He would give us a good-night kiss before going off to his bedroom and we prayed that Laddie the dog wouldn't bark or snarl at him.

While he said we couldn't have a dog — "another bloody mouth to feed!" - Dad never said we couldn't have the neighbour's dog. So although officially we didn't own Laddie, we did have the neighbour's permission to adopt him. To be honest, we were usually awake because our bedroom window overlooked the 'Black Dog' car park and most nights our late evening's entertainment would be viewing the drunken antics of people leaving the pub, singing, or arguing. We would sit and watch their capers for hours while dipping into the crisps Dad had given us. When we got bored of car park watching, we would practice high diving off the top of a chest of drawers in our bedroom, landing safely on the bed after a nifty tuck.

It wasn't a particularly great height though and we could only do it in Dad's absence, as landing on the horsehair mattress supported by rusty springs made a hell of a noise which could be heard throughout the whole house. For months we pestered Dad to buy us a wardrobe (as that would be a much better springboard for diving) and in typical DIY fashion he finally built us one. Making use of the alcove space, several pieces of wood and a piece of dowelling rod, the whole thing was completed in a matter of hours and it was finished off by hanging a curtain for use as a makeshift door. Unfortunately, it only lasted the one night because the first time I stood on top of it, preparing to carry out another spectacular high dive, the whole thing collapsed and I ended up in a dishevelled heap on the floor, surrounded by clothes and broken pieces of wood. That was the end of the wardrobe until Dad found time to build another one and we had the common sense to realise that the materials he was using couldn't bear our weight.

We had secret dens and rope swings situated all around our estate. Prince Charles had Gordonstoun but we had our very own version of an adventure playground. The bigger the rope swing the better and we would swing Tarzan-like across roads and rivers. One of the rope swings, sited on the top of a small hill opposite the tip, would swing right across the road and could actually clear the height of a double-decker bus. The key was to wait for the bus and, as it approached, daringly swing out to 'walk the roof' then swing back to safety and hopefully land in one piece. Once committed, though, you had passed the point of no return and there was no turning back until the deed was done. But dangerous as it may have been, it somehow encouraged a sense of adventure. Although regrettably, in my case, one day my hands slipped and I let go of the rope, fell onto the tip at the other side of the road and sustained a broken arm. Dad had to be contacted at work while I was admitted to Rochdale Infirmary.

He sat with me until I drifted off under the anaesthetic but wasn't overly pleased at having his wages docked for being absent from work. Not only was walking around the streets with an arm in Plaster of Paris like a badge of honour, it was also quite handy for chalking out hopscotch squares! When the news filtered through to PC George, he very quickly had the swing cut down, but he still didn't know about the one in the Big Dell that crossed the fast-flowing Spodden River.

Ah, the Big Dell, or 'Healy Dell' as it is known, which subsequently became a nature reserve. Back then it was a paradise for all of the kids on the estate - not only because it was just minutes away from our homes but because its expanse was huge. It had spectacular waterfalls, beautiful scenery and a viaduct which seemed to be sky-high. We could lose ourselves in the Big Dell for hours on end in the Summer playing on rope swings, building dens, bird watching and generally just being intrepid explorers. We could easily vanish for 12 hours at a time, exploring the dense woodland. Some days we would walk our way out of it by climbing the steep banks, ending up on the Cobbled Road at Lane Head. The Cobbled Road to us was just 'the cobbles' but as an adult I learned about its amazing history. I knew a lot about, for example Tutankhamun and Egypt, from my school lessons but nothing about the cobbled section of Rooley Moor, which was right on my doorstep. How could I not know the history of this section of road that we walked, played, and raced on so often?

It was built by dozens of mill workers during the cotton famine of the 19th Century, which is impressive in itself, but what amazes me more was that the mill workers had been building roads as opposed to spinning or weaving cotton.

During the American Civil War, 1861-1865, US President, Abraham Lincoln stopped all exports of cotton until slavery was abolished in the USA and thus created a famine of cotton for the Lancashire mill workers.

Thousands lost their jobs as a result. But despite losing their livelihoods, the mill workers accepted and supported Lincoln's decision to stop exporting cotton until slavery had been abolished. During that period the mill workers had only two options - to either build roads or starve. So, they built roads.

The connection between Rochdale and the American civil war came as a total surprise to me but the selflessness of the mill workers in supporting and fighting for the abolition of slavery and the human rights of others did not. They were certainly engaged and informed about the abhorrent nature of slavery, but how was my question and it was then that I learned of Frederick Douglass.

In 1846 at the age of 28 Frederick Douglass arrived in England from the USA and spoke on 7 occasions to an audience of thousands - mostly mill workers - in a public hall in Rochdale. He spoke about his life as a slave in the USA and about slavery itself. His speeches educated and informed the people of Rochdale and the surrounding mill towns about the evils of slavery and no doubt he influenced the selfless behaviour of many Lancashire Mill workers during those cotton famine years.

Interestingly he came to Rochdale a fugitive slave but left and returned to the USA a free man - His freedom was secured by raising funds to buy him out of slavery and a third of the money required was contributed by Rochdalian John Bright MP.

Cotton Famine Road, is an amazing living memory and in my opinion the history of how it came about should be taught in every school in Lancashire because this extraordinary chapter in Rochdale's history is something to be proud of.

As children, we walked the road often as it was the beginning of so many journeys for us and the starting point for many other paths we would take. We could swim in the Wam Dam, throw rocks in Ding Quarry, sunbathe on the open moorland, or continue walking towards Stacksteads in the Rossendale Valley and be mesmerised by the spectacular views. All of that in a pair of pumps, because we'd never heard of - nor could we have afforded - sensible walking shoes. Most weekends and during summer holidays we would be uncontactable for hours. But as long as we were home before the street lighting came on, our parents were happy.

During our intrepid exploration of the moorland, we would fuel up on food before we set off or refuel en route and have a picnic. These were not lavish spreads and usually only consisted of what we could get from our parents' food cupboards on a given day — and without them noticing. Stealthy food raids occurred when parents were at work but it was only rarely that Dad wouldn't notice the missing items. I could guarantee the moment he went in the pantry he would immediately notice what was missing and shout: "I'm only going to ask this once and I want a proper answer! Who's had the tin of pineapple rings out of this cupboard?" No answer. "Oh, I suppose it's that Mr Nobody again, is it? No-one ever sees him but he lives at this bloody house!" Still no answer. Similar questions were being asked by parents up and down the estate: "I'm sure I bought a tin of corned beef last week," or, "how is it possible that we're out of butter on a Tuesday?" As crafty kids, we learned that the best response was either to say nothing or simply: "I don't know."

Dad's interrogations about the missing food items rarely resulted in the answers he wanted, nor did the pineapple rings miraculously reappear. Instead, all the kids would congregate on the estate at a designated place (bus stop, pub car park, little dell or football field) and share stories of those who had been caught raiding the pantry and those who hadn't. For those with suspicion hanging over their heads like the Sword of Damocles, we created cover stories for them quickly in case a collective of parents started questioning us on the street. Then we'd start planning our next expedition, now knowing which pantries we could raid the following day. On days when pantries were empty (usually Wednesday) we dined out on rhubarb and goosegobs (gooseberries) dipped in sugar. If we were particularly diligent in our planning we could also make spo. A local delicacy with two basic ingredients - Hard liquorice (sold as a laxative at the chemist) and water. The liquorice we dissolved overnight in a bottle of water, and hey presto, we had pop and also regular bowel movements.

The saga of the missing pineapple rings wouldn't be mentioned again in our house, at least until the next time, but I guarantee that every parent knew exactly where their missing food had gone. It would have been the topic of conversation on the bus going to work the following day but they just couldn't prove anything. Hence the no answer ploy, even when they'd follow up with: "Hello, am I talking to myself?"

Summertime and weekends were also times when we would visit the grounds of Sam Heap's Dye and Bleaching

Works, a short walk from our estate, to search out the new delivery of acid! Huge glass containers - Carboy bottles - of industrial acid were delivered to the factory and, for safety reasons, would then be placed in open-topped metal mesh cages ready for future use within the factory. If word of a delivery got out, usually via one of our parents, we would descend mob-handed on the delivery site that very evening, ominously collecting bricks from the tip on our way there.

On arrival, though from a relatively safe distance, we would compete with each other to see just how many of the Carboys we could break with the bricks, just so that we could watch them explode and spray their toxic contents everywhere. Even now, it makes my hair stand on end just thinking about it. Carboys and Indians! We had to complete our mission in one night because our nefarious activities would guarantee the presence of PC George the following evening. Once the coast was clear though, we could return to Heaps to play on the walls of the large storage tanks that contained veritable lagoons of dye.

On hot summer evenings, the sunbaked dye formed a crust on top of the lagoon and, when we weren't racing along the top of the walls, we would spend time throwing bricks into the tanks to break through the crusty top that had formed. Eventually, after much deliberation amongst parents and the factory hierarchy and following the unfortunate death of a child who drowned in a vat, there was no more playing at Heaps as the tanks and the Acid area were securely fenced in. We could still play in the little dell near Sam Heaps though, making more dens and catching sticklebacks and tadpoles near the lodge.

Our local shops cooperated with the whole community by giving everybody tick — or credit - but the usual rules applied. Tick had to be paid back on Thursdays (pay day) and you couldn't turn up at the shop with an excuse because it had to be paid off in full.

It was never a particularly pleasant experience visiting the shops, especially when there was a distinct possibility that you had been placed on their 'Debtors List' — and less so if you knew that you already featured on it. The list was a system employed by some local shopkeepers to encourage people to pay off their outstanding debts as agreed. If they didn't, then their names and outstanding amounts would be taped to the shop's front window for all to see. It was Lancashire equivalent of going viral in the pre-Facebook days. At that time, the list was often a more popular read than the Rochdale Observer. Fortunately, the Stanier's escaped the humiliation of appearing on the list, although God only knows how or why. I can only assume they took pity on us, even though, like many other families, we exceeded our credit limit on more than one occasion.

Many a time you would walk into the shops only to be faced with a ferocious argument going on at the counter with one of our neighbours, head usually adorned with rollers and colourful headscarf, vehemently disputing their appearance on the dreaded list. They would complain vociferously about alleged irregularities in the shopkeeper's inventory of previous purchases of boiled ham, tins of corned beef, pineapple chunks or packets of cough-inducing Wild Woodbine/Park Drive cigarettes. The arguments would escalate into the use of loud, juicy profanities and threats of shop windows being put in if their names weren't removed from the list of shame. However, the shopkeepers were always dogmatic in such matters and kept accurate records of all purchases, the details of which could rarely be disputed.

43

They knew unfailingly what items had been purchased and precisely how much was owed. Usually, though, after about 20 minutes of haranguing, shame and embarrassment won the day and a compromise of part payment, or a payment plan, would be reached, with a promise from perpetrators to be more vigilant about settling future payments. Humble pie had to be consumed in copious amounts, particularly as the following day something else might be needed on tick. As you would stand there drinking in this amazing theatre of life, you just knew that as a knock-on effect, one shopkeeper's gain was another's loss and that someone else wouldn't be getting paid what they were owed that week. Swings and roundabouts.

We were all in the same boat when it came to living hand-to-mouth. When it happened to be someone collecting debts at our door, they were particularly unfortunate because on those occasions the house went into the well-rehearsed lockdown and blackout ploy. We all hid behind the sofa in our house, Dad hurriedly ordering us into the silent mode until the collector either took the hint or lost the will to live, departing with their tails between their legs to try their luck somewhere else.
The coal man was a frequent victim of unpaid bills. He was inevitably unlucky because it was a matter of routine to dispute with him just how many bags of coal had been dropped off that week. He always went for the compromise of people only paying for one bag, even when they both knew full well that two had been dropped in the coal shed. More often than not, we heard Dad declaring: "I'm not paying for two bags when you only dropped one," which he then validated by saying that his neighbour was in at the time and had seen it. This was usually followed by a quick vault by one of us over the back fence to

inform the neighbour, with a request for them to back up Dad's story when he called on them - that's if they in turn dared answer the door after being tipped off the coal man was on his way. How those tradesmen survived I'll never know.

My refusal to 'nip to the shop' on particular day was, in part, due to us tottering on the precipice of the family name being placed on the Debtors List. I knew for a fact that we had exceeded our allowance.
Dad, however, disagreed and interpreted my refusal as being down to sheer bone idleness, but I genuinely knew that we were very close to being added, hence my reluctance to go. Dad and his exotic cuisine had pushed us to the point of debtors' shame because of his frequent purchases of cheap pineapple rings and peach slices.

Pineapple rings, coated in batter and deep-fried in chip pan fat, were always considered to be a delicacy in our house, particularly for Sunday morning breakfasts.
According to Dad, "Everybody in Hawaii eats them all the time," so how lucky were we? Since it was highly unlikely that I'd ever get to Hawaii to see that for myself and confirm his fanciful statement, I proceeded to eat them not just because they were delicious, but more out of sheer hunger.

Obviously the 'exotic' menu had nothing whatsoever to do with us being piss-poor and on full collision course with the 'Debtors List,' nor having no bread, bacon, eggs or beans that morning. On the plus side, our friends and neighbours were most impressed by our tropical leanings, even though I never heard any of them say that they'd had pineapple rings themselves. Dad did make a mean Rag Pudding though. These were huge suet dumplings, filled with mince and onion and wrapped in a sewn cloth, or pillowcase, then boiled for hours on end. That sort of food clung to the ribs. The only problem was that someone in the house had to lose an item of clothing to wrap them in, which caused endless discussions in our house. The shame of the Debtors' List was one thing, but a shirt with only one sleeve - that was something entirely different. The fear factor alone made me shudder as I pictured removing my blazer at school only for an entire classroom to observe my naked arm.

Anyway, to address Dad's interpretation of my laziness and dislike of walking to the shops and to prove a point that we could still get tick at the shop, he instructed me to meet him at the top of the factory steps the following day. We arrived at the shop and there in all his glory was PC George in the process of taking a statement from the shopkeeper about an incident that had occurred on his premises the previous evening. It was alleged that someone had attempted to steal his car and had caused damage to his garage in the process. "Evening Ernie," said PC George, totally blanking me as he continued to document the crime, which didn't take long. Within five minutes of us being in the shop, PC George concluded his investigation. In his opinion: "There are some right bastards knocking around," and without doubt someone definitely had attempted to steal the shop owner's car and damaged his garage in the process.
Everyone in the shop agreed with PC George, shaking their heads in solemn commiseration as the PC left the premises to conduct his investigations and hopefully apprehend the guilty 'bastards'. It was normal run-of-the-mill stuff for PC George but provided me with an opportunity to experience a masterclass in Northern soft-soaping. Collectively the customers sucked up to the shopkeeper, lavishing him with praise, flattery, sympathy

and empathy, but none of what they said rang true with me. It certainly worked a treat though because the shopkeeper didn't need any further persuading about giving tick to everyone in the queue, even those already on the infamous list.

Soft-soaping is not a natural trait of Northerners but it's clearly in their skill set, alongside the much-preferred straight-talking and steadfast honesty. So, armed with a bag of onions (on tick) and a frozen jubbly, we left the shop, wreathed in triumph and heading straight for the butcher's shop to buy some tripe.

Now in my humble opinion, tripe on any level is disgusting. When boiled with milk and onions, however, it is putrid. Still, when money was scarce and you had hungry mouths to feed, there wasn't a great deal of choice. But I refused, point blank, to eat it on any occasion it was served up, usually opting instead for something like banana and sugar butties or crisp butties. If I was lucky, it could be leftover food from the day before being given a new lease of life. Dad never threw anything away - and I mean anything.

When we got home that particular evening, Dad started preparing the disgusting concoction that was tripe and onions, while I went to look for my brother and the other so called bastards to warn them that PC George was pounding the beat on the lookout for a car thief. He was not, at that stage, looking for a group of kids and what he didn't know wouldn't hurt him or us. If he did find out then there would certainly be consequences for us because, no matter what, our parents would not back us up if we were caught doing anything wrong.

So, what was the background to this crime of the century? In essence, it was all down to the ancient art of nicking apples - or 'apple-ing' - another one of our favourite pastimes in the summer. Unfortunately for the shopkeeper, he had the best apple tree around and so every year without fail we stripped it like a flock of ravenous parakeets.

On this particular occasion, it had been my turn to climb to the top of the tree to reach the biggest apples, only to slip and find myself hurtling towards the garage roof, still clutching my ill-gotten gains. Thankfully, I managed to avoid breaking either of my legs on landing, despite ignoring the usual warnings from all parents when caught climbing trees to "get down now before you fall and hurt yourself!" Much to my relief, upon crashing through the flimsy Asbestos garage roof, I instead soft-landed on the roof of the shopkeeper's Ford Cortina. Once I'd slid off the car roof and caught my breath, I realised to my horror that I was locked inside the garage. Not to worry though, as the gang arrived to save the day by smashing the garage window so I could make good my escape, heroically still clutching the apples. Fortunately, the true identities of the 'Rochdale Robbers' were never revealed and Dad helped the shopkeeper repair his garage window and roof. In exchange for more tick, obviously.

Had Dad and I not stopped off to read the invidious Debtors' List and gone into the shop that day, I would never have known what a close-call I'd had with the long arm of the law. Relieved by the news that we were all in the clear and that PC George suspected someone else, it was time to head home with jumper and hat in hand to suffer that putrid smell of tripe and onions.

******

CHAPTER THREE

'Terminated by Tripe'

I had a sixth sense about the inherent dangers of eating offal - after all, my maternal grandfather had succumbed to 'termination by tripe' when I was only five years old. Although we were not in contact at that time, perhaps the knowledge of my Grandad's demise lay tucked away deep in my mind.

The fatal day for Harry Green (whom I had only met very briefly early on in my young life) occurred in January 1957, at the comparatively young age of 52.

Unfortunately for Grandad Harry, a piece of tripe lodged itself in his throat, blocking his airways and causing him to collapse. A family member found him unconscious on the settee in the front room, his face blue. All hell broke loose and an ambulance was summoned quickly.

When it eventually arrived on the scene, desperate attempts were made to dislodge the tripe and get Harry breathing again. When it refused to budge, he was hurriedly placed into the ambulance with frantic resuscitation efforts continuing all the way to the hospital.

Unfortunately, it was to no avail: my maternal Grandfather succumbed to the blockage and passed over the great divide. It was undoubtedly a tragedy particularly for such a relatively young man - and made even sadder by having 'Terminated by Tripe' as his epitaph.

Anyway, Grandad Harry, may you rest in peace.

Despite his early death, Harry had led a very colourful life and by all accounts was a bit of a character and a spiv, but who nevertheless had reputable ways of earning money. In all cases, however, he required payment up front and in cash. While he owned a business supplying and fitting sun blinds for commercial properties, his more lucrative jobs were removing camouflage paint from industrial and residential properties following the end of the Second World War. The paint had been applied to many essential industrial buildings to prevent the Luftwaffe (the German Air Force) from identifying them and subsequently bombing them during air raids. Similarly, some residential and industrial properties that didn't have blackout curtains also had their windows painted black to stop light from showing through. It was everyone's responsibility during the war not to leak any light that would reveal to German pilots that they were flying over built-up areas.

Once the war was over, however, all of the black and camouflage paint needed removing and Harry was successful in winning large contracts to carry out the work. What a lad! He had a gang of men working for him who would be hoisted up the side of buildings in baskets to remove and strip the paint using caustic soda.
Financially, it was a very lucrative time for Harry. But he didn't believe in banking his hard-earned cash, instead keeping it hidden in a suitcase under his bed and, to eliminate the risk of his money being stolen, visitors were not allowed.
However, he did have a second home in which to receive guests - a caravan parked up behind the local pub which he used frequently after pub closing time. I am reliably informed that after Harry had made enough money, he ran off to the Isle of Man with a busty redhead and a suitcase crammed full of £5 notes. Several years later, he returned to Rochdale both without the money and his female companion.

His passing was well documented in the local press:

Collapsed While Eating Tripe – (Evening Chronicle)

No Inquest Following Post Mortem

On Friday evening an ambulance was called to the home of Mr Harry Green (52), of 96 Tweedale Street, Rochdale where he was found in a collapsed condition on the settee. On the way to the infirmary artificial respiration was applied and on arrival there an obstruction, a piece of tripe, was removed from Mr Greens throat but, he was found to be dead. After receiving the results of a post-mortem examination the Rochdale County Coroner (Mr A.S. Coupe) has dispensed with an inquest.

I don't really have any memories of meeting grandfather Harry but oh how I wish I had. Any knowledge of my maternal ancestry was lost on the same day my Mother left us, although research for this book has provided me with some of the answers. I didn't meet my maternal Grandmother, Alice (Marsden) Green either, as she died in childbirth in her early 30s and sadly, following her death, the whole family was broken up. Harry found it impossible to raise his five children - including my mother - on his own. As a result, the four youngest children were separated and either adopted or fostered to family or friends of my Grandfather.

In the case of my Aunt Hazel, she was adopted, aged two, by a family in Southport, while my Uncle Roy, aged three and a half, was fostered by one of my Grandfather's cousins. Separate foster homes were found privately for my Mother Dorothy, aged 10, and her younger brother Fred, aged 9. My Uncle George, being the eldest child, was fortunate enough to be able to remain at home before eventually starting work in Grandfather Harry's sun blind business.

Uncle Fred was placed with my grandfather's brother, my Great Uncle Fred, who was described by everyone who knew him as being a gentleman and an educated man. Young Fred settled in the home provided for him but as soon as he was able to, he left and went his own way.

Sadly, years later at the age of 56, my great Uncle Fred committed suicide by gassing himself in his kitchen. Once again and with all my heart, I wish to this day that I'd met him but at least I have comfort in knowing he existed and that, by all accounts, he was a good man.

His passing was well documented in the local and national press.

Man gassed himself because he felt he had failed in job - *(Daily Mail)*

Fred Green was a perfectionist - and it was his pride in his job which finally killed him, it was said at an inquest yesterday. Green, a 56-year-old electrical engineer, worried because he cost the firm he joined as a boy £300 to fly to Caracas, Venezuela to test machinery.

His nephew lorry driver George Green told the Rochdale inquest: "He blamed himself when he discovered that a defect in the machine he had been sent to repair in South America arose from his own workmanship." He said his uncle became very worried, restless, and unable to sleep when he returned from the trip. Later he gassed himself in the kitchen of his home in Bury Road Rochdale where he lived.

Blameless

Mr Green said, "My Uncle was the worrying kind.
He thought it was his fault that he could not put the

machine right. He was very upset when he came back. He had been with the firm 37 years and said that a man of his experience should have checked properly, but what he should have checked he did not tell me." Last night Mr Frank Whipp head of the giant electrical firm of Whipp and Bourne Limited, Rochdale said: "It was not his fault. He is in no way to blame for any trouble. Mr Green was sent out purely to test and commission the switchboard. When he got back he was depressed. He was very conscientious and had no reason to worry."

Green's Foreman, Mr Bob Ridehaugh, said, "He was the best man I had. I worked with him for 34 years and he was always keen and meticulous when doing a job." "I don't know what happened when he went to South America but when he came back he wasn't well," said another workmate: "Everybody throughout the firm knew Green as a first class man. He had a good word for everybody and was tops at his job."

******

CHAPTER FOUR

'Things are going to change around here, lads!'

Dad was born in Heywood, Lancashire as one of six children - George, Frank, Ernest, Gladys, Winnie, and John. At a relatively tender age he was a fully-fledged participant in World War Two where, along with his brother Frank, he was involved in the horrendous Arctic convoys. Having survived the war - and he really did only just survive, having on one occasion ended up in the freezing sub-zero temperatures of the Barents Sea – both he and Frank returned home. Four years later, he married my mother, Dorothy. They set up home at 227 Rooley Moor Road, Rochdale and eventually nature took its course with my brother and I arriving on the scene.

There wasn't an idle bone in Dad's body, he was always doing some sort of work, paid or unpaid. He loved life and his lads - but not his job at the Turner Brothers Asbestos Factory.

Turner's was one of the largest Asbestos factories in the world and I'm happy to say the site has long since been shut down and abandoned. But its legacy continues to this day as it has yet to be decontaminated. Locals once referred to the neighbouring woods as 'the snow trees' because Asbestos was blown there from the factory's extractor fans. By the 1980s, the devastating effects of the highly toxic material were known, with *The New Statesman* reporting that on several roads close to the factory, "every second household had lost a family member to Asbestos-related diseases, such as 'Mesothelioma.' A cancer which mainly affects the lining of the lungs and which is rarely possible to cure.

Dad and his brothers, Frank, and George, had all worked at Turners, as had several of my Aunts and older cousins but I didn't see much evidence of job satisfaction during my visits there. Working conditions were poor at best and most workers were on piecework, which meant their Thursday pay packets reflected how many pieces of work they had achieved in a week. Pieceworkers were under constant pressure to earn a decent wage as soon as the foghorn sounded, so if their machine broke down, it was a complete catastrophe for them.

I did, however, observe a fair degree of happiness all around the sheds, presumably because they had job security and were earning money to support and improve their families' lives. There was also a camaraderie that I have seldom witnessed since. Everybody supported and helped each other in the factory, just as they did on the estate, because they were all in it together and making the best of a tough situation, but with smiles on their faces.

As children, every adult we spoke to had to be addressed by their title – Mr, Mrs, Miss, Auntie or Uncle - even when they were not blood-related sometimes. That rule changed only on the day you were old enough to drink in the pub with them or work alongside them in the factory. At that point you were officially considered an adult.

As I got older, I would often stand at the top of the factory steps waiting for Dad, or occasionally even go into the factory itself. It was like watching an LS Lowry painting come to life when the home-time buzzer sounded. Swarms of people vacating the factory premises all at once, chatting, laughing, complaining, walking, or running. It was a hive of activity as the workforce headed back to their homes and families on the estate.

Receiving a wage packet certainly helped make ends meet and gradually our parents were able to provide us all with a better standard of living than they had experienced growing up. I remember our first black and white TV, which always closed transmission at the end of the day with the Epilogue. We would sit there until broadcasting ceased and the TV was turned off, our eyes remaining glued to the screen as the white dot slowly vanished into infinity as the valves inside the TV cooled down. Each time we secretly wished that another programme would come on; programmes such as 'Z-Cars,' 'Dixon of Dock Green,' 'Steptoe & Son,' 'The Saint,' 'Opportunity Knocks,' 'Sunday Night at the London Palladium' and the fantastic (to us anyway) 'Fireball XL5.'

Dad was a grafter and worked every hour he could to bring money in. After he bought a second-hand car he became a bit of a 'Del Boy', buying wholesale goods from shops, mainly clothing, and selling them on to everyone on the estate. Most weeks he would arrive home with his car jam-packed with goods, especially coats and anoraks, the car roof rack piled high with boxes. I suppose these days he'd be called an entrepreneur. The stuff he sold was very popular and, without fear of contradiction, I can say that at least three-quarters of the neighbourhood wore 'Ernie coats'. I have no idea where he found the time or the energy to do all that work and still look after my brother and me.

When he wasn't working or selling coats, he was also the Secretary of the local Community Association, the primary purpose of which was to organise sporting events for kids and community events such as fêtes and he would never give up his job as a Barman. I can honestly say, without a shadow of a doubt, that my brother and I walked that estate feeling very proud because our Dad was Ernie Stanier and everybody knew and loved him.

Because of his hard-work we continued to prosper financially and Dad loved his second-hand Ford Popular, which made us feel we were special. Not everyone was fortunate enough to own a car in those days. Even though it wasn't particularly roadworthy and the bodywork wasn't all the same colour - and more often than not it was off-road being fixed – Dad loved it. He and his brothers Frank and George spent hours tinkering with it - repairing bodywork, bleeding the brakes etc - and Warran and I would hang around them for hours, just watching them work.
Uncle George was the proud owner of a three-wheeler Reliant Robin, which once ended up in the middle of a grass roundabout on our way home from Blackpool when the brakes failed. Fortunately, we were following behind and were able to rescue them. I can still remember my Auntie Connie shouting at Uncle George: "Let me get in Ernie's car because I'm not getting back in that bastard flat iron without brakes!" Meanwhile, the remainder of the traffic on the road was at a complete standstill, watching the drama unfold and grinning in wry amusement.

One day, Dad announced, "Things are going to change around here, lads, we're going to have a lodger." Initially I thought this was just another one of his money-making schemes, but I was wrong. Our new lodger was Brenda, the divorcee living down the road at her mother's house with her daughter, Barbara. Brenda – or Mrs. Jackson as we knew her - was no stranger to us and was always very polite when our paths crossed in the street. We also knew Barbara because we played together in the street sometimes and Warran was in her year at school.

We were slightly nonplussed about the whole idea, but it was the word 'lodger' that really threw us; what Dad was saying effectively was that he and Brenda were going to be living 'over the brush' at our house. We already knew from the bush telegraph that Dad was seeing Mrs. Jackson and from the vantage point of our bedroom window we could confirm the gossip. For six months we had watched Dad and Mrs. Jackson leaving the 'Black Dog' at closing time together, so the announcement didn't come as any great surprise. They would laugh and joke with each other as they walked across the car park towards our house, occasionally falling into the privet hedges before making it to our front door. However Mrs Jackson was never there in the morning when we got up, but there was still evidence of her presence, such as empty 'Cherry B' and 'Snowball' bottles littered around our living room, or fag ends with lipstick in the ashtray.

Within weeks the announcement became a reality, with Barbara continuing to live with her Grandmother down the road. That seemed slightly strange because I thought that the whole idea was for us to be one big happy family living in the same house.

Things were definitely changing at home not only was Mrs. Jackson now living there, but because we also now had all manner of strange female hygiene products in the bathroom. It felt like there were rubber girdles, bras, and nylon stockings everywhere, particularly in the living room. And it took me ages to work out why there was talcum powder on the rug, in front of the coal fire, every morning and evening, but just one check through the crack in the kitchen door was all I needed to find out.

It was like watching an act from 'Cirque du Soleil' as Mrs. Jackson stepped inside a rubber tube whilst applying lashings of talcum powder to smooth the journey of the girdle from her ankles and up over the hips to her waist. Gradually, the rubber tube would compress and smooth out all her 'problem areas' on its journey north - but such was the effort that she needed to pause for a cig break before putting her nylon stockings on and then check if the seams were straight at the back.

But if Dad was happy in his new relationship, it was a small price to pay — even though it certainly wasn't normalising our family in any way if that's what he was planning. Discussions took place about the all-important and delicate question of titles. Would Mrs. Jackson become our Stepmom and her daughter our Stepsister, and did it mean that we now had a Step Grandmother too? It was all so complex and confusing, but my brother and I just got on with it. They were, after all, only titles.

After a period of time, Mrs. Jackson did want us to call her 'Mum' and Barbara did become our 'Sister,' despite the fact we had different surnames. However, it certainly didn't mean that Brenda was a mum in the proper meaning of the word. We saw her more as a Governess and we would privately refer to her as Mrs. Jackson or Brenda. She was not in any way, shape, or form like our surrogate Mother, Mrs. Dawson, and she definitely didn't have a sense of humour, which didn't help matters because humour was pervasive throughout the Stanier family.

Other than to my Father, she wasn't overly affectionate towards anyone. Or maybe she just held back any affection towards my brother and I – and her own daughter, Barbara, for that matter. She was definitely a disciplinarian and certainly of the opinion that my brother and I needed training. Over time, and once she'd got her feet under the table, she imposed new house rules and monitored our every move to ensure we didn't transgress or step outside her imposed boundaries.

I was now expected to eat porridge for breakfast every morning instead of my preferred slices of toast. Warran would eat both bowls, leaving me to go to school hungry. The porridge saga continued for months until Dad changed the rule back to toast for me - not least because Warran was coming out in heat lumps after consuming both bowls every morning and had to visit the GP about his heat rash (source unknown at the time)!
Having failed in her attempt to change my breakfast choice she then imposed the new rule of eating breakfast at our newly inherited Grandmothers house, but alas, this ruling didn't last long either. Thats because in my young impressionable mind Grandma Kitty's culinary skills were borderline macabre.

She started cooking early mornings or should I say boiling - Pigs heads, Pigs trotters, Cows tongue - Edible offal of all descriptions. The smell during the boiling process was horrendous and once my nausea progressed to projectile vomiting the ruling quickly changed. Kitty enjoyed every-thing she boiled and to watch her eat a pigs trotter or cows heel (without dentures) was like observing a competitor in a noisy gurning contest. As was watching her slurp hot tea from a saucer rather than the cup she'd made it in. Apparently the surface area of saucer compared to that of the cup cooled it down much quicker.

Brenda interrogated us regularly to try to find out what we were up to out on the street and who we were mixing with. I'm surprised she didn't try waterboarding us to get the answer because our reply was invariably, "Nothing," and "No one."

She even resorted to listening outside our bedroom door, but that failed because all conversations between my brother and I were tailored to suit her needs. We absolutely knew when she was listening because stairs three and seven leading to our bedroom always creaked and if Laddie was staying the night he would also be alerted. If stair three creaked she was checking that we were in bed and sleeping, but if seven creaked it meant that she was outside the door listening to our conversations and checking that we weren't eating Toffees (sweets). No sweets or food in the bedroom was another new rule she imposed on us, as was no watching the pub car park from our bedroom window. Bedrooms were for sleeping in only and not for food consumption nor watching the closing time antics in the pub car park from our prime vantage point.

Our tailored conversations would be repeated to us by Dad which only confirmed our suspicions that Mrs. Jackson had been earwigging outside our door. It was challenging, but she would never match the skills we had gained from the 'University of Street Life' on a Council Estate.

It seemed to us that she wanted to control our every move and we didn't trust her at all. I can't count the number of times she would say to my Dad, "What those two need is a bloody good hiding from you!" but she knew that it was never going to happen, much to her evident frustration. He just didn't believe in physical punishment and his methods of punishment were far more effective.

You always knew exactly where you stood with my Dad; he had clear and unambiguous standards about what was right and what was wrong. Both Warran and I knew that once his rules had been breached, the inevitable consequences would follow - especially on those occasions when he wouldn't accept our responses of "Don't know," to his every question.

Not always did he accept 'Don't know,' and silence from us when trying to get to the bottom of things. If deemed serious, then his usual routine was always predictable: he would calmly sit us down for the 'W' interrogation - 'What,' 'Why,' 'Where,' 'When,' and 'Who?' interspersed with the occasional 'How?' This could last for hours, if not days, if he had cause to summon witnesses. The interrogation could be more painful than the consequences as he carefully sifted the chaff from the wheat in order to get to the truth.

Only then would the punishment follow, usually us being grounded for days or missing out on a social event.
Physical punishment was never ever an option for him - he never so much as raised a hand towards us at any time. The worst part, though, was the emotional blackmail he employed. He concluded every interrogation by asking if we loved him, always followed by us saying "YES,"
followed by his, "Then don't do it!" coupled with a swift reminder about what Social Services might do should they find out.

The fear that Social Services might put me in care and separate me from my Father and brother usually did the trick. Until the next time. Then I'd immediately go into rehearsal mode just in case a Social Worker visited me at school about my errant ways. "Yes, No, No and No, everything is fine - can I go now?" However, most visits were not about my errant ways, but usually to offer me an activities holiday at a local children's home. I never did accept the offer. I had more than enough activities on the estate in Summer and I never did trust the woman in the green tweed suit or her colleagues.

Unlike my Father, Brenda's frustrations would spill over into explosive anger to the point of rage - but never in Dad's presence. Then, she'd look for a reason to justify her explosive behaviour and it was always down to us. The two things that always made her react explosively were us not addressing her as Mum, and the word 'no'. Eventually, to avoid the drama, we addressed her as Mum when required, but to us she would always be Mrs. Jackson or Brenda. It was a difficult ask to call her mum because my brother and I knew our Birth Mother was still out there, somewhere, and, despite the family silence about her existence, we would constantly be reminded by our peers at school of that fact — usually when we were in conflict with someone at school. We had no idea whether what they were saying was true, we just knew it was emotionally painful to hear the likes of: "Your Mother left you because she's a prostitute!" or, "You don't even know who your Mother is!" or, "She's a down-and-out and an alky!" or even sometimes that she was in prison, followed by a detailed list of her alleged offences. By and large, we became emotionally resilient towards the name-calling and their attempts at bullying - and we were no strangers to fighting back physically and verbally when it happened either.

We couldn't show weakness because, if we did, we would be forever known as soft touches and the bullying would continue unabated. But we never shared these experiences with Dad and we coped, not least because we had the backup of our school friends from the council estate when it all kicked off. Should one of us sustain a black eye during these conflicts, questions would inevitably be asked when we got home.

Often the response was, "Oh, I banged into something," to which the guaranteed response from Dad would be, "Well, it looks to me like you were talking when you should have been listening, lad!" Or "You should get your feet stuck in em next time".

Although displaying outer strength and putting on a brave face was of paramount importance during all the confrontations concerning our Mother, the emotional inner turbulence they triggered could continue for days afterwards and sparked spontaneous sibling debriefs. Such meetings were held privately, usually at bedtime, and at a whisper so no one else could hear. Occasionally they continued into the early hours of the morning and always with great vigilance about the creaking of stairs three and seven. After the debrief, we often lay there speculating about our Mother's whereabouts and what might have happened to her, even worrying that she might be in harm's way and my brother would always conclude our debrief with, "Don't worry I'll look after you."

As a general rule, we didn't backchat or argue with Mrs. Jackson and were always polite, but she did expect total capitulation and for us to do as she wanted without question. Unfortunately for her, we hadn't been raised that way and we questioned everything and anything, particularly why she would eat oranges in the bedroom when the 'No eating' rule applied. We had the evidence because she would wrap the orange peel in newspaper and covertly burn it on the coal fire the following morning.

On one such morning, I set out to expose her hypocrisy. As she placed the parcel on the fire on her way to the kitchen, I jabbed it with a poker. Immediately the parcel fell apart and, sure enough, there was something attached to the poker. But it wasn't orange peel. Try as I might, I couldn't remove it and Mrs. Jackson returned from the kitchen to find me running around the living room like an Olympic torch bearer with a blazing sanitary towel stuck on the end of the poker! Quickly removing myself and the blazing sanitary towel from the scene, I headed off down the road to seek refuge with Kitty and Barbara.

At any given opportunity, Warran and I would willingly despatch ourselves to their house as a sanctuary away from Brenda. In time I discovered that it wasn't that Barbara didn't want to live with us as a big family; she did - she just didn't want to live with her Mother!

The repercussions from the blazing sanitary towel were addressed once my Dad got home, resulting in me being grounded from playing out with my friends for several nights. Dad probably said, "I don't know what possesses you at times, our Graham," because that phrase was used a lot in our house. I took the punishment without question because I knew there would be no point in humiliating myself by mentioning my suspicions about Mrs. Jackson eating oranges in bed and disposing of the evidence on the coal fire.

Our personal hygiene also came under the spotlight as she scrutinised us getting washed and brushing our teeth, which we had done perfectly well prior to her arrival, but apparently not well enough. I drew the line, however, at her dental hygiene practices should our teeth be slightly off-white. On those occasions she would march into the living room with wet toothbrush in hand then thrust it up the chimney to collect soot, before liberally sprinkling the blackened toothbrush with salt. "Now clean your teeth," she would say, to which I replied, "Soot and salt? No thank you!" and then it would all kick off again.

Mrs. Jackson could not contain the jealousy she felt about the relationship we had with our Dad and envied the love between us. At every given opportunity she would do her level best to sabotage it, but all to no avail. She would complain bitterly (and for many years) about how much time Dad would spend with us, almost as if we were diverting his attention away from her. She even resented Dad watching Warran at his weekly football matches or going with me to my swimming competitions, but he still did. Over the years she had the opportunity to change her behaviour towards us and, for that matter, her own daughter, but she didn't because, in her eyes, she knew best. Her philosophy that, "Children should be seen and not heard and do as they are told," never changed. Having said that, neither did we!

By the age of 11, it was time for me to take the education exam known as the 11+, but as it was already a given that only Meanwood School's top boy and girl were going to go on to Grammar School, I couldn't see the point. Predictably, the rest of us went off to a Secondary Modern.

It proved to be a whole new world of education. Discipline was imposed with an iron hand in an iron glove by all of the class teachers and it was common procedure to be rapped over clenched knuckles with a ruler, be strapped on the palm of your hand or, even worse, slippered on the buttocks, usually by the PE teacher, if you put even a step out of line. The punishment was commonplace for misdemeanours such as answering teachers back, fighting in the schoolyard or messing around in class. While the basics of reading, writing and arithmetic - the 'Three Rs' - got pummelled into us daily as they had been at junior school, we were now able to expand our knowledge of Science, Art, Geography, History, English Literature, Music,

Cooking, Woodwork, Metalwork and ballroom dancing too. - You can only but imagine how the ballroom dancing went down.

The onset of partial independence for me and some of my friends - particularly Ste, She, Flynny and Scon – happened when we were 11 years old. It meant we were finally old enough to have a paper round and earn some money and, although we didn't particularly enjoy the early morning walk to the paper shop at 6.30 am - and in all weathers - we did enjoy payday on Fridays. More so, we enjoyed our Christmas tips from the customers, which almost quadrupled our weekly earnings. And during the lead up to Bonfire Night, we also benefitted from a healthy discount on the fireworks the paper shop sold. The paper shop sold 'all manner of things' - lucky bags, catapults, kites, pea shooters, spud guns, water pistols, cap guns, footballs, but not throwing arrows.

These prized possessions we meticulously made ourselves. They were effectively long garden cane darts with flights made out of playing cards and competition to see who's arrow travelled the furthest was fierce. However, no matter how aerodynamic the arrow the technique of launching it from a string wrapped around a notch 2/3rds up the body of the cane was everything.

Bonfire Night was celebrated just as much as Christmas on our estate and we needed a constant supply of fireworks from the paper shop, particularly bangers, especially for playing 'ghost up the drainpipe.' The banger would be carefully placed inside a drainpipe and, once exploded, it would send shockwaves throughout the entire house, startling the residents. As we ran away, we would hear a chorus of shouting voices telling us what they would do once they got their hands on us. It was their own fault in our opinion - they should have given us a 'Penny for the Guy' when we knocked on their door.

We would lovingly build our bonfire over several weeks until finally its pyramid shape stood taller than the adjacent houses on Daniel Fold. Once built, we would guard it with our lives, on constant lookout from the den for potential 'bommy' raiders who were building their own similar structures around the estate or neighbouring estates on Cutgate and Greave.

When we weren't on guard, we were searching, day and night, far and wide, for wood through dells, gardens, and public areas - and some not so public areas — to get enough to ensure ours was the biggest 'bommy' around. Only when it was built and ready to burn did the adults get involved, supervising us as we collectively set the bonfire alight from all sides. It was a great family event and our parents were welcome guests, as they brought with them trays of treacle toffee, parkin and black peas. It was only a one-night celebration but we could make it last days by fueling the bonfire daily with more wood, cooking spuds in the burning embers.

My paper round could be backbreaking work sometimes, due to the sheer weight of the bag on some mornings, particularly if it carried magazine supplements as well as newspapers. On those days, we just looked forward to slipping each newspaper through the letterboxes so that it would lighten the weight on our backs and shoulders. Once all the papers had been delivered we had no time to dawdle. It was a quick sprint back home to get washed, changed, and ready for school and then meet up again on the bus to be in time for the school assembly at 9 am.

Whenever we could, we would sit upstairs on the back seats of the bus, engulfed in cigarette smoke. The bus terminus was at the top of the estate, so we often got first pick on the way to school, but the journey home was always a case of grabbing any available seat. That said, if an elderly adult got on the bus and there were no seats free, we always gave up ours for them. It was an accepted rule, as was never making eye contact with the bus Conductor. They could spot the face of a non-paying passenger from a distance that even owls, falcons and eagles would envy. "Fares, please!" they would shout before staring you down with eyes that burnt right through to the back of your head. When the Conductor was patrolling and on the lookout for non-payer, we would keep our eyes well and truly glued to the window in order to avoid them.

Window gazing was compulsory. Unless of course we were sitting on the bench seat upstairs at the back of the bus. Then, it was a case of eyes looking straight ahead or at each other but never at the Conductor and being constantly vigilant about keeping legs firmly together and feet planted on the ground to hide the non-paying kids hiding under the bench seat. No one wanted to be under the bench willingly but, on some days, needs must. Many a time we would be covered in fag ash and someone's discarded cold and greasy chips by the time we left our hiding place to divvy up our money, including bus fare savings, to buy a packet of 10 No 6 cigarettes at the newsagents. Buses were full of windows but no doors, except for the one on the drivers' cabin, the only exit from the bus being the open platform downstairs. The moment the Conductor rang the bell signalling an imminent stop we would head downstairs and gather on the open platform, ready to 'back-drop.'

This was a skill that we learned from an early age and practiced daily. Not everyone grasped the concept, but most did. We would stand on the platform while the bus was still moving, clutching the steel pole, or grabbing handles for balance, and then slowly edging backwards with our backs to the open road until only our toes were in contact with the platform floor. Once the bus decelerated to a speed we felt comfortable with, we would let go of the pole and drop off the bus, landing on our feet on the road. The trick was to maintain the right momentum as you ran with the bus and slowed down at your own pace, carefully avoiding those who were dropping off after you and ensuring you didn't 'cruckle' on landing if you wanted to avoid a broken ankle.

Some days there could be six of us leaving the bus that way, even with the Conductor hollering, "I'm going to stop you doing this!" after us. Our reply was often, "Yeah, you and whose army?" and then we were gone. It was fun watching people drop off the bus when it slowed down on hills and before reaching bus stops, but when an Inspector got onboard to inspect tickets, people backdropped like lemmings off a cliff to avoid him. It truly was an art form.

There were also times when the lower deck of the bus would just erupt en-masse with laughter. It was a sign that someone had mistimed their exit, gone base-over-apex and were left watching their dropped shopping rolling down the hill. Those steel poles and grab handles on the bus platforms were also a blessing in disguise if you had roller skates on and were exhausted because you could grab hold of them at a bus stop and, as the bus slowly moved off, it would pull you up the hill.

The evening paper round was a doddle compared to the morning one, as the load was much lighter and my round was on the route I would take to get home. The lead topic of conversation between us at that time, other than the Moors Murders, was always how we were going to spend our wages that week.

70

The Moors Murders dominated the lives of many of us on the estate for a long time, not least because we were all shocked and in total disbelief that five children had been kidnapped and murdered in and around the Manchester area. It felt too close to home and we were being made fully aware that evil existed close to us, which in turn triggered greater parental vigilance all round. Rules about playing out were strongly enforced from that point onwards. Parents needed to know where you were and who you were with at all times. Everyone had to be indoors after dark — and woe betide anyone that broke the rules. "Don't be late! Don't talk to strangers! Don't get in a car! Don't walk home on your own!" To which our stock response was, "Will I 'eck as like!" - and we didn't.

We had previously lived a carefree existence on the estate and to a large degree it continued. However, until Ian Brady and Myra Hindley were arrested and taken into custody, strict rules were imposed to protect us from potential harm. Unlike other rules set down by our parents, these ones could not be broken and they were adamant that 'mumming' would be cancelled until further notice.
This was a devastating blow as we made a fortune as mummers on New Year's Eve. On Mummers Night we'd blacken our faces with butter and soot, wear hats and usually someone else's old clothes as disguise, before walking uninvited and unannounced into neighbours homes to clean.

Much like a home invasion really, only the invaders couldn't be identified or speak, just make a constant humming sound whilst cleaning – 'Out with the Old and in with the New.' Only on payment could we speak, and then only to wish them a Happy New Year. If we encountered locked doors we simply knocked and rushed past as the door opened and often to the cries of, "Bloody hell fire it's the Mummers," Once in their homes it was always a done deal that we were staying, as superstition ruled they would be cursed with bad luck if they threw us out. They could only avoid payment if we spoke, and believe me, that was never going to happen. 'We were quids in.'

One thing we could not afford was to be put in detention after school, making us unable to do our paper rounds. While it was a motivator for most of us to behave at school, it was never a guarantee and if school detention loomed large then the paper boys and girls had to take the other option - 'the Strap.' This was the Headmaster and his Deputy's preferred punishment for most misdemeanours at school and, on some days, it was like a conveyer belt of strapping - particularly for group punishments when an individual culprit could not be identified.

The Headmaster would carry out rigorous interviews to identify culprits prior to strapping but loyalty between the kids was everything and most interviewees   responded to the interrogation questions with, "Dunno, sir." And their loyalty paid off because it meant they went in the Headmaster's queue for punishment, rather than his Deputy's queue.The Headmaster's was the preferred queue as he was short in stature and couldn't quite get the height necessary to inflict pain with the strap. Even when he stood on tiptoe and leapt from the floor with each downstroke he failed in his mission. Being taller and more than enthusiastic in inflicting pain, his Deputy had much more success. Sometimes when the Deputy Head (who also did 'fart patrol' during assemblies) was visibly angry. You could see his neck veins throbbing as he uttered the words, "Impudent young boy/girl!" as he brought the leather strap down across the palm of the recalcitrant's hand. The phrase he least liked after "Dunno Sir" when enquiring about why we had done something was "Ferralaf Sir". For some reason this enraged him.- "For a laugh!, For a laugh!, Well we'll see who's laughing after this shall we".

There were countless misdemeanours requiring physical punishment, particularly the pastime of 'high peeing' in the boy's toilets at lunchtime (pupils would regularly compete with each other, in front of peers, to see how high they could pee up the urinal). More often than not, the boy who was successful in peeing out of the open window above the urinal was declared the winner. That misdemeanour, along with fighting and smoking on school premises, resulted in the highest number of straps being received. Fewer straps were given for backchat to teachers, inappropriate uniform, and bad behaviour in class. Having an umbrella open and wearing an anorak with the hood up on scorching days in double math's and asking for all windows to be closed because you felt cold, was all deemed inappropriate behaviour. For some though, getting out of double math's was worth the pain.

The music class was always chaotic because all of us wanted to play the only set of drums in the class. Listening to classical music often solicited the response of "It's shit, sir." Singing was also not very popular. Occasionally, when someone important was visiting during our music lesson and the teacher was forewarned, he would ask us to sing for them rather than play instruments. That made perfect sense because although our singing was bad, playing instruments harmoniously was a total disaster. He also made specific requests of certain pupils in the class to lip-synch the words during the visit,

73

as he knew full well that sabotage was likely. Often those individuals obliged, but not always. If our teacher was absolutely determined to avoid embarrassment, he would ask someone to perform a solo piece on a recorder - but only if it was their personal recorder, as school-issued ones were usually covered in spit and no one wanted to touch them.

Deliberately singing out of tune during morning assemblies was also a popular ruse. Several boys would also purposefully — and it has to be said, quite cleverly - fart on cue during the assembly, particularly when there was a silent pause in the proceedings. Trying to find the 'phantom farters' was always a problem for those teachers in detection mode, as each boy strenuously denied committing the offence. "Not me, sir!" and, to be fair, how could it be proved? I can't recall if girls ever got accused of that particular noxious deed. Perhaps girls just didn't trump? It wasn't the sort of question you ever asked them.

Visits by the school nurse were also commonplace and God forbid if you left the examination room with a bottle of lotion for head lice, because you would then be ribbed about it for the rest of the day. There were also routine eye and hearing tests, as well as immunisation programmes for poliomyelitis, chicken pox, measles, scarlet fever, and other dreadful diseases, all of which were doing the rounds at the time.

On a positive note though, we had the enthusiasm to learn and most of us were quite bright, even though in our heart of hearts we knew we were only being raised as factory fodder.
Once you'd got the 'Three R's' under your belt, the other subjects needed to be of some interest, otherwise

attention spans vanished into thin air and led to nefarious behaviours being employed to avoid the class.

For instance, I loved Geography, particularly when we studied Egyptology and the life of Tutankhamun. What I didn't know about King Tut could be written on the back of a postage stamp. Our teacher, Mrs. Blackman, was very impressed with my Egyptian leanings. Not so much, however, with my classmates 'She' and 'Flynny,' who couldn't have cared less about Egypt and at any given opportunity would try their level best to be dismissed from the class. They achieved that by repeatedly asking which house number Tutankhamen lived at because they were sure they'd delivered newspapers there! Eventually, they achieved their aim and were ordered out of the class.

Conversely, I disliked Physics because I just didn't get it - and knew I never would. Sometimes I could kick myself for not having absorbed the complexities of logarithms (and yes, I'm being a bit sardonic here!). The teacher of that tortuous subject would put me in 'Team Idiots' for every lesson, alongside Teams' Rutherford, Faraday, Newton, and Einstein et al.

Most lessons would start with him handing out rubber bungs and wooden rods with which to build a model of whatever atom he had in mind on that particular day. 'Team Idiots,' being idiots, would instead use our great imaginations to construct grotesque animal models. On completion of the set task, 'Team idiots' would then become target practice for the teacher as he carefully removed every bung from the model and launched them at us, hitting his selected target with every throw, after which we were hoofed unceremoniously out of the classroom.

A team effort was also required to get removed from Algebra. On the occasions we were thrown out of class, we headed for the smoker's area behind the playing field. Firstly, though, we had to visit the Headmaster's office for the laying-on-of-the-strap ceremony and would then swagger around school showing off the red marks on the palms of our hands, which we displayed like badges of honour.

Anyone lucky enough to be thrown out of class on the first period after lunch could also vanish for the rest of the day, their attendance for the afternoon having already been marked down. When that happened, we would head to a friend's house and just chill for the rest of the afternoon. If it were cross-country running for the games period, coupled with a rainy day, it was a given that we would vanish. On the days we weren't able to avoid it, we'd only run until we were out of sight of the PE teacher and then we'd hide behind a hill, wait for the group to return, then join in on the home leg trying to appear suitably exhausted.

No one ever missed Art class because it was so much fun. Drawing and painting provided us with a break from all the academic lessons. Our art teacher, Dorothy Smith, was a legend and the person everyone went to when they were troubled. Don't get me wrong though, most of what we produced in the class would not be found hanging on a proud parent's fridge at home - that's if they were fortunate enough to have a fridge.

Education didn't stop at school however because, now that I was 11, I'd also been given formal clearance to light the

fire at home. That had previously been Warran's job, but he had been 'promoted' to food preparation - well,
peeling spuds anyway. So, once Dad had taught me the mysteries and complexities of how to set the fire properly, I was ready for the off. Setting the fire consisted of
twisting and tying newspaper into tightly bundled knots and filling the fire grate with them, then placing kindling wood on top of the paper before setting light to the paper and adding lumps of coal/smokeless fuel as the fire took hold. If the fire ever proved difficult to catch (start), there was always the fire shield to draw the fire. I loved doing it - in a non-pyromaniac way - and welcomed the added responsibility.

Good kindling wood was a crucial element of fire-lighting. The wood was soaked in paraffin at the local hardware shop to virtually guarantee it would catch alight. Once the wood was burning, the rest was easy. On the first morning of my new job, and before Dad left for work, he gave me the money to buy some kindling on the way home from school. As I set off from home however, it was clear that Warran and his mates were about to sabotage my efforts to buy the wood, persuading me to either give them the kindling money instead - or die, basically. That left me with a bit of a problem but they'd already found a
solution, informing me that there was plenty of kindling wood freely available on the local tip. So I caved in and parted with the money.

After my paper round, and in the pouring rain, I began the long journey to the tip with my friends. Once we got there, shock horror, there was not a scrap of wood to be found - not that it came as a great surprise to me. But hope springs eternal and out of the corner of my eye I spotted a car tyre, a joy to behold because it was something that burned. Without further ado, I devised a cunning plan. I would wheel the tyre home, strip it down with our wickedly sharp bread knife, then use the rubber as a substitute for the wood. What could possibly go wrong?

Once back home, I had enough time to get things organised so that I could impress my father with a cheerful and welcoming, blazing fire when he got back from work. After stripping the tyre and with a fire grate full of rubber and paper, the experiment began. Because the thick pieces of rubber stubbornly refused to catch fire, I made what seemed to me at the time to be a logical assumption. I decided that, like the kindling, all the rubber needed was a splash of paraffin. I soaked the rubber and paper in the liquid and it worked a treat - the fire caught and blazed away merrily. I had achieved my aim. But my unbounded joy at my success didn't last. Once I'd lit the paper, the roaring flames immediately rolled out of the fire grate and within minutes were licking at the frame of the mantlepiece. No problem, I thought, because the flames would soon die down and a quick wipe of the mantelpiece with a damp cloth would soon sort things out. That was until the flames then spread to the flock wallpaper on the chimney-breast wall. By now, the flames were inching menacingly up the wallpaper and reaching ever closer to the ceiling. Suddenly I was scared.

Such was the ferocity of the flames that the treasured glass ornaments on the mantelpiece were cracking with the heat. Some paperwork on the mantelpiece also went up in flames, disintegrating before my mortified eyes. My new responsibility wasn't going too well.

Sitting on Dad's brand new and much-prized PVC sofa, with matching red velour covering and cushions, I desperately pondered my next move. Before I could even consider the options, I was being bombarded by blazing rubber pellets, flying at me and past me and scoring direct hits on the treasured sofa. The fire was spitting the rubber out with such regularity that I had to run into the kitchen for cover, watching through the crack in the door as the flaming bullets continued to score direct hits on the sofa, leaving tiny smouldering smoke trails as they did so. Not only was the back of the prized furniture covered with tiny burn holes, but thick putrid grey smoke now filled the living room. It was a total disaster.

Warran charged in like General Custer leading the 7th Cavalry, with the ingenious solution of throwing a pan of newly peeled potatoes, which were being steeped in cold water, onto the blazing fire, thus encouraging the remnants of the fire to flow onto the hearth rug. Surely things couldn't get any worse, could they? Panic reigned supreme. Within seconds though, my fear had notched up to the maximum level as I saw my Dad back dropping off the bus and sprinting towards his now smoke-filled home.

As he hurtled through the front door, Warran and I rapidly beat a retreat via the back door, hurdling all of the neighbour's garden fences like Olympians. We headed for the safety of the hills, bypassing Barbara's house because even she couldn't offer refuge this time.

As darkness fell, we could hear Dad and the recently summoned PC George shouting our names across the fields where we hid, quivering, in our den. Our trepidation knew no bounds as we were approached by the two shadowy figures and, on being discovered, there were no hugs to be had, only Dad's usual statement of, "I don't know what possesses you at times," followed by orders to, "Get home before me, get washed and changed and be in bed by the time I get back!"

It was a long, tortuous night as I laid in bed wracked with the guilt. All I wanted to do was talk to Dad and explain everything, but I guess he was similarly trying to work out in his own mind what had happened. My biggest fear was him giving me the silent treatment the next morning because sometimes when he was angry he would punish me by keeping our communication to a bare minimum. That's when I would know for certain that he was beyond angry. Accordingly, I got the silent treatment for days until one morning the torture finally ended, after I responded to Dad's interrogation with a full explanation, including the lie that I had lost the firewood money. There were strong words of advice after the questioning. "Just use your bloody loaf next time," meaning I could've burnt the house down because I wasn't thinking. There would, however, be punitive action, with my paper round money being donated to the Stanier Sofa and Rug Recovery/ Replacement Fund for many months after. Oh, and my transistor radio was also confiscated for weeks.

Dad was always suspicious of my transistor radio, which he himself had bought me and which I loved. But he thought it influenced me unduly. I'm not sure why though, because I only ever listened to music on Radio Luxembourg under the bed clothes so that he wouldn't hear it.
Listening wasn't allowed at bedtime on a school night but that rule was often broken - and the radio confiscated just as often, with the radio's batteries also removed just in case I discovered his hiding place.

The only times the radio ever left the house was when I went to Scout meetings on a Friday evening, when I'd listen to Radio Luxembourg on the bus journey home, and also when I had to go to Sunday School. I say I had to go to Sunday School, because I had no choice in the matter. It was a statement of fact, "You're going to Sunday School, so get ready, my lad." It wasn't such a big deal, and it was only for a couple of hours, but I got bored very quickly and most of the time excused myself from class and listened to the radio outside until sandwiches and cordial were served. Scouts, on the other hand, I enjoyed and Dad was pleased about me joining — but probably less pleased knowing he had to pay for the uniform, including my woggle and knife.

Tying knots and learning new skills kept me off the streets for one night each week and occasionally for weekends as well when we went away on camping trips. Even better, the summer brought with it a week-long adventure holiday. 'Bob a Job' week, though, was hell.
To earn a 'bob' (a shilling), we had to go door-to-door soliciting money from neighbours in return for manual and menial labour tasks, and oh boy, did they take advantage of that. Somedays I could spend hours cutting a privet hedge, tidying up someone's garden, running an errand or worse, running several errands, just for one measly shilling.
However, I quickly learned never to go to old people's bungalows during 'Bob a Job' week. No point really, because all they would say in response to "It's 'Bob a Job' week. D'ya want owt from shops" was: "I'm not giving you money for running my errands. You did 'em for now't last week - now bugger off!"

Because of the financial sanctions imposed by the Sofa and Rug Fund, it became necessary for me to replenish my financial losses, usually from the pockets of Dad's trousers hanging by a pair of braces on the back of his bedroom door. How else would we get to the pictures on Saturday for the 'Tanner, (sixpence) Rush'? We would all descend on the Regal Cinema en masse with our mates from the estate for a couple of glorious hours every Saturday for the matinee performance.

Those who didn't have the entrance fee sneaked in through the lavatory window, which was opened immediately once one of us got into the cinema legitimately by purchasing a ticket. The Usherettes would often complain that we were making too much noise and being disruptive, but the harassed Manager's threat to stop the film and send us home if we didn't behave soon restored peace and quiet.

******

CHAPTER FIVE

'Just pull over!'

The sentence I never wanted to hear from Dad on Sundays during the summer was: "Let's go for a run out in the car and have a picnic!" Even worse still were the horrors of travelling with the extended family in convoy. It was stress on a grand scale from the moment it was mentioned. Food had to be prepared and the car checked at least 20 times for roadworthiness, then loaded with enough stuff to last us a week when we were only going out for about six hours. It was like preparing for a pandemic.

I also dreaded the words: "What the bleeding hell has happened here, our Graham?" on Sunday washdays. I knew what he was referring to. "Jesus Christ, how do you get bastard ink all over your school shirt like this - and I mean ALL OVER!" I dreaded the question but dreaded even more the punishment of having to vacuum the whole house after the ink-stained shirt had been discovered. Somewhere in the deeper recesses of my mind I had convinced myself that by burying the shirt deep in the washing basket, Dad wouldn't notice. "Another bastard boil wash," he would say as he manhandled the washing machine and mangle out of the pantry to do an unscheduled boil-wash.

I couldn't be bothered to explain the finite details of why my school shirt was covered in ink. Furthermore it was never a good time to imitate his actual punishment instructions "Run round the house with the hoover NOW!" or say, "It won't suit me," if he asked me to "Put the kettle on and 'mek a brew." It just happened sometimes, normally in an English lesson where it was compulsory to write using a fountain pen. It was known as the 'Quink

Wars', named after the type of ink we used. It usually started once a targeted person had been randomly selected to receive a direct hit of Quink ink. Sometimes to the face, often to their white shirt (when not wearing a blazer) and always in copious amounts.

The surprise ink attacks could come out of nowhere and at any time. Once a direct hit had been scored, time was of the essence for the target person to pass it on, meaning they had to pick a classmate and score a direct hit on them in order to lose their own target status. Some days, covert 'Quink Wars' could last for an entire lesson and rarely did the teacher catch anyone launching an attack, although occasionally she would question why half the class looked like Smurfs as we departed her classroom.

That was something that Dad didn't need to know and the excuse that my fountain pen had leaked wouldn't work either. "Don't know," was usually the best explanation for both of us - and let's be honest, Dad knew anyway! Linda's Mum also knew her daughter would be covered in ink after English lessons, despite her repeated requests for it not to happen. "Mum said you can't throw ink at me today." She would normally be the first target.

The preparations for Sunday runouts in the car took hours. Once the boot reached maximum capacity, the rest of our equipment would be loaded inside the car until every available inch was taken up with stuff. There would be blankets, chairs, Tupperware containers, flasks, maps, a compass, car part spares, a spare tyre, Sammy the tortoise and, last but not least, Dad's boiled sweets tucked away in the glove box. Although usually by the time we eventually set off, the once bulging bag would have become an empty paper bag that had once held boiled sweets.

Before we set off, Dad assumed the role of a weights and measures expert, carrying out a risk assessment before inevitably concluding that the car was roadworthy and light enough to reach the top of every hill we would encounter on our foray into the unknown. I say unknown because I can't remember a time when we actually arrived at our intended destination. The journey always descended into mass chaos, particularly if we were in convoy, because not one of us was a decent map reader despite the firm belief that we were. We would take sharp left turns instead of rights and blindly follow signposts into oblivion. The convoy of following cars would be on two wheels at roundabouts trying to catch up with the lead vehicle. Then there would be frequent stops whilst we waited for Uncle George and Auntie Connie in their Reliant Robin, which always had difficulty keeping up with us.

Dad would also have to contend with the indignity of other irate drivers honking their horns and hurling abuse at him as they drove past our chugging little motor. He was totally confused by their reaction to his driving as he considered it to be impeccable. Little did he know that it was nothing to do with his driving skills - the adverse reaction from other motorists was a result of Warran and I giving them two-fingered salutes from the back seat of our car!

The car windows would fog up until no one could see out of them and then, as the car rocked along, all unsecured picnic items would be launching themselves at our heads from every direction. You soon developed an instinct to hold on to anything and everything, especially when Dad hurtled around a bend on the road. Without the statutory requirement for seat belts in those days, it was an achievement not to injure the person sat next to you. As for Sammy the tortoise, he was on the roller-coaster from hell.

Then there was the inevitable hill. Nearly every time we encountered a steep incline we had to get out and push that bloody Ford Popular up it because it was struggling to make the crest. We then had to run manically after it as it descended the other side, before jumping back in whilst it was rolling along. Dad's knuckles, meanwhile, were white from gripping the steering wheel.

There would also be the inevitable stop to change a flat tyre, which would be the moment our picnic location was selected, usually with the words, "I'll just pull over." Invariably it would be in a busy lay-by and far too dangerous for children to leave the car, but at the very least we could wind the windows down and see the outside world, despite the fact there was very little to see other than a busy main road and occasionally a field full of grazing cows. Who wants to see a field of cows eating grass and passing humongous amounts of excrement every couple of minutes, which would slowly turn into sunbaked cow flaps surrounded by squadrons of flies? Not really the desirable view when you're tucking hungrily into a picnic.

Our picnic locations were never ideal and you could be guaranteed to suck in lungs full of CO_2 every time there was a traffic jam. But, undeterred, we would continue pretending that it was an amazing experience watching cows voiding their immense bowels of endless quantities of cow-flap and traffic hurtling by, rocking our car, as Dad struggled to put the spare wheel on.

I couldn't mention 'cow-flap' in front of Dad ever since an incident with our mate, let's call him George, the upshot of which was that Dad had to buy George a new pair of shoes. George's Mother, turned up at our house spitting feathers, and hurtled a pair of shoes, full of cow shit, at Dad. As usual, I'd had a hand in it, metaphorically speaking. I had no defence because I'd encouraged George to fill his shoes with cow-flap in order to help him grow. It had worked, he was inches taller when wearing the shoes! Apparently, the smell from the 'fallout' in their living room was horrendous and it took weeks to get the remnants out of their much-prized carpet. Dad's usual comment, "I have no idea what possesses you, our Graham," followed by his sardonic smile and shaking of his head, which meant that at one level he approved but at another level he didn't. I always trod a fine line.

Our family picnics were never on a grand scale because the Stanier's kept it very simple. Forget hampers, plates, glasses, napkins, cutlery, pastries, and a salad made up of spinach leaves, rocket, cherry tomatoes, peppers, avocados, olives, and feta sprinkled with pine nuts and walnuts, assorted meats and/or cheeses. Our salads were much simpler, consisting of a celery stick, a whole tomato, chunks of cucumber and a piece of wafer-thin ham, presented to us on a Tupperware plate with neatly folded toilet roll for use as a serviette, the whole lot smothered with lashings of Heinz salad cream. That's only if the bottle was still intact and we weren't already wearing its contents from it ricocheting around the car during a hairpin bend manoeuvre.

On Sundays when the picnic had actually been planned in advance, we could also enjoy a hard-boiled egg with our salad. However, picnics were rarely that well planned, with the exception of the packing element. Après salad there'd be Eccles cakes washed down with gallons of tea, although how much tea was available was entirely dependent upon how many flasks had been broken during the journey there!
Following our sumptuous picnic, we would then pack up in preparation for making the return journey home, facing

the same challenges and dilemmas of map reading, car breakdowns and hairpin bends that we faced on the way. It didn't matter though because at least Dad could tell his mates that we'd had a family run out on Sunday. Of all the things we did with him, that was my least favourite because his stress levels went right through the roof.

I would much rather have been playing out on the estate and enjoying the summer weather, particularly when it was nice and we could go off and collect wire and cables from the tip and factory grounds, burn off the rubber and then weigh the copper wire in at the scrap yard in exchange for cash.

Sammy the tortoise always came with me on our days out, but if we were going on holiday to Blackpool or elsewhere, Ginger the cat and Mickey the budgie would also have to accompany us in the car. I insisted and, unlike the hat, there was no compromise. Dinky the rabbit wasn't a good traveller so would have to stay at home and be looked after by a neighbour while we were away.

******

CHAPTER SIX

'Childhood holidays – Blackpool'

It was always routine that on our first day in Blackpool, all the cousins were given a choice about what beach toy they wanted, even though for financial reasons the choice was limited. It was either a bucket and spade or a ball and they had to last the whole holiday. That, of course, never happened. Rubber balls would be punctured by Warran and my cousin Malcolm, who booted them everywhere and at everyone. Buckets and spades quickly lost their appeal and were instead used as weapons against each other. Spades became swords and buckets were used for water bombing.

Our cousins Barbara and Freda, who were older by a couple of years, were designated childminders. Unfortunately, they had no control over us whatsoever, not that they particularly cared. We would play merrily on the beach with balls, buckets and spades and swim in the polluted sea, under supervision from Freda and Barbara, who'd receive hard cash instead of toys but were stalked constantly to share it. We'd stay on the beach until the sun disappeared over the horizon and even longer if we could drag it out. The physical evidence of us playing out for hours in the sunshine was apparent most days. There were no sun creams offering protection for us because, to be honest, I don't think they existed then.
It was just calamine lotion if we succumbed to the UVA/UVB rays and perhaps, if you were lucky, a dollop of Ponds cold cream to help ease the pain of sunburn.

It always seemed like the whole of Rochdale had packed their suitcases and toddled off to join us in Blackpool. We would be surrounded by our friends and familiar faces from our estate whenever we were on holiday there. Some days, Barbara and Freda would have to supervise us on the Crazy Golf Course which always got very competitive and usually descended into arguments between us. These disagreements often resulted in my cousin Neil throwing his golf club away, complaining that he wasn't playing because someone was cheating, but we expected it from him because he was always very competitive and yes someone was always cheating.

Susan, his sister, and our younger cousin, would despair at our behaviour. Malcolm and Warran often taunted Neil, who would then run off to find Freda and Barbara to report everyone. The girls were usually nowhere to be seen but could eventually be found sat on a bench eating ice cream, with boys wolf-whistling at them. I wish I had a pound for every time I heard them proclaim in an exaggerated way, "I've got a boyfriend thank you," or "Honestly, these boys," as they feigned embarrassment whilst rolling the waistband of their skirts ever higher. They would threaten us with dire consequences when we all got home, promising to tell our parents about us misbehaving, cheating and not playing 'nice.' That was never going to happen though because they'd have been more at risk of us telling our parents that they'd abandoned us on the Crazy Golf course or were on the beach seeking out admirers.

To get to Blackpool, we would travel as a huge group on the train, piling off excitedly at Blackpool railway station, dragging our heavy suitcases beside us and heading for our boarding house, en masse. You could almost sense the Landlady's dread as she opened the door and saw us all stood there, squealing, and wriggling with excitement.

Each morning after breakfast and before heading for the beach, we would all go for long walks along the promenade with our parents, listening to their stories about what had happened the previous evening in the club or pub. They relived their joy and laughed out loud about how good a night they'd had and what last night's 'turn' was like. If they had been awful, they just laughed even louder.

In the evenings, we would all dress up in our Sunday best and have dinner together in the guest house, then the promenade again before bedtime, when the adults would go out for the evening. It was pandemonium when our parents went out because our excitement and energy just couldn't be contained. There was always mischief afoot. We had pillow fights before bedtime every night and we couldn't sleep for excitement, thinking about what the next day held for us. Blackpool: shamefully brash yet fabulous. It was our very own version of Las Vegas.

There was so much to do there. Amusement arcades were everywhere, trams, donkey rides, fish and chip shops, pubs and bingo halls and even open-air dancing on the piers for adults. On a dull or rainy day, we could spend hours in the amusement arcades and at the Pleasure Beach.

The highlight of the holiday was the final evening, when we would all go with our parents to the pier, dressed up to the nines, to see the summer show. The following morning, though, there was the sadness of leaving it all behind, but at least we had the excitement of the train journey home to look forward to.

When we couldn't afford to stay in a boarding house on our seaside holiday, we would go for the next best option which was a caravan park, usually several miles outside of Blackpool. The caravans were always basic and it was almost like stepping back in time. There was no inside toilet and having a strip wash at the kitchen sink — with water warmed in a pan on the two-burner hob - was back on the agenda. If I close my eyes now I can instantly recall being hit by the heady aroma of dampness, Calor Gas and San Izal Disinfectant when the caravan door was first opened. The only upside of being in a caravan was that you were master of all you surveyed and could come and go as you pleased. In a boarding house, once you went out after breakfast and the front door closed behind you, you weren't able to return, on pain of death, until early evening.

Another delight of those dated caravans were the gas mantles. Gaslight was the order of the day as electricity was not available. I was mesmerised by the delicately constructed gas mantles and we needed at least one replacement a day, while most families only needed two for their whole holiday. The gas mantle was the only form of lighting in the whole caravan and I was constantly trying to work out how it worked. For those of you unfamiliar with gas mantles, they were the precursor to electric light bulbs and were powered by Calor Gas.

Dad would buy two new ones on arrival at a caravan, placing them precariously over the gas light feeder. Within seconds of turning the gas on and lighting it, there would be a ball of incandescent, hissing light. If there were two mantles burning, they illuminated the whole caravan. I would wait with anticipation for Dad to light them each night because it was like watching a magician performing a magic trick. Once he'd lit them, he'd leave for the pub with strict instructions for us not to touch them.

Obviously, his dire warning was for safety reasons and also because mantles were difficult to fit and very delicate when alight. Just one touch at the wrong time and they crumbled into a flaky powder, becoming immediately unusable. But it's like being told not to touch wet paint - what do you do?!

Without fail, each night after Dad had left to go out, I would give one of the gas mantles a poke and because they were very delicate they disintegrated on being touched. I was fascinated by them and despite the first one crumbling, I would then try the second one — with similar unfortunate and disastrous results. Dad would eventually arrive back at the caravan, inevitably in pitch darkness, falling over anything that was on the floor and mumbling about the "Shit gas mantles!" that the shop had sold him, before drifting off to sleep. The following morning there would be the usual interrogation about the broken mantles. I would normally own up but on the occasions I didn't, I would stand innocently behind Dad in the caravan camp shop while he asked the shopkeeper for replacements for their faulty goods. Occasionally he got one, but most times he didn't and had to pay.

Dad would sometimes fancy a change of holiday location and that meant Fleetwood. This was in stark contrast to the busy and illuminated Blackpool and, unsurprisingly for us, not as exciting. We did still get to go to Blackpool for the day though and also visit the Isle of Man by boat. We would wander around Douglas for the afternoon, where Dad would order kippers to be sent by post to relatives, after which we'd head back to Fleetwood. The following day it might be a trip to Knott End. Living the dream!

Dad was a great saver and was always tucking some money away for holidays and the proverbial rainy day. He always had money put to one side that no one knew about. He was a member of what was known as the '13 Savers Club' at work, which involved a group of thirteen men putting an affordable and fixed sum of money in a pot every week, with the total amount collected subsequently paid out to one of the Club members that same week. It meant everyone in the Club received a lump sum of money four times a year. Dad also did the football pools every Saturday and I wish I had a pound for every time he'd say, "When we win the pools, son." He always had high hopes that he would win one day and, like millions of others, diligently checked his coupon each week, watching the football scores on TV. I can't remember a time when he got even a small pay-out, but I do remember the time when he and his mates won big on the Grand National horse race.

They'd been putting a small amount of money aside for months before the big race and had accumulated a substantial sum to place an each-way bet on a horse called Jay Trump (no relation to Donald)! Dad sat and watched the whole race on TV, the veins standing out in his neck, screaming encouragement to Jay Trump throughout the whole race. When it finally won, Dad did several laps around the house faster than the winning horse, thumping the air with his fists. I thought that this would equate to a pools win but it didn't. What it did mean, though, was that we'd have more money to spend on holiday that year - that and not having to pay the rent for two weeks. Council house tenants didn't have to pay rent during the 'Wakes Week' holiday, when perhaps half to two-thirds of the council estate's residents were also at the seaside.

Everyone being away from home at a specific time would, you might think, be a robber's charter but that wasn't the case. Your house would be watched by those neighbours not on holiday, and in reality we didn't really have anything worth robbing. As the late Sir Ken Dodd once said, "Who's going to steal a mangle?" Mind you, there were the gas and electricity meters, which had coin boxes to tempt those with light fingers. If your meter did get robbed then it could be a mutually beneficial situation because the crime would remain unreported until the man from the gas or electricity board came to empty the meter. In the meantime, residents would feed the meter and joyfully keep the coins as they fell out of the damaged equipment through the space where the coin box used to be.

******

CHAPTER SEVEN

'Bogies'

Cars always had to be at the ready and Dad and Uncles Frank and George spent hours repairing them at Frank's garage. Warran and I would spend hours on end helping them, although, to be fair, we weren't that much help. But we could do simple things like pushing brake pedals up and down whilst the brakes were being bled. The most exciting times, though, were our visits to the scrapyard. On those occasions, we would go mob-handed with Dad, Uncle's, and several of our cousins. It was a regular haunt of ours, particularly at the weekends when we were searching for parts to patch up cars, or 'bangers,' as they were commonly referred to. To be honest, those vehicles were a liability on the road.

The scrapyard was packed with discarded vehicles and we could just wander around and play, unhindered, for hours. Standing side-by-side and stacked on top of each other, the cars covered a huge area. As soon as we got there, the adults would start to dismantle anything and everything with their spanners and screwdrivers. Items ranging from gearboxes to spark plugs and light bulbs were fair game.

Our job was to fill our pockets with all the car parts that had been removed and then sneak out of the scrapyard, our trousers and coat pockets bulging with vehicular treasure. An older cousin would then help us leave the premises with our ill-gotten gains, hopefully unseen by the owners. Meanwhile, Dad and both Uncles would present themselves to the scrapyard dealer with a couple of spark plugs in their hands, innocently asking, "How much?" There were two things you needed to know about the scrapyard. Firstly, make sure the two German Shepherd dogs were firmly tied up, because no way could we out-run Samson and Delilah - and secondly, get ready to do a runner if Joe the scrapyard dealer was heard to say, "Hang on a minute, Ernie!" because that meant he had become suspicious.

During our visits to the scrapyard we were also constantly on the lookout for pram wheels and, if we found any, we would throw them over the perimeter wall to be collected later. Alternatively, we could scavenge them off the local tip. Pram wheels were a much sought-after commodity, particularly in our neighbourhood as they were a key component of the bogie. Just thinking about it, I suppose that a bogie without wheels would be a sledge?

I can remember the time I saw a Silver Cross pram without its wheels, sitting forlornly on the tip, with an irate woman screaming, "If I get my hands on whoever did this, God help them!" But then her daughter shouldn't have left it near the tip when she was playing with it. Back then, you definitely wouldn't want to be on the receiving end of a Mother's anger and frustration because, without doubt, the culprit would be the recipient of a severe and justifiable ear-ringing head slap. Mums in particular would hunt you down mercilessly if they knew you were responsible for a misdemeanour and, if caught, the inevitable clout or two around the head would follow. It was no good ducking to avoid the 'incoming' either because most Mothers were far too fast for that.

Nor was there any point in you going home and complaining that you'd been 'lug-holed' because any such conversation would be shut down straight away. In my particular case, if I went home to complain that someone's Mother had dispensed justice for nothing, Dad would just reply: "No-one just hits you for nothing, lad. You must have done something wrong. Now get out and play!"

There were times, however, when Mums could turn into lionesses protecting their cubs. The uproar that these spats entailed quickly became a spectator sport as women set about each other, arguing loudly either on the street or in the pub car park. Forgiveness always seemed to be the order of the day though, because come the following morning, the combatants would be sat next to each other on the buzz (bus) going to work chatting away as if
nothing had happened. Whatever the situation or event they seemed to have an amazing life skill of remaining connected to the person they had previously been in
conflict or disagreement with. - "Ive just given Him/Her a piece of my mind and He/She wont forget that in a long time either" - "Ive said my piece and thats enough". - "No hard feelings". Problems were sorted very quickly and didn't fester.

If by any chance anyone missed the 'set to' the previous evening, there was always an opportunity to learn about it on the bus the following day.

"Did you hear all that commotion last night?" "NO!"

"Mavis and Florrie had a right doo on't road and it were all over summat and nothin." "What Happened?"

"Well, Mavis said to Florrie about so and so and thingy and she kept harping on about this, that and the other. So Florrie said I'm not having this and she right laid into Mavis and then Mavis is agate and then Florrie's agate and it all kicked off."

"What happened after that?" "They both went to bingo."

"Oh and Mavis won the jackpot and shared it with Florrie 'cos they were sharing books that night." "Oh right."

But back to bogies. They were very basic and constructed from four pram wheels attached to a plank of wood, on which you would sit while holding on to a length of cord attached to the front wheels that you used for steering the 'dream machine.' If you were riding pillion, your passenger clung on to you like grim death, the wind whistling through your collective hair. You could race your bogie opponents down a local hill, which also happened to be the main road on which buses travelled regularly. The hill was, conveniently, the same one we used for sledging in the winter.

We would set our bogies off from the bus stop at the top of the hill, start the descent and build up a suitable head of steam for about a mile. The road didn't level out until you hit a three-way road junction. Without good steering you could only travel in a straight line and, having no brakes, would thrash across the junction without stopping. It was in the lap of the gods as to precisely where you would come to a halt. Usually, the only way to stop bogies before the junction would be to put both feet on the ground, scraping off the soles and heels of your shoes in the process, (presumably that's where the term 'foot brake' comes from)?

Conversely, we would attempt a manoeuvre that would ensure you crashed into someone's much-treasured privet hedge at the speed of sound but were at least guaranteed a soft landing. The more skill you acquired, the more you could use your body to steer the bogie. Sometimes we were able to level off into an avenue away from the main road and then gradually slow down. There would inevitably be a near miss incident with the 12a bus or the Rag and Bone man if the lookouts weren't being vigilant. Our friends would run after the bogie as it hurtled down the hill and anyone wanting to 'ride' the hill next had to drag the bogie behind them back up the incline. We had a beltin' time.

In the evenings the use of bogies was banned, largely because of their low visibility without lights and frequent near misses with the 12a bus. Instead, there were youth clubs on and around the estate where we could socialise with friends in the evenings. There were no organised events to speak of but it was a great meeting place, with snooker tables, table tennis, darts, and music.

That's where I had my first experiences of drinking alcohol and puffing on cigarettes. We would daringly consume a litre of cider on Friday nights between us and then I'd sneak back home to get into bed before Dad returned and walk soberly through the living room to avoid a breath check from Mrs. Jackson.

She could often be found sat in front of the coal fire surrounded by her newly washed underwear, waiting for it to dry, nylon stockings secured by ornaments on the mantlepiece, hanging either side of the fire; brassiere front and centre of the mantlepiece resembling the Giza pyramids, her voluminous knickers drying on the hearth, with the guarantee that her rubber girdle and suspenders weren't far away. It is almost like an early Victoria's Secret shop window display. She could sit for hours waiting for her clothes to dry, reading the problem page in her Woman's Own magazine, puffing on Park Drive cigarettes and flicking fag ash everywhere.

Occasionally she'd pass the time counting how many chocolates she had left or marking the fluid level on her lemonade bottle with a pen to ensure that no one else drank it. That was her code for, "This is all mine and no one else had better touch it!" Anyway, we had Dad's ginger beer and if I wanted chocolate or sweets I could just go to the 'Black Dog' and ask Dad - that's if they could get hold of him and he wasn't busy behind the bar or entertaining the regulars with his rendition of 'Oh Please Diana.' He sounded nothing like Paul Anka but he didn't care.

Dad used to make ginger beer - his 'Eau de Rochdale' – using all sorts of bottles, which I would refer to as Bottle Bombs. He loved brewing it, but no matter how many times he prepared the recipe there was always the distinct and ever-present possibility of exploding bottles. Once filled, he would store them in a cupboard under the sink, fermenting away and bubbling evilly. Whenever I stood at the sink doing the washing up I had to exercise constant vigilance just in case the cupboard doors were blown open by an exploding bottle or two. The chance of a bullet-like cork hitting you just didn't bear thinking about and certainly kept you on your toes. If I was in bed and heard something akin to a military exercise taking place in the kitchen, I would know that it was Dad's ginger beer bottles exploding and that the kitchen was definitely out of bounds until things had quietened down.

'Ernie's Ginger Beer' was a potent but non-alcoholic brew. For Dad, it was more of a hobby but even over the years he never did quite perfect it. He would try all sorts of combinations to stop the bottles from exploding or firing their corks across the room like Exocet missiles. He would tilt the bottles at various angles, leave them upright, change locations from dark to light areas, put them in cupboards or the pantry. Alas, it was all to no avail as havoc was inevitably wreaked, resulting in ceiling lights getting broken and cupboards damaged. Anxiety reigned supreme every time he declared that he had completed another batch and we knew that we would have to keep dodging the ginger beer bullets. The only thing that was lacking in our house were hazard warning signs.

Interestingly – and perhaps a bit suspiciously - Dad didn't drink much of the ginger beer that he'd made. He just liked brewing it and either gave most of it away to friends and family or donated it to the many community social events that he'd organised. Dad and his mates were always busy planning football matches, fêtes, and days out for everyone on the estate. He was inordinately proud of the fact that he was Chairman of the Spotland Reform Football Club and equally proud of his ginger beer production.

******

CHAPTER EIGHT

'A letter to my 15-year-old self'

So, you're 15 years of age and driving everyone to distraction with your moodiness and your constant moaning about how you've been hard done by, how life is unfair and nothing's your fault. Here's the life memo you didn't receive, 'Life is neither fair or easy," so get used to this fact and don't fall into the entitlement trap.

Yes, it's a difficult age and life can be unfair but, to be honest, you were never going to be fully prepared for the realities of adult life leaving school at the age of 15 without any formal qualifications. Not the best start in life but it is what it is. You never did understand how your future employment prospects would be so blighted by your lack of formal qualifications and it's OK to feel deeply let down and angry at the system that educated you. They told you how bright you were but then failed you and your contemporaries by not providing you with an opportunity to sit final exams and therefore gain the all-important formal qualifications before leaving school.

Do please try to understand though that you were raised in an education system devised simply to provide factory fodder, and that without any formal qualifications it will always be an uphill struggle to compete for jobs with those that do have them. This is not your fault, but nevertheless your pain is real.
You never did envisage that just one weekend after leaving school you would be clocking on at 7.30 am each morning and working, surrounded by lethal Asbestos, in an unskilled job alongside your Dad. But remember it was never his dream for you either — it was always his

intention that his sons would do better than him in their working lives and not have to follow in his footsteps.

As a single parent, he has raised you and your brother on a proud council estate and worked hard all his life to provide and meet your every need, so please remember that he has never let you down.
You need to stop the moodiness because he doesn't deserve your attitude right now. I know this is easier said than done because you don't believe in yourself at the moment and don't feel you have the capabilities to find employment outside the factory setting - but believe me, one day you will.

You must, however, also understand that the process of change is slow and you have to be central within that process if you are to reach the goals you have set for yourself. There will be struggles on your journey which will also bring with it more unhappiness, frustration, and resentment about how your life is panning out. There will be times when you lack the motivation and drive to change your circumstances because you feel powerless - but keep hope alive. - It is these moments of discomfort that will teach you the greatest lessons in life.

Believe me, you will tire of the "poor me" talk and also realise that your Father is absolutely drained by your constant moaning and blaming everyone and everything for your predicament. Listen to your Dad when he says you need to take responsibility for moving your life forward and believe him when he says your current job situation is only a means to an end and not necessarily your job for life. He's also right when he says that, "At least you have a job and you are earning money and that is a positive thing."
 On life's journey you will still face knock backs and

rejections. Please don't despair when this happens - because it will - just hang on in there because the break you are hoping for will eventually happen. Accept that your life will not always be perfect and don't be defeated by any future challenges and problems that you'll face in life and always seek help and support when you need it, because you won't have all the answers or solutions and that's fine - others just might.

Be realistic about your goals and expectations, stay focused and work hard but remember life and achievements are a gradual climb and there is no rush to get there. Importantly, education and knowledge are precious commodities so value them both because they will open your mind to things you would never otherwise have known.

When you do get the right breaks and opportunities, grab them with both hands and don't let go. You are without doubt unknowingly privileged and one day you will realise that your father's investment of love, care, support, and warmth shaped you, and that the safe and secure environment he and the community provided for you is what will make all the difference. This cannot be taught in schools.

It's unlikely you will receive any financial inheritance from your Dad however, your emotional inheritance will be akin to being a billionaire, and you, and your friends from the estate will bask in the wealth of that emotional inheritance for life. They will also be your friends for life.

Finally, don't compare yourself to others or their achievements, because like them - you are unique.

******

CHAPTER NINE

'Leaving school'

Before leaving school, we were all offered career guidance by some well-meaning professionals who came into the school to try and point us in the right direction. It was patently obvious that my particular advisor had not spoken to the teacher, Mrs. Blackman, and tapped into the fact that I was an expert on Tutankhamen and therefore destined to be an archaeologist, excavating tombs in Egypt's Valley of the Kings. Neither did she seem particularly interested in the fact that I'd been in the top form throughout my senior education, top of the class in French every year and in the top 10 overall for most subjects. Descriptions such as 'bright,' 'attentive,' 'academically promising,' and 'good scholar,' were littered across my school reports, had she cared to read them, but depressingly there seemed to be a distinct lack of paperwork on her table. Maybe she only focused on the subjects with comments like, 'could do better,' or 'needs constant encouragement and supervision,' or, in the case of Physics, 'lacks any interest altogether.'

My Dad had made a point of attending all the parents' evenings and rewarded me handsomely for good school reports. Like me, he had high hopes for my future employment prospects. Sadly, the school's Careers Adviser didn't offer me the opportunity of a lifetime but did have some suggestions. Well, two to be precise as she metaphorically 'gave me the middle finger.' The options on offer were the Army or a factory labourer. Clearly not being happy with either option and being a child with a need to know the whys and wherefores of everything, I questioned the lack of them.

However, my protests were ignored and there was nothing more to discuss; it was going to be the factory option. There were a lot of choices about which factory I could work in and apparently I was one of the lucky ones as many were short of labourers. The choices were endless. I could work as a labourer in the dye works, rubber works, spring works, cotton, or wool factories or, if I were really lucky, the Asbestos factory. It was as clear-cut as that. I would end my job as a paperboy on Friday and by the following Monday I would be clocking on as a Labourer at the Asbestos plant with no time to experience a life of leisure between school and work...as if that was ever going to happen!

The education 'Ladder of opportunity' and any thoughts about social mobility had come to a grinding halt. Maybe I had ideas way above my station, as the saying goes. It was all very confusing to say the least because the environment in which I had been raised made me imagine that the world was my oyster once I left school. Like most of my friends on the estate, we were confident, articulate, streetwise, educated and we certainly didn't lack self-esteem. Crucially, though, we did lack formal educational qualifications which meant, presumably, myself and many others were classed as not being good enough for any other work opportunities.

It was the rude awakening our parents warned us about. Untapping the potential of working-class children was certainly not the buzz word of the time and any hopes and aspirations we may have had quickly evaporated during my long walk home that evening. Feeling embittered and angry with the occasional bout of crying, my Father didn't utter any profound encouragement such as, "Your revenge is to be successful one day son," but what he did say was, "F**k 'em son, you're going to be all right, your Dad'll see to that."

I didn't hold out much hope for Christine the girl behind me in the Careers Advisor's queue either. While awaiting her turn, she was gripping her recorder and practicing 'Three Blind Mice,' no doubt hoping to impress. She didn't succeed and went on to choose the Cotton Mill.

My first day at work was memorable, not least because it felt like the longest and most exhausting day of my life. It was certainly the huge wake-up call I had long been promised. After arriving at the Personnel Department, I was greeted by a nice lady who asked me to sign a few pieces of paper and hey presto, I was introduced to Mick, my Supervisor and mentor. Within hours I had grasped the basics of the job, which was moving various forms of Asbestos in huge trollies around the factory. The weaving and spinning sheds needed a constant supply of the material because those machines never stopped and needed feeding throughout my eight-hour shift.

I knew instinctively on my first day on the job that it wasn't for me but, on a more positive note, I was earning a wage and on top of that the banter within the sheds was amazing. There were lots of familiar faces around the factory, including many family members, and once I had mastered the routes and the wonky wheels on the trolley, there was always time to sit around and have a laugh with everyone. More importantly, I was earning enough money to pay my way, with enough left over to be able to socialise with my friends at the weekend - which usually involved underage drinking at most of the pubs in Rochdale town centre.

I could also catch up with my brother Warran, who had now left home and was living independently. I missed him enormously but was pleased that his car mechanic apprenticeship was going well and that he was enjoying a life travelling up and down the country and driving stock cars with his boss.

Barbara was now living with us full-time and, although she could never replace my brother, we bonded as if we were true biological siblings - not least in our dislike of her Mother. Coincidentally, she was also working at the Asbestos factory with me.

Months passed by and Dad kept using his usual rhetoric about the job being a means to an end every time I mentioned how much I disliked it. But to what end was the question I wanted answering. Don't get me wrong, factory work was important but working in the Asbestos factory just wasn't for me. My biggest fear was getting trapped there for life like many of the men I was working with, including my Father.

Eight hours can be a long day when you're not happy at work and I dreaded the request to work overtime.
However despite my point blank refusals to work it, I somehow or other worked every hour on offer. As soon as my Dad heard of my refusal or in his words 'bone idleness' there was definitely 'trouble at mill.'

He'd seek me out like a heat seeking missile and I'd receive the usual lecture, "Money doesn't grow on trees lad, you need money to keep a roof over your head, food in your stomach and hard work never hurt anyone," and then to my supervisor, put him down for overtime Mick.
I'd stand in shocked silence giving him my death stare, but to no avail, as he'd just smile and say " Whats with the face - it'll stay like that one day lad" and then "I'll put extra sandwiches in your lunch box tomorrow.
In retaliation when I get home I would discreetly seek out his newspapers and finish his crossword puzzle.

"Hey, smart arse, how many times have I told you not to touch my crossword!" "I know Dad, but how many times have I told you about the factory and overtime but apparently we can't always have everything we want in life, or so I'm told." " Thats enough smart arse" would be usual response" to end that conversation.

I could sense his disappointment that I'd followed in his footsteps. For months he encouraged me to apply for apprenticeships, but I didn't because the only ones I was aware of were at the Butchers and the Undertakers, both valuable jobs but just not for me. It didn't take long before I had that feeling of having no purpose in life and being stuck in a rut, questioning myself and underestimating my capabilities of finding employment outside the factory setting. I had dreams of a career helping people, possibly in social work, and even though I'd expressed those ideas to Dad, we both knew that without formal qualifications it was going to prove difficult, if not impossible. By then I had developed a burning resentment towards the education system that I believed had failed me by not affording me the opportunity to gain formal qualifications before leaving school.

It wasn't going to be a level playing field when it came down to job and career opportunities and that irked me enormously and I would dwell on it often. I would dread the walk to the factory work each morning, as did Barbara, but then she did see it as being a means to an end working there because she had a plan. She'd reached the momentous decision to elope to Gretna Green in Scotland to get married.

That was mind-blowing for me because Mrs. Jackson was going to lose the plot should that happen, but Barbara was hell-bent and determined. Barbara's being headstrong and her Mother expecting unquestioning obedience from all children was always a volatile situation anyway, but for this particular plan we were going to need a bomb disposal team.

For 18 months she'd been in a relationship with a musician named Dave. She was head over heels in love and would ride pillion on his motorbike at any given opportunity. With guitar strapped to her back she would go to all his gigs when he performed across the north-west. In short, they were inseparable. Her Mother on the other hand did everything in her power to separate them.

Dave was never allowed into our house, or anywhere near it for that matter, because according to Mrs, Jackson, "He was a bad un!" She disapproved vehemently of Barbara's choice of boyfriend and on the occasions when she found out that they were seeing each other, all hell would break loose in the house, with Barbara grounded for weeks on end. On these occasions, yours truly was the messenger boy between Barbara and Dave because I thought he was cool. He didn't have a 9 to 5 job with a guaranteed pension and gold watch after 50 years' service, but he loved his music and being a musician. In Mrs. Jackson's eyes, however, he was a waster, bone idle and not good enough for her daughter - but more importantly, not good enough to be her son-in-law.

Dave was neither a criminal, dangerous nor age-inappropriate, but one of his downfalls was not being afraid to speak his mind to Barbara's Mother, particularly when she hurtled abuse at him. In the early days of their relationship, the arguments between Dave and Mrs. Jackson were monumental and on several occasions escalated to him being physically attacked by her and sustaining injuries.

Barbara had considered all her options before making the decision to elope; she was definitely not prepared to wait several years for parental consent so that she could marry the man of her choice. Nor was she prepared for her Mother to choose the man she should marry. She felt that the only option open to her was to elope to Gretna Green where they could marry legally without her Mother's consent. With her mind made up, the plan to elope was hatched.

Over the preceding weeks, Barbara would start removing clothes and belongings discreetly from our house until, once all her plans were in place, they were ready to leave. As we both walked to work on the day of the elopement, she was met at the bottom of the road by Dave so that they would have at least eight hours' start before anyone found out they had gone. I had no worries for Barbara as I waved her off because she was her own person and once she'd made her mind up to do something it was done. She was also an intelligent, kind and a beautiful person, inside and out, and eminently sensible – I loved her. I was so excited as I waved them off that day, but equally heartbroken because I had no idea if I would ever see her again.

"Where is she?" I heard that phrase several times that evening but didn't respond, despite the fact it was an open question. By then Mrs. Jackson and I had developed an unspoken mutual agreement of not saying much to each other. A similar agreement had also been reached by most of my Aunts and Uncles with Brenda. The evening went on and curtains were being drawn back every time a bus arrived at the terminus, but there was still no sign of

Barbara. Her Mother was getting more and more agitated about what she was going to do to her daughter when she finally got home. The one thing she was convinced of - and yet didn't really know how - was that I was definitely somehow involved.

The last bus arrived at the terminus at 11.05 pm with still no sign of Barbara, so it was coat on for Mrs. Jackson and off to Dave's parents to 'skull drag' Barbara out of their house. Within the hour she was back. With my best game face on, I asked if she'd located Barbara. With spittle hitting my face from several metres away she told me that she had. Dave's parents had been fully aware of the plan to elope and they shared their joy with Mrs. Jackson when she arrived at their door. I said nothing and left the living room for the sanctuary of my bedroom. The volume of Mrs. Jackson's furious voice from downstairs permeated through every room in the house.

The following morning, PC George was downstairs taking notes and promising not to leave any stone unturned to find Barbara. He occasionally sneered at me and I smiled back at him, but within the hour Dad and Mrs. Jackson were heading for Gretna Green, hoping to stop proceedings before they obtained a marriage licence.

In just 48 hours Barbara was tracked down and brought home while Dave was left stranded in Scotland. It was bedlam in our house the evening Barbara arrived home. She and I were forbidden from speaking to each other as we were, "As thick as thieves!" according to Mrs. Jackson and a disgrace to the family we had brought so much shame upon. We obviously didn't see it that way and just left our catch-up chat until the morning on our walk to work, gaining light relief by giving Mrs. Jackson the two-finger salute behind her back at any given opportunity.

One thing was clear though, Barbara would marry Dave with or without her Mother's consent – and that's
precisely what she did. Just a year later she married Dave, with Warran and I as her ushers. Our Dad gave her away but her Mother never conceded and continued with her hatred towards her now son-in-law, which at times was unrelenting, especially behind closed doors. My sister had found her husband but all her Mother wanted was to lose her son-in-law as quickly as possible. There was to be no compromise. Barbara loved Dave but her Mother, without any logical reason other than that she disliked the fact he was a musician who spoke his mind, literally hated him.

******

CHAPTER TEN

'The Army'

Working at the Asbestos factory was finally taking its toll on me and I genuinely could not muster any enthusiasm for the work. Routinely I would wait for Dad to come home from the pub and have that never-ending chat with him about what I was going to do with my life. On one of those evenings, he came up with the suggestion of joining the Army, "Because at least you'll get a trade, son." I pondered on that for several days. Warran was not of the same opinion as Dad and thought I was a pillock for even considering it, but I was certainly giving it serious thought.

Later, Dad and I went off to the Army Recruiting Office in Manchester and it genuinely did seem like the better option as, apparently, I would get to see the world. Pictures of soldier's water skiing particularly whetted my appetite. Before I knew it, I'd signed the necessary paperwork and we left the Recruiting Office with my start date to join the Junior Tradesmen's Regiment, based at Dundonald Camp in Troon, Scotland. Dad and I just needed to have one more chat before I joined the Army in three-months' time, a chat he was definitely not ready for - or maybe he was.

He finally arrived home that night and, once again, I was waiting for him. He immediately sensed that I was nervous, a clear sign that something was amiss:

"Whats with the face" - "What have you done now?"

"Nowt."

"Penny for your thoughts then, Lad."

"You don't want them."

"I do."

"I'm gay."

I didn't receive a huge reaction from Dad, which I assumed was because I was using the word 'gay' instead of 'homo,' which was the more common parlance for homosexuals in our neighbourhood. There was, however, the usual intensity beaming from his eyes which meant he was listening, while at the same time mentally preparing to interrogate me further, which duly followed. To be fair, I really didn't have much more to say to him after my big announcement and I certainly hadn't planned any responses for the interrogation. Other than my sexuality had not been influenced by anything I had listened to on my transistor radio.

It didn't take any strength or courage on my part to tell him because I knew that no matter what my sexuality was, he would never abandon me or stop loving me. There did, however, follow 30-minutes of searching discussion as he played detective, trying to find out exactly why I had made my disclosure. He finally felt comfortable that I hadn't just told him to avoid joining the Army and he adjourned our meeting until the next day, concluding, "I don't have a problem with it son, but it's not bloody great either!" As he walked away shaking his head he could be heard muttering, "Bloody hell fire Our Graham, what's next with you lad!"

The following evening and before Mrs. Jackson arrived home, we stumbled clumsily into our follow-up conversation in the living room. Dad may not have had a problem with me being gay but he did have a problem with people wanting to physically harm me. He and I had already absorbed sufficient information from the mainstream media to realise that they portrayed homosexuality in negative terms at every opportunity. It was viewed by many as being wrong, sinful, a crime and even a mental illness. The sad reality was that homophobia was rife in the 1960s and my being attacked because of my sexuality was a distinct possibility — and my Father's worst fear. That's what he'd meant by it, "Not being great." My Dad was not naive in such matters and he, and indeed everyone around me, knew about the violence perpetrated towards gay men at the time, violence that was driven by hatred and that sadly went largely unreported and, therefore, without any consequences for the perpetrators. Shamefully, it was allowed to continue unabated and unchecked.

There were several uncomfortable silences between us during the rest of that evening and later on I spotted him from my bedroom window, sitting alone on the steps at the bottom of the path. He was motionless, just staring into the distance, chain smoking and occasionally burying his head in his hands.
Instinctively, I knew something was wrong and that he was upset. After about 30 minutes I quickly descended the stairs and sat beside him. He turned towards me and spontaneously I just hugged him tightly. It was obvious that he was upset and he hugged me back even more tightly, declaring that he, "Didn't give a f**k about [me] being gay," but asking me to promise one thing.

My promise to him that evening was that I'd tell him if anyone ever dared threaten or actually physically harm me because, if they did, he would, "Swing for them." Then

117

came the request. He practically pleaded with me not to join the Army. In his opinion, my announcement changed everything. On the one hand he didn't want to wrap me in cotton wool but, on the other, he worried about the safety of his 16-year-old gay son living miles away from home and without his protection. He took no comfort from my assurances that I could look after myself, but he also knew that once my mind had been made up, I would be going. I had to go and seek out this opportunity, and to be honest, neither one of us could face another year of my tantrums and outbursts about working in the factory. It would also put an end to my underage pub crawls at the weekend and I could finally rest my angry face. My Dad would also benefit from less lip, door slamming, sulking, whining and my death stares.

The following morning I caught the bus to work and sat upstairs with a friend from school, who also worked at the factory. I was eager to tell her news of my future Army career, but she was clearly not interested. She was, however, more than intrigued to find out when I first knew I was gay. Once I'd recovered from the shock that she already knew and wondering how, she then proceeded to tell me that my Father, in his wisdom, had informed the whole of the pub's darts team the previous night — and anyone else in the pub within listening distance, including my friend's Dad — that I was gay. I later learned he had said something along the lines of, "Our Graham came home with a belter tonight. He's gay now!"

Apparently there was much merriment and amusement amongst the Tap Room men and it didn't take long for the news to spread to both the Snug and Entertainment Room, where all the ladies would be assembled waiting to be entertained by that night's 'turn.' Surprisingly, it seemed no-one was particularly fazed by the revelation.

Thinking back, I shouldn't have been surprised by the reaction. The council estate had a close-knit community and the people living there all made sure they looked after each other. It was that tradition that made working-class people strive and work together, regardless of their background, race, sexuality, or religion. Yes, I may have been gay, but I was their gay and as such was afforded their love and protection. The alternative of course was that they didn't believe me and thought I'd said it merely to garner attention in some way. Whatever the reason, from that point onwards I continued to live my life openly and honestly until departing for the Army - though in no way living a 'gay lifestyle,' whatever that was.

I had no idea where 'gays' lived anyway. I had read that there were a few in London and maybe, just maybe, there might be one or two in Scotland, because that's where I was heading, but first I had to speak to Warran about the 'gay thing.' His response was typical, "I know - and so does everyone on the bloody estate." Clearly Dad's big announcement had spread far and wide and had taken less than 72 hours to do so. Warran wasn't fazed either but he did assign one of his friends, 'Sunshine' as my protector should he not be around when I was socialising in town.

My sexuality was rarely discussed again but at least I'd had the opportunity to lessen my burden by getting it off my chest and had also ensured that, at the very least, my Father was fully in the picture. My impending departure to join the Army was also rarely discussed but, on the day he took me to the railway station to catch the train to Scotland, he spoke of nothing else. He really didn't want me to go. There was a moment as I sat on the train looking at my Dad wringing his hands and attempting to smile when I could have changed my mind, but it quickly passed and soon after he was waving me goodbye as the train pulled out of the station. As the train departed, I opened his present and card:

'Keep warm my beautiful son, it's cold in Scotland.

Love, Your Dad.'

I cried buckets while staring out of the window, wearing my present - a new ear-flap hat.

—

To say Dundonald Camp was a shock to the system would be an understatement. On my arrival the first thing that I noticed was the distinct lack of any lake for water skiing! God knows how many times I would subsequently ask myself, "What is the point of this?" This was not going to be like the Boy Scouts that was for sure.

There followed months of basic military training, learning how to handle and shoot weapons, and physical training, which primarily involved running cross-country while wearing a backpack and marching to the sound of a bellicose Drill Sergeant roaring "Left, right, left, right, mark time, get those knees shoulder high, lad!" If I wasn't doing that, I would be applying spit and polish to my boots to make them shine (known as 'bulling') and learning how to fold my clothing and make my bed using an ancient tortuous military technique referred to as 'boxing blankets.' Our efforts were subsequently inspected and then destroyed by the Platoon Sergeant for various minor and insignificant infringements of the rules. On some occasions, we would find ourselves marching around the parade square at 4 am wearing pyjamas, boots, and heavy greatcoats, just because someone in the Platoon had committed a minor transgression the previous day.
After that, of course, came even more training.

Vital subjects such as how to survive under arduous conditions. We would set up camp on some desolate moorland, sleeping outside in sleeping bags and having to wash and shave in freezing rivers. The Permanent Staff had cunningly devised tests such as spinning us around on a block and tackle strung high up above a ravine, tests that came under the remit of 'External Leadership Training' and 'Confidence Building' - but with no sign of learning a trade. To me it just felt like mindless punishment. There was, however, some respite as fortunately I excelled at hockey and playing in the hockey team and taking part in practice got me away from some of the horrors of basic training. Boxing was also another sport that would get you out of some elements of basic training. Luckily, I was also good at that, despite not having boxed previously. Boxing was entirely different to street fighting, where you got someone in a headlock, threw them to the ground, then sat on their chest asking them threateningly whether they gave in.

My whole military experience lasted nine months before reason intervened and Dad purchased my discharge — or 'Buying [me] out.' You pay to learn. I left Troon with a deep sense of relief. I knew, as did the Army, that there wasn't a Field Marshal's baton tucked away in Stanier's rucksack and I was relieved to return home, catch my breath and have a rethink about the way forward. The 'only gay on the estate' was back and the way ahead, as far as I could see then, was the factory. Mrs. Jackson's disappointment that I was back was palpable but Dad's name was on the rent book. It was my home and he wanted me there. To say I was the only gay on the estate was something of an assumption on my part but there was no way I was going to carry out a local survey in order to check out that particular fact.

The following week saw the hard work and repetition start again as Dad found me a job at the print works and I was back in the daily routine of clocking on and giving my Dad the 'poor me' speech every day. I can't remember how many jobs I had over such a short space of time in textile factories, but there were a lot of them. I was never unemployed - there was no way Dad would allow me not to have a job - but I did unofficially start working part-time.

I'd take a couple of days off every week and, while this impacted enormously on my take-home pay, I was coping better with my reduced hours.However, it definitely didn't solve my problems and the arrangement ended abruptly when Dad unexpectedly returned home one day while I was supposedly meant to be working. He caught me napping on the sofa following my sumptuous lunch of potted meat sandwiches on thin sliced white from my lunch box.

Secrets were hard to keep on the estate and of course someone had told him about my self-imposed part-time work schedule. He instructed me to, "Get your coat on now!" and then frog-marched me down the road in silence until, finally, we ended up on a building site. He asked whether Joe was around, to which Joe obediently appeared in his hobnailed boots - covered in cement dust - and from that moment onwards I was officially working on a building site as a labourer. But at least it was summer. It wasn't a baptism of fire either because most of the people working on the building site I knew from the estate.
It was banter all day long and I'm sure Dad lived in the hope that one day I was going to come home and say I want to be either a plasterer, carpenter, electrician, or builder. That didn't happen but I wasn't moaning either because I loved working there.

Most of the day I was driving the dumper truck, transporting building materials around the site while also utilising it at lunchtimes to go and collect everyone's lunch. I could go missing for hours collecting their food but waiting around for the sandwiches to be made was the worst part. Not just because the guy took ages to make them in the kitchen of his end-of-terrace house but because, on a busy day, there was always a long queue. He was also quite deluded about how amusing and witty he was and never ceased in his attempts to entertain anyone waiting in the queue who was willing to listen. "Oh, nancy boy's arrived," was his usual greeting to me, which even his most loyal audience tired of after a while. But this didn't put him off and so each sandwich he handed me was accompanied by one comment or another, "There you go, nancy boy," or, "Where's your handbag?" I didn't ask him to stop because I knew that wouldn't have achieved anything but I did seek revenge by insisting he made several sandwiches twice as he'd put brown sauce on a bacon butty instead of red. My mistake, but his loss.

There did come one day, however, when he didn't address me as 'nancy boy' and on that particular day, I couldn't help but notice he looked slightly under the weather. His nose was bruised and swollen and his nostrils packed with ribbon gauze, topped off with a moustache dressing across his top lip. Concerned, I asked if he'd been in the wars but he didn't reply. Instead I was met with glaring eye contact and absolute silence, which I put down to him feeling pain and discomfort. But as I was leaving the kitchen, he suddenly asked, "Did you tell Tony the Plasterer I called you nancy boy?" I replied, "Not to my knowledge." Nonetheless, he didn't call me nancy boy again after that. I never did find out why he looked under the weather that day and nor did I ever question Tony.

123

Occasionally I would do some labouring on the building site, but not very often because if, I had any spare time, I would be making brews for everybody. The men on the building site had also worked out pretty quickly that I wasn't compatible with hard manual labour and that hod-carrying was never going to be my forté. Then the reality of working on a building site in winter set in and, along with it, my determination to make some changes because, no matter how many times I pulled out the 'poor me' act, nothing ever changed, even if Dad did continue to listen patiently anyway.

Finally, there came the kitchen table meeting-of-all-meetings, when Dad agreed I could go back into education and study part-time. And so, on my way to get the lunches one day, I parked the dumper truck outside the college and picked up the paperwork I needed to enrol for GCE O-Level courses. The only setback was that I would have to continue working because I needed money to survive. But I wasn't the only one, as my sister, Barbara, was now living on the breadline.

******

CHAPTER ELEVEN

'The opportunity'

Having arranged to meet Barbara on a Saturday morning, my news about college quickly paled into insignificance when she told me her plans for the future. As we sat in the café sharing cuddles with her beautiful new baby daughter, she revealed her decision to emigrate and start a new life in Australia. My first reaction was to question the excessive lengths she would go to escape her controlling and interfering Mother but, as always, her mind was made up and her plan was already in place, her husband Dave having already left for Australia that morning.

They were not alone in their move as at that particular time Australia was perceived by many to be the land of opportunity and prosperity - and because the Australian and British governments were subsidising the Emigration Scheme at a cost of £10 per person (Ten Pounds 'Pom'), including accommodation in a migrant hostel on arrival, it was also affordable.

But rather than jumping straight on a plane at the first chance like thousands of others in the UK, Dave and Barbara had decided on a more cautious plan, with Dave going first and Barbara and the baby following once he was settled in employment and had found a house for them all to live in. All she needed to do now was let her Mother know, hence our meeting. Having all the right answers ready for the inevitable questions that would be fired at her was vital. We also had to pre-empt her Mother's inevitable demand that she move back home.

We planned meticulously for the meeting so that when the moving-back-home discussion did inevitably come up, we countered it well. I had already agreed to move into Barbara's home and together we could just about pay the rent and cover any overheads. Needless to say, I didn't pack my college application papers the day I left Dad's house to move in with her. They had to go on the back burner along with my hopes and dreams for a while, or until such time as the letter from Dave arrived and Barbara was safely on her way to join him in Australia.

Spring arrived and so did Dad and Mrs. Jackson with our much-needed weekly provisions. We sat down at the kitchen table for the usual debrief and the occasional vociferous outbursts from Mrs. Jackson about 'Dave the Waster,' how he had buggered off leaving Barbara and the baby and how Barbara would never see him again. I suspect that Mrs. Jackson was secretly hoping and praying that that would be the case, but sadly for her it was not to be because Barbara had more news for her.

Dave had been in touch and had given Barbara the go-ahead to travel out and join him in Australia. It was another opportunity for Mrs. Jackson to vent her spleen but Dad and I left them both to it and went into the living room because he had something he wanted to show me. He had circled an advert in the Rochdale Observer and asked me to read it because, he said, "It's got your name written all over it lad!" The local hospital was recruiting for Student Nurses for which applicants needed three GCE O-Levels to apply. However, it also highlighted in italics that there was an opportunity to sit a Nurse Entrants Examination should you not have the required qualifications.

I read the advert over and over again, thinking each time that I'd got it wrong and the bit in italics would somehow disappear, but no, there it was right in front of my eyes, the opportunity I'd been waiting for. The weekend couldn't end soon enough because I was desperate to 'phone and ask for an application form, even then still worrying that I had read the job description incorrectly. It turned out what they were actually offering was effectively an apprenticeship in Nursing. Within the week I was contacted by the School of Nursing with an appointment for an interview, which would be followed by the entrance examination.

I didn't feel particularly confident as I boarded the bus on the morning of the exam. I wasn't overwhelmed by nerves either, but I did have a fear of the unknown, particularly as I had no idea what the exam would be about. I sat nervously outside a room in the School of Nursing with a group of other interviewees until my name was called and the interview commenced.

The interview panel was made up of three daunting women sitting in a row in front of me wearing white coats, all of them Nursing Tutors. I knew immediately that this interview was going to be far harder than the entrance exam but I had to be honest with them and say I just wanted a career helping people. At the back of mind though, a little voice was saying, "Please don't ask me any questions on human biology because I know nothing." - It was not taught at my school. Thankfully, they didn't and after what seemed like a very long interview, I entered another room to sit my hour-long entrance exam.

Waiting to hear back from the hospital was excruciating and I checked the post twice a day for the next couple of weeks in the hope of receiving a letter to confirm whether I had been successful. Finally the all-important letter arrived and - success - the job was mine. I will never forget the mixture of joy, hope and happiness I felt that day. To say I was on cloud nine would be an understatement. My Dad was as cool as a cucumber when I called him, but I knew that he was over the moon for me as well.

The letter informed me that I could start in the next School of Nursing term in September, which was perfect timing as Barbara had also confirmed she and the baby would have left for Australia to start her new life by that time. I was beyond ecstatic on hearing the news and couldn't wait to start State Registered Nurse (SRN) training. I was also offered accommodation in the Nurses' Home so, at last, I could live independently.

Over the following weeks I felt a mixture of emotions - joy at having an amazing opportunity, but also moments of fear and doubt. I was also worried that everyone in the class would be much brighter and more intelligent than me, especially as most of the other students had been given a place through the formal qualification route. There was no sense of my being an imposter though and, for the most part, I really did believe I could be successful if I put the effort in. Fortunately I was also consciously aware of the occasional moments when self doubt would kick in and then have a serious word with myself.

On my first day, I arrived at the Nurses Home to be allocated my room for the next three years, which was situated in the male section on the first floor. It had a single bed, washbasin, wardrobe, a wall light and very little else. I was then given a guided tour of the home by the Warden, who proudly took me around all the facilities such as the mailboxes, shared bathroom, kitchen, lounges, pay-phone, and dining room. Then came the inevitable rules. No visitors unless they were signed-in by the Warden, no visitors allowed to visit your room and definitely no overnight visitors. The front door would be locked by 11 pm - after that time, access to the Nurses Home was only via the Night Sister. No cooking in the room, definitely no loud music and all shared areas had to be kept clean and tidy at all times.

That same afternoon, members of the new September intake were called to the School of Nursing to be informed about the training programme. At that point, looking around the room, my perception was that not many Student Nurses in the group would be able to identify themselves as council house children — maybe one or two others maximum. Oh well, onwards and upwards!

The SRN training programme was three years in total, very similar to an apprenticeship scheme. To start with, we would spend six weeks in the classroom studying anatomy, physiology, clinical & hospital procedures, hygiene and, importantly, hospital etiquette -Pre Training School. Then, for the next three years, we would undergo an intensive cycle of practical training on the wards under the guidance of a Clinical Tutor or the Ward Sister, followed by more segments of teaching and training. The following day it all became a reality. During my first six-week induction period in the classroom, I knew immediately that I had to get to grips with anatomy and physiology very quickly as most of the Student Nurses in my class had studied it at college, whereas my understanding of both topics was sadly lacking.

During my initial training, I burnt the midnight oil to ensure I was ready for the lectures the following day. Learning something new had never been a problem for me, in fact I loved it and I engaged with the same learning

process I had been taught at school, i.e. to read the study material once, put the book down and then summarise without looking back at the book. It's how I practiced remembering and recall. Sometimes the process had to be repeated, other times not - but it worked for me. If I was in a lecture, I engaged with a similar process, making copious notes then rewriting them in an abridged version and summarising without referring back to my notes.
Being prepared for the wards though, that was something else. Not only were there plenty of rules, more importantly, there were people to be very afraid of.

We were not allowed to address patients or colleagues informally when we were working on the wards and could only use their title and surname — and in the case of colleagues, often just their surnames. The Sisters and Assistant Matrons were to be feared and they expected exacting standards from everyone, enforcing rules and regulations rigidly to achieve those standards. Consultants and Matrons were seen as godlike figures to us Student Nurses - and in most cases behaved as if they were as well!

Despite the rules though, I loved it from the first moment I stepped on to the wards and I happily absorbed everything I was taught. It felt like I had been raised to be a carer and that role was deeply embedded within me. There was no limit to what I could learn. Surprisingly, I also retained most of the learning without difficulty. It was like my brain had suddenly kicked in and, before I knew it, I was in my second year, having successfully completed training in medicine, surgery, geriatrics, and paediatrics.

Any transient thoughts or doubts about my ability to compete with my peers had subsided after that first block of training, when it became apparent that those with formal entry qualifications were no brighter nor more intelligent than I was. The phrase 'educated at the university of life' now made more sense to me, as did the word 'compassion' because, for me, that was far more important. I was gradually becoming aware of the rewards of being a Nurse, not least the fact that I found the work to be very fulfilling on a personal level. I thought that I was genuinely making a difference to the lives of patients every day. I felt appreciated by them and that feeling was great.

As students, we also worked extremely hard on the wards, being constantly at the beck and call of patients, doctors, and ward sisters alike. Without doubt, we were the main workforce and the workload was very demanding. As a result, the blocks of training in Nursing School, where the emphasis was placed on education, were at times a welcome relief from the wards. I was constantly knackered and overdrawn at the bank every month, but I was loving every second of it. It certainly wasn't financially rewarding, but then that wasn't my priority. I was looking more for the opportunity to gain knowledge and qualify as a Nurse and then advance my nursing career. More importantly, I always kept at the back of my mind the thought of how extremely proud my Dad was going to be of me once I had qualified as a State Registered Nurse (SRN).

We were rotated around the wards regularly and with each secondment came fresh challenges, but there was always a deep sense of community between the Student Nurses, particularly those who lived in the Nurses Home. Every ward was different; some you looked forward to and others you didn't, particularly as there were a few permanent staff members on the wards who lived up to their reputations as ogres.

All of the wards had their own cleaners, porters, ward clerks and domestics — all of whom could console you if you were confronted by one of the ogres because they dealt with them on a daily basis. Nora, one of the ward cleaners, was often in trouble. She never did master the intricacies of the floor buffing machine and would be dragged along by it on numerous occasions, whooping like a cowgirl at a rodeo and frequently being told off for doing so. We all thought Nora's floor buffing was hysterical, but the Ward Sister clearly did not.

Getting a second stripe on my uniform was a nursing milestone and indicated that I had progressed both in my training and education. It facilitated more secondments to specialist wards such as orthopaedics, ENT (Ear Nose & Throat), A&E (Accident & Emergency), Theatre and Psychiatry. But it was also a milestone in other ways too, particularly because of my new neighbour in the Nurses Home.

All the windows on the ground floor of the home had blocks of wood attached to them to ensure they only opened a maximum of six inches. It was presented as a security measure but I'm certain it was primarily to prevent anyone climbing through them when they got home after the 11 pm curfew. A screwdriver was therefore just as essential to us as a stethoscope, as removing a pair of window blocks became a requisite for being able to go out for the evening. A visit to the Night Sister was out of the question, particularly if we arrived back in the early hours, drunk and dishevelled.

I would generally stick to the rules, but lapses became more frequent after my new neighbour arrived. He moved into the room opposite mine while I was working a late shift. On arrival back at the Nurses home at 9 pm, I was greeted by loud music sounding from his room and dirty plates, empty bottles and general litter piled up outside his door, which had a handwritten 'Do Not Disturb' sign attached to it. It sounded like a party was going on inside there – and he or someone else had clearly used the kitchen and bathroom as well, as both areas had been left in a similar mess.

After much deliberation about whether or not to confront him about the noise, the music suddenly stopped at about 11 pm, just before the Night Sister arrived to lock up. Happily, I was then able to settle down before my early shift in the morning. However, around midnight I was awoken by a knock on my door and, on opening it, came face to face with my new mystery neighbour, Henderson Western Karloff Clinton - or Hendy for short. He was wearing a stocking cap on his head and holding a pot of moisturiser in his hand, which he applied liberally to his face as he spoke to me. He asked me how to get out of the Nurses Home after midnight, because all the doors were locked. I explained that, as it was after the curfew, he needed to call the Night Sister using the 'phone situated next to his room, then I quickly closed the door and went back to bed.

Several minutes later I heard the sound of breaking glass outside my room. I opened the door to see what was going on, only to find the fire door wide open and the key that had previously hung behind safety glass now hanging freely and swinging on a chain. Hendy was stood on the fire escape, still holding the pot of moisturiser, waving someone off. He then turned to walk back to his room and, glancing in my direction as he walked past my door, said, "The Night Sister can kiss my black arse!" Mortified, I quickly closed my door - there was no way I wanted to be involved in the incident - but I went to bed smiling and thinking, "Things are about to change around here." The following morning as I left my room, the Warden and several Nurses were huddled around the open fire door debating the 'break in, break out.' I thought it wiser not to get involved and quickly ran down the stairs to grab breakfast before heading off to work.

There had been similar incidents previously during my stay in the Nurses Home and, much like the others, this one sounded like it was going to be blown way out of proportion. One such incident that was particularly memorable was the attempted murder inquiry when someone apparently tried to murder Jack, the Kitchen Porter. A butter knife did indeed fall from a first-floor window, narrowly missing Jack, who was having a sneaky cig outside the kitchens. It fell from the room of one of the Irish girls. It turned out that she'd thrown it out of sheer frustration because it was too blunt to cut her Christmas cake.

On that occasion, Matron had carried out a full 'attempted murder' inquiry, so the latest 'break-in' was not going to be any less dramatic. Sure enough, I was summoned to Matron's office later that day along with several others - including Hendy – and we trooped in there en masse. Matron was most concerned that the Nurses Home had been burgled the previous night and that valuable items of property and furniture could have been stolen from our rooms. Several notices had now been placed around the building advising people to check their personal belongings. They told us that something similar has happened before and on that occasion, due to the vigilance of the Night Sister and Warden, the burglars had actually been caught red-handed.

The culprits had managed to escape in a car, but apparently we could all have easily been murdered in our beds! "What a busy night," I thought - and all I'd seen was someone breaking the rules by having an overnight visitor and breaking the key glass. I knew to keep my mouth shut though because the last time someone broke the rules in that way, they got the sack - and I didn't want that to happen.

Later that evening, Hendy knocked on my door yet again, but this time he wanted to thank me for keeping quiet. I warned him that he needed to be a bit more careful because Matron did not take prisoners and the Wardens were excessively vigilant, reporting all that they saw and heard. He took my advice on board and over a cup of tea I introduced him to the method of removing the window blocks with a screwdriver. From that moment on we became firm friends and broke the rules together. The mystery person he was waving off from the fire escape that night turned out to be his boyfriend, who'd helped him move in earlier in the evening. Hendy was flamboyant and a breath of fresh air, with his engaging Bajan personality and endless energy. His love for life knew no bounds and when he partied he was always the centre of attention. He was already a qualified Nurse, having completed his Enrolled Nurse Training in London and was now joining my year group on a shortened training programme to qualify as a State Registered Nurse (SRN).

His wisdom knew no bounds, not just because of our seven-year age difference, but because of his lived experiences. He was to teach me so much about life, particularly his live and let live philosophy - that we should all live in the manner we want to, regardless of what others may think of us. He was my best friend and a magnet for other friends to join us and he educated me endlessly about civil rights and injustice and almost verbatim he could recite snippets of the famous MLK, "I have a dream," speech. I was to learn so much from him.

My Dad visited me often at the Nurses Home, bringing monthly food parcels which were important for my survival, and it wasn't long before he met Hendy either. It was not in the formal way I had anticipated but rather a much more dramatic one. As I sat with Dad in the first floor TV room, I started to hear Hendy shouting my name and demanding my attention. Within a matter of seconds he made a full theatrical entrance, looking resplendent in a short, blue dressing gown, hair braided in cornrow, covered with a stocking cap - moisturiser cream dotted around his face and clutching a crumpled scarlet jumpsuit.

He wanted to know if he could borrow my iron and, without even acknowledging my Father's presence other than with what appeared to be a small curtsey and some nervous laughter, he exited the room with my room key. A further explanation would definitely be required if my Dad were to recover fully from his shock, but there was no time to explain anything to him as Hendy soon returned.

This time he was wearing his skin-tight jumpsuit and asking both me and Dad for our approval of his evening wear - which could only be described as quite loud. I approved, but Dad was hesitant - and not just about the jump suit. Hendy calling me 'sister woman' was probably like a white noise inside my Dad's head and more than he could handle in one evening. Hendy eventually left, saying goodnight by blowing Dad a kiss and informing us that the corned beef and rice was ready to eat. All Dad could say was, "He's not catching the bus like that is he?" and, "What's corned beef and rice?" Dad soon found out what corned beef and rice was - and no, Hendy was not catching the bus.

I knew that no amount of reassurance would ever stop Dad worrying about me coming to physical harm because I was gay. The only way I could deal with it was to be economical with the truth and promise him that I was constantly vigilant of haters and keeping out of harm's way. It wasn't easy for him because he knew that pretending to be someone else or denying my sexuality just wouldn't be me. Actually, I truly liked being me and felt comfortable being gay. However, I was uncomfortable about having to be guarded and not be able to talk about something I felt at ease with. That's not to say I wasn't a people pleaser - naturally, I wanted people to like me - but I learned to accept that in life, not everybody would and that, importantly, I had no control over what others thought of me. It's a hard lesson to learn, but then I was raised in the school of hard knocks. The more valuable lesson is to go where love and kindness can be found.

The threat of physical violence was real and tough for both me and my Dad but I was determined never to believe the haters' view that being gay was intrinsically wrong. I would never experience the shame they wanted me to feel. Quite the opposite in fact. I felt only pride and happiness towards my sexuality and celebrated it at any given opportunity, much to the annoyance of those who wanted me to hate myself.

The biggest lesson I ever learned from Hendy was to find the strength within me to challenge prejudice and call people out when they made homophobic remarks — be it directly or indirectly. In that sense he was a good teacher but sometimes I found myself having to judge when it was appropriate to call them out. The night I was being hunted down by a group of drunken men while crossing the North Sea on a ferry to Denmark was not the right time. It was a serious threat as they were very determined in their quest to, "Throw the queers overboard!" To avoid our fate of drowning in the sea in complete darkness that night, my friends and I hurried back to the safety of our cabin where, to avoid detection, we sat as quietly as possible, only occasionally breaking the silence in whispers. The search party could still be heard loud and clear as they shouted out their profanities, calling us, "Fucking queers!" - but at least we were safe from being thrown overboard.

'
On spotting them in the dining room the following morning, we all expected an apology for their threatening behaviour the night before, but instead there was more verbal abuse. This time it was in hushed tones but still loud enough for us to hear. I didn't wish to talk to them about their hate but I was openly honest about what I thought of them, publicly and directly to their faces. Thankfully, the remainder of our trip to Denmark passed without incident, and we had a great time.

That incident and other near-miss experiences would never be shared with my Father, nor any of my family for that matter, because I didn't wish to burden them.
Instead, I constantly reassured Dad that I was safe and had a small group of friends that were both gay and straight living in the Nurses Home and that we all looked out for, and supported, each other. That part was entirely true and over a short period of time it became a much larger group of friends. Many were from the Caribbean and Ireland. Several were fierce dykes, but what we all had in common was our love for each other and of Aretha Franklin, James

Brown, Otis Redding, The Temptations, Isaac Hayes, Rufus Thomas, and anything Soul. Soul music was most definitely the soundtrack to our lives. We loved its sound and we played it, sang along with it, and danced to it at every opportunity. We could even relate to many of the lyrics because some of those words rang true in our own lives and even described situations that we could interpret as actually happening to us.

However, there was always going to be a group of haters to contend with, even in the Nurses Home. The best plan was for minorities and their allies to keep together and look out for each other and so that's what we did. We needed to be seen and couldn't afford to be afraid and with allies like the McNulty sisters, Madeline, Christine,Janet, Margo and Joan et al we could cope.

Dad continued to call me several times a week from pay phone to pay phone, just to check that I was OK, and we would also meet up once a week in Rochdale town centre for my driving lesson. There was no way that he could fund the driving lessons and so his contribution was bringing food parcels monthly to the Nurses Home instead. He even added two tins of corned beef, a packet of rice and a Bounty bar to the food parcel after meeting Hendy. Don't ask me why a Bounty bar, that was just my Dad. He had clearly formed a mental association with that chocolate bar, Barbados, sun-drenched beaches, and coconuts - much as he had done with pineapple chunks being eaten by Hawaiians for breakfast (deep fried, obviously).

Unbeknown to Dad though, I was socialising weekly in Manchester's gay scene and it was so exciting as all the clubs were, of necessity, exclusively secretive. It was like a hidden subculture in the back streets of the city, with our own meeting places and bonds of loyalty to each other. Entrance to the clubs could only be gained by introduction and through facial recognition by the Doorman as he peeped through a hatch in the door. The only setback was that we had to be very careful and cautious when entering and leaving so as not to draw any attention to the fact it was a gay club. Often, we'd sit in the car until we were sure the coast was clear, then make a dash for the club door. Later, when leaving, the Doorman would make sure all was clear for us and we'd dash back to the car again. It was important not to be complacent at any time because visibility could also bring danger. Some gay venues, however, were becoming more visible no matter how cautious we were.

That was never more obvious than the night we became trapped inside a venue that had a growing reputation as a gay club because a gang of drunken football fans had launched an attack on the premises using bricks. The club's blackened out windows on the ground floor were being smashed and the attackers were battering down the door shouting loud profanities. It was terrifying and I couldn't have felt more vulnerable knowing that we were locked inside the club with no escape, as people screamed hateful remarks at us through the smashed windows. Everyone in the club went up to the first floor to avoid the bricks and glass, but the hatred and bile being spewed out could still be clearly heard. Thankfully, no one was physically injured and the football fans eventually dispersed, boarding the coaches waiting to take them home. Nevertheless, it was a horrifying experience.

Those were the days when we didn't have security on the club doors and I didn't see the Police that particular night either, but who knows - they might have been inside the club, just not wearing uniform. Plain-clothes Police Officers came into the clubs and pubs regularly to perform their surveillance operations and harass us, so we were always wary of their presence. Despite their efforts to be covert, however, they stood out like sore thumbs and the coded message would quickly circulate that 'Lilly Law' was in.

We didn't behave any differently when socialising in the presence of the Police but we had to be very careful about men dancing too closely together (licentious dancing), which was often the case for the last dance of the night. The allegedly covert officers would slowly move towards the edge of dance floor to observe the final dance but, sadly for them, would often leave disappointed as they watched dykes and gay men smouldering together on the dance floor. 'Grab a Dyke' on the dance floor was standard on such occasions and helped the club survive one more night without the threat of being shut.

The drag queens on the other hand had a field day and would do their level best to make 'Lilly Law' feel uncomfortable. Often during their lip-synch performances, they would leave the stage and stand beside one of the officers, directing every song lyric at them. That announced the Police's presence to absolutely everyone in the club, particularly to those who hadn't received the coded message. The officers' embarrassment was profound, especially when a drag queen would let rip with a number like, "Kiss me, honey, honey, kiss me," directed at them, or end their performance with Dame Shirley Bassey's "This is my life," also sung directly to them. If they were feeling particularly daring, or in some cases just pissed, they would even ask the plain-clothes officer for the last dance.

Things could be much more intimidating outside the club, however. If the Police approached a large group of gay men embracing it would often result in them having their names and addresses taken and then being cautioned about their behaviour. If it were a more manageable group and particularly one involving feisty drag queens - it would result in them being arrested and transported to the police station, running the risk of them being charged with a Breach of the Peace. Drag queens were the ones most likely to be taken to the station because the Police could only have so many Dusty Springfield's, Shirley Bassey's and Dorothy Squire's on their list when asking for names and addresses. In the case of the all white drag act 'The Mimer Birds' Diana Ross or any principal member of the Supremes was never the best choice of name to offer up.

Everyone gave a false name and address if possible, but not knowing what the Police might do with this information was a huge worry. Disclosing my name and address to them would immediately identify me as being a Nurse and also raise the possibility of them contacting the hospital, which could have a major derogatory impact on my career, particularly if I were to be charged with causing a Breach of the Peace. Fortunately, this never happened but the repercussions would have been most serious. Having a police record could ultimately have ended my nurse training programme and resulted in my dismissal. I frequently gave the Police my well-rehearsed false name and address, which was word perfect. And it had to be, because the idea of running away from the Police in four-inch platform shoes and flared trousers was unthinkable!
That said, there were certainly occasions when we had to run for our lives in those platform shoes - and had there been Olympic medals awarded for it, we would have been on every podium claiming gold. Over the years we must

have run miles to avoid queer bashers and, fortunately, on most occasions we outran them. Their verbal abuse would often start long before any potential face-to-face encounters, which was handy because it gave us the opportunity to hitch up our flares before running so as to avoid tripping on the start line. The silent haters were more concerning as there was no prior warning, it just happened. Undoubtedly the gays won the word count in the exchange of insults during these confrontations but not always the fight and, if push came to shove, platform shoes were quickly removed and used to defend oneself.

Verbal abuse was common when walking the streets and the rule of thumb was always to avoid confrontation with the mindless haters at all costs - if only to escape physical injury - and pay no attention to the abuse being hurled from a distance. But when it came to face-to-face confrontations we stood our ground and, if hands were laid on us, we would fight back with every ounce of strength we had. We much preferred the verbal abuse to be hurled at us from a distance and preferably from moving vehicles (as long as they didn't stop). At least on these occasions we could avoid a fight and turn up at a club looking half decent. On the nights when we couldn't avoid the fight, we arrived looking decidedly disheveled - or in the words of the sisterhood that awaited our arrival, "Girl, you look like the wreck of the Hesperus - what happened?!" Once our ripped attire, shoddy appearance and breathlessness was explained, benevolent club owners would provide brandy free of charge and the sisterhood went into impromptu caring mode. We were a family, a community and we protected each other fiercely and we were bang on trend with our pronouns She/Her. However, we didn't identify as female.

There was safety in the clubs but they were clearly being targeted by the Police and it felt like they'd been instructed to look for any excuse not only to harass and arrest gay men, but to shut down the clubs too.

Undeterred and choosing not to accept the haters or the oppressive attitude of the 'Boys in Blue,' we continued to be visible, albeit with carefully designed safeguards in place to protect ourselves. Regrettably, the aggressive manner in which we were being pursued by the Police, continued for years. Substantial amounts of the force's resources and money must have been expended on the surveillance and harassment of gay men.

Weekends in Manchester were still fun though and I looked forward to them when I wasn't working nights at the hospital. I would practically stagger off duty most mornings after a 12-hour night shift and could never get into the routine of sleeping during the day. Night duty was arduous work and, on most shifts, the ward was only staffed by a single trained nurse or, in my case, a Senior Student Nurse, plus an Auxiliary Nurse. Often it was just the two of you looking after 24 to 30 patients. If you were lucky you might have a 'Runner Nurse' galloping between wards to help you out during busy times. There was also the constant presence of the Night Sister or Nursing Officer throughout the night who would pop in unannounced to check that all was well, supervise the drug round and check that we weren't sleeping. As if we had a chance!

Most night duty shifts in my second and third year of training were on male medicine, not my preferred choice as I much preferred the surgical wards. I absolutely knew I would be working on Roche 3 ward, the busiest on the medical block, especially at night. It was the Night Nursing Officer who had rota'd me to work on Roche 3. My relationship with her started off reasonably well but then after only a few weeks suddenly went south. I had no idea why until one morning a grinning Hendy eagerly awaited my arrival in the breakfast room to tell me.

Apparently, I was a rude young man with no manners or respect and terribly common. I was certainly common as I lacked any significant status within society generally and I 'owned that' status, but the rest came as a bit of a shock until Hendy enlightened me. Through tears of laughter, he told me the gossip circulating of an incident that had occurred between me and the Night Nursing Officer several weeks earlier. It had been embellished massively and bore no resemblance to the actual truth, but as it led to me being perceived as a bit of a hero, I didn't correct it either. I remembered the incident quite clearly but didn't recognise the context in which it was being delivered. The word going round was that there had been a huge confrontation between myself and the Night Nursing Officer, during which I had wished her dead. What actually happened was that she'd informed me about her holiday to Naples that summer and I'd replied, "Oh, see Naples and die."

I could see where her misinterpretation might have come from but all I was doing was repeating a commonly used phrase about Naples, meaning that the Italian city was so beautiful, it was a place you must see before you die. She clearly hadn't understood it that way, concluded that I'd wished her dead and then shared her version of our conversation - and my impudence - with others.

She wasn't exactly a chatty person and was ever so slightly self-absorbed, so at the time, I thought our Naples conversation had been a huge success. It was certainly an improvement on prior ones we'd had about her magnificent dinner parties and courgette recipes.

They never did interest me but I was always attentive and engaged throughout them, even during times when I felt like I was dying on the inside, which often happened halfway through her giving me her detailed courgette boat recipe*. According to her, her courgette recipes were always a big hit — and topic of conversation - with her dinner party guests. She may have been the envy of many but not me I'm afraid and, sadly, we were never to fully recover from our little Naples contretemps.

- *For any 'courgette aficionados' out there, apparently you halve a courgette, scoop out the pulp and fill the scooped-out hole with tomatoes and stuff, then wrap it in foil and bake it in the oven.*

As we all assembled in Turner Hall to await our ward allocation it was a racing certainty I'd hear her bellow, "Stanier - Roche 3 Ward!" punctuating her announcement with a menacing glare in my direction. My allocation didn't bother me that much but it delighted the other Night Nurses who were sat waiting and watching for the moment she executed her act of revenge on the impudent one. As soon as the words left her mouth, you could hear ripples of laughter around the room and all eyes were on me as I thanked her and met her glare with a beaming smile. She knew that I preferred surgery but what she didn't know was that Roche 3 was actually my preferred choice for night shifts on medicine. I genuinely didn't mind working on the ward because it was always busy and the shift went by so quickly. It was the usual Nightingale Ward of about 30 beds, occupied by men with various medical conditions. But it was also the intake ward for suicide attempts by drug overdoses, which kept me busy most of the night, especially at weekends.

Such patients would be brought in by ambulance, usually in the early hours of the morning. They were quickly assessed by the on-call doctor and for most patients, we would carry out a gastric lavage - stomach pump - procedure to remove the ingested substance before it could be absorbed. At weekends, we could admit up to three patients in the early hours of the morning and, with only a maximum of three staff on duty, it was always busy. Dealing with these emergencies kept us on our toes and we still had to meet the needs of the other 26-plus patients on the ward. Some nights we didn't even get a meal break and ate on the go if and when we could. Even then, often all we had to eat was the patients' leftovers from the day before that had been hidden in the fridge for us.

In most cases, the overdose patients we'd admitted during the night would be gone by the following evening, either because they had signed themselves out or had been transferred to the psychiatric unit for ongoing assessment. But their vacated beds would almost certainly be filled again with emergency admissions during the night shift.

Throughout my training, there were wards and departments I enjoyed working on more than others, but I loved A&E because of the constant flow of walking wounded or wheelchair-bound patients. Casualties arrived throughout the day with a wide range of injuries — from fractures and lacerations to sprains and head wounds - all of them needing treatment. After an examination by the Casualty Officer followed by X-rays and lab work, they were usually either passed over to the wards or to the nursing staff for treatment within A&E. The department was divided into two sections, one for treatments — mainly staffed by students and a few trained staff - and the other for emergencies such as cardiac, respiratory, and cardiovascular problems. Those patients were usually admitted on a   stretcher, having arrived by ambulance. In the main, the emergency side was run by qualified staff who were proficient at dealing with these traumas and the use of the crash cart. You could only stand and watch in awe as the qualified medical and nursing staff beavered away saving lives.

It was an exciting place to work and the experience I gained there was invaluable. Amidst all the drama, there was still time to mischievously insert bogus treatment cards among the genuine ones and then just wait and watch. Students could be heard all around casualty calling for 'Teresa Green,' 'Ben Dover,' 'Hugh Janus,' and 'Betty Swallocks,' to name just a few. Great fun until the Nursing Officer walked through and heard a nurse bellowing out 'Hugh Janus!' and saw all the people in A & E falling about laughing. That led to the inevitable investigation by
Matron, but fortunately the offenders weren't caught.

Then there was the plaster room, where people would have Plaster of Paris applied to stabilise their fractures. Most of the time we would practice on each other and sometimes went off to the pub still wearing plaster casts. The operating theatre, however, was not one of my favourite places to work because most days I was
seconded to the sterilisation room where I would spend the whole day packing swabs and instruments ready to be put into the autoclave. On the plus side, it gave me the opportunity to repair the constant rips in the soft top of my friend Vincent's Triumph Herald, using the silk sutures I'd 'borrowed' from the storeroom.

Most people knew I had no interest in the operating theatre and several times the surgeon asked me to leave because I was leaning on the diathermy machine, bored and chatting to someone. I wasn't all that keen on running around the theatre chasing swabs either, not when there was a perfectly good bowl within the surgeon's reach where he could easily place them. Then would come the swab count before an incision could be closed. We had to ensure all of the swabs were accounted for before the closure and inevitably that would cause delays, not least if there was one missing. On those occasions, all I could hear was a voice in my head saying, "If you didn't throw them around the operating theatre it wouldn't be a problem, dickhead!" Surgeons were generally rude and didn't really want us there, always treating us like a necessary evil. It's called a theatre because that's just how it operated. It was one drama after another and the principal players loved it, while the supporting cast stood around chatting and running around collecting swabs or autoclaving; thus it ever was!

ENT – (Ear, Nose and Throat) – was a conveyer belt of tonsillectomies on surgery days and I swerved the optical department and moved on to psychiatry, which was certainly an eye-opener. The Psychiatric Ward was similar in layout to the General Wards but different in as much as many of the patients were wandering around in their own clothing rather than pyjamas. While there was still practical nursing to do, a lot of my time was spent observing. It was helping people in a whole different way, talking them through things, helping them to cope, particularly the depressed, anxious, and suicidal patients. Wherever you looked on the ward, there were so many kind, compassionate and empathic nurses using an amazing skillset and I learned a great deal just listening to them. I got it, I just got it — talking helps. Therapeutic conversations were going on everywhere, every day, and not just in sessions with the Psychiatrists. Then with eyes wide shut, I was seconded to a ward to observe

149

Electro-convulsive Therapy, and later to a department to observe Electrical Aversion Therapy, after which my eyes were firmly wide open.

The therapy came as a massive shock to me. Observing a gay man sat in a chair with electrodes attached to his arm and legs was certainly not what I expected. Observing him being given a shock via the electrodes each time he was shown a picture of a naked man to stimulate him, then not being given a shock when shown pictures of naked women, was jaw-dropping. I genuinely could not believe what I was seeing. They were trying to shock the gayness out of him. They actually believed his sexuality was a mental illness and they were electrocuting him to facilitate feelings of pain fear and disgust about his sexuality.

I left the room bewildered, haunted and angry by what I had just witnessed and it seemed that no one wanted to discuss it with me. When I arrived on the ward several days later, however, I was able to actually have a conversation with the man himself because he had just transferred from a general ward following a suicide attempt 24-hours earlier and I knew him. I had vaguely recognised him during my observations of him receiving the aversion therapy and then the penny dropped. I had admitted him several times on Roche 3 ward and performed numerous gastric lavages on him. He was sat alone on his bed not making eye contact with anybody. I had absolutely no idea what to say to him and any attempt on my part to exchange a few pleasantries just fell on deaf ears. Over the next few days however, his mood seemed to be improving slightly and he was certainly socialising more on the ward.
Through the grapevine I learned that he had stopped his Electrical Aversion Therapy.

The Ward Sister called me to the office to officially inform me this was the case, which meant my second observation session was also cancelled. She then asked me whether she could tell him that I was gay and I consented. I don't know when she told him but when I arrived back on the ward two days later I had a new friend, because that's how it felt; it was a friendship. I may not have had the skillset of the trained nurses, but I could certainly be a friend and perhaps that's just what he needed.

As we sat in the sunshine outside the Occupational Therapy department that day, he bravely told me of his greatest fears and I sat quietly and listened. He told me that he had reached such levels of despair coming to terms with his sexuality and felt that he had no hope of anybody, including his family and friends, accepting him as a gay man.
His fear of being rejected by his family and friends and the sense of shame he felt about his sexuality was profound and his greatest fear was anyone finding out. He enlightened me about why he had consented to Aversion Therapy and explained that attempting to change his sexuality was his only option because otherwise he risked losing everyone and everything. Sadly, this was not the first time he had tried to end his life. In the past week, however, he had finally accepted that Aversion Therapy - or anything else for that matter - would never change his sexuality.

My sadness for him was profound and overwhelming. I genuinely could not understand how parents could reject their child because of their sexuality. But I also understood that his fears multiplied each time he spoke. Not only was he afraid of his parent's rejection but also the rejection of all his family and friends and being left entirely alone in the world. As we sat in the sunshine that day, he continued to pour out his fears until it was time to go back to the ward. I said very little that day but felt burdened by all his anxieties and had no idea what I was going to do. But then the light bulb moment happened because I knew he was definitely not alone in the world.

The following day, I handed him a gay newspaper in which I had circled the phone number of a support organisation for gay men - just as Dad used to circle job opportunities in the Rochdale Observer for me - and encouraged him to call. Several days later he did.

I was sad when he was eventually discharged because we had become good friends, but he knew that he could contact me should the need arise and he did so on several occasions. He would update me with his progress reports and we'd chat about life in general, until one day the phone calls just stopped.

I would still think of him occasionally and wonder how he was getting on. Then about a year later in a gay pub in Manchester, I saw him across a crowded room socialising with a group of friends, and the very sight of him filled me with joy. As he went to the bar alone, I approached and stood next to him and he spontaneously hugged me before we'd even spoken. When we did get to talking, it was not about the past, it was just about the present and how happy his life was with his boyfriend, who he pointed out among his group of friends. That was one of my greatest achievements up until that point in my life - and all I'd done was listen to someone and be a friend to them. We caught up regularly on the gay scene after that but we never, ever spoke about the past.

In my final year of training I'd progressed to the more advanced level of nursing and so I was no longer on basic nursing duties and working under supervision. Instead, I was now expected to take responsibility for a 30-bed ward when there was no Sister or Staff Nurse on duty. Simultaneously, I also had to study for upcoming practical tests and my final written exams. This certainly curtailed my social activities but I was willing to compromise anything - even my social life - in order to achieve my all-important goal of becoming an SRN.

It was also decision time because I had to consider which area of nursing I wanted to specialise in. It had to be surgery, but that also meant choosing Miss. Kelly, an Irish Senior Nursing Officer whom I'd known since my first year of nursing. She had an incredibly powerful personality and was an influential figure within the hospital. In my first year, her authoritative manner terrified me and I never dared speak to her directly - in fact, I made every attempt to avoid all contact with her during my first secondment to surgery. As a Junior Nurse I just got on with my duties whenever she was around, doing my utmost to avoid meeting her searching gaze.

Her reputation preceded her and she was renowned for her no-nonsense attitude towards all the staff within her sphere of authority. She had an unfailing human sympathy for all of the patients but demanded high standards of nursing care from all her colleagues. If you failed to meet and maintain her exacting standards, she took no prisoners. She was eagle-eyed, a true disciplinarian and never missed a trick. But as my training progressed, I worked under Kelly's leadership on several occasions and in doing so developed the utmost respect for her. At times it even felt like she had assumed responsibility for being my legal guardian, as she did with all of the Irish nurses.

Even when I wasn't working on her wards she would stop me in the hospital grounds or even in the dining room, asking in her beautiful broad Irish accent, "What's this I've heard about you, Stanier?" Usually, that meant she'd been told by the Night Sister that I'd been out on the tiles, had stayed out late or had been caught climbing through a window at 2 am. Either that or I had been fooling around generally. I always reassured her I wouldn't do it again, which guaranteed that I would at the very next opportunity.

While working on my final surgical secondment before my exams, it was Miss. Kelly who asked me to apply for the surgical staff nurse's position should I qualify. I was truly honoured that she would want me working on her wards. We had a great working relationship but had our occasional disagreements during her ward rounds. Having said that, whenever I needed her support she was always there by my side, particularly when the Consultants and Doctors were being officious, overly demanding or uncooperative. They also feared the might, knowledge, and influence of Miss. Kelly.

With my final exams just three months away, I went into lockdown because nothing mattered more to me than being an SRN. First, though, I had to pass my hospital finals, which were similar to a State mock exam. I wasn't nervous about either of the exams but I also knew that after three years of arduous work, failing wasn't an option, so I had to be ready. History showed me that, from previous final exams taken at our hospital, only around 60% of us would pass first time, with a guaranteed option of sitting the exam a second time. And so most evenings after work I locked myself away in my room for a couple of hours, revising every possible question that could come up on the day.

As always on the day of the final state exam, our nursing colleagues were lined up on the roads wishing us all the best as we made the long walk to the school of nursing — and at that point I was really nervous, if not terrified. My whole life depended on me passing the two final written papers, each three hours long. All my practical exams and hospital finals were out of the way and this was the moment for me to shine and hope that my recall of everything I knew was going to be accurate. The exams went on forever, or so it seemed, but finally it was pens down and my fate was in the hands of the marker. Frustratingly, I would have to wait at least six weeks for the results. Over the coming days, I regularly pondered my answers on the exam paper and could only reflect on what I should have written, and not what I had. The wait was agonising.

My results were being delivered to Dad's house but with strict instructions that only I could open them. On the day they were due to arrive, I sat quietly in the living room waiting for the postman and then, finally, I heard the envelope land on the doormat. I immediately went into panic mode and could do nothing other than stare at the envelope for ages before eventually scooping it up and placing it on the arm of the chair - before freezing up again. I started to regret my decision to open the envelope myself and just wanted Dad to be there to do it for me, but alas he was at work.

Eventually I plucked up the courage and opened it. I immediately scrutinised it for where it would say that I had failed, because surely I had done so. But no, I'd done it - I had passed. I charged around the room, cheering myself on and knowing in my heart that this was the best day of my life. All I wanted to do was to share the news with Dad. I left the house at breakneck speed and ran all the way to the Asbestos factory clutching the letter, heading straight for the Rubber Shed where Dad was supposed to be working that day - and closely followed by Bert the Security Guard, bellowing that I wasn't allowed in without a pass. Apparently this was the new rule.

Dad was nowhere to be seen in either the Rubber Shed or the Spinning Shed, which meant he could only be in the Weaving Shed. Then suddenly there he was, standing alongside two other men in the corridor. The first, wearing a white coat, was my Uncle George and the second, in a grey charge-hands coat, was Uncle Frank. They all turned in my direction, hearing the commotion as I ran down the corridor towards them being pursued by Bert and by now in floods of tears (me, not Bert)! All I could hear was the echo of all three men asking, "What's up with our Graham now?"

I couldn't speak as I reached my Dad, hugged him, and handed him the letter, which he proudly read aloud. By then we were all hugging each other; my excitement and pride at my achievement was overwhelming and interrupted only by my Uncle Frank telling Bert to "Fuck off!" Both Bert and I did 'fuck off' eventually. I say eventually because every one of my family working at the Asbestos factory that day was summoned to the corridor to hear the good news before they allowed Bert to escort me off the premises.

For the remainder of the day I made frantic phone calls informing everyone about my success, the celebration only tinged with deep sadness when I heard that some of my colleagues and friends had not been so successful. Then, another moment of joy as Dad and Uncle Frank came home and walked me to their garage - where there stood my very first car, bought as a present for passing my exams. It was an old and battered Hillman Imp – which broke down all the time - but I didn't care because now I

156

could be mobile and on the road. "But what if I hadn't passed, Dad?" I asked him. "You were always going to pass lad!"

The gift of a car was also an apology from Warran, Dad and Uncle Frank for their behaviour several weeks earlier when I had tried to buy a Mini. Buying a car for the first time was always going to be a daunting process for me because I didn't know a thing about them, other than how to drive one. To save a lot of hassle on that front I'd asked my brother to come along with me but, when I met up with him, both Dad and Frank were also sat in his car eager to help. I was happy they all wanted to help me through the purchasing process but things took a turn for the worse when we all got there.

The Mini was sat in the seller's drive when we arrived, looking resplendent from a fresh waxing and polishing. As I waited for the seller to answer the door, I could see out of the corner of my eye both my Dad and Uncle Frank stood on the front and back bumpers. They were rocking the car like a seesaw... and then the dreaded thumping noise. As the guy opened the door I barely had time to say a word before Dad called me over to soberly inform me that the sub-frame was, "Knackered!" He was absolutely correct, the sub-frame was indeed knackered and was clearly unable to withstand the willful rocking motion they'd administered, as was obvious by the car now listing to one side like a sinking ship. The seller looked aghast, protesting loudly that the car hadn't been like that prior to our arrival, but he was reassured by Dad and Uncle Frank that subframes on Minis were always a problem, and with that sage advice, we made our excuses and left.

Speechless doesn't even begin to describe my reaction that morning as I sat in the back of the car mortified; the three of them congratulating each other on their fault-finding mission. I may be wrong, but my guess would be that the Hillman Imp was already parked up in Uncle Frank's garage the day I went to view the Mini and maybe its sub-frame was weak - but we'd left it completely knackered.

I swear I spotted a tear in Miss. Kelly's eyes when I arrived on the ward the following day as her new Staff Nurse on the surgery wards. Waiting for my arrival, she was the first to congratulate me, saying that she had high expectations that I would have the same leadership style as hers. I tried but failed her on that one! We all grafted hard and worked exceptionally long hours under Kelly's leadership and never wavered in our exacting standards of nursing care. She would carry out her ward rounds at least twice a day, visiting every patient on the ward to check that her demanding standards were being maintained. Everything had to be 'Ship shape and Bristol fashion' prior to her arrival - or else!

It was often the case that we didn't have time to complete all the tasks on time and took shortcuts. That was fine, as long as she didn't catch you. She did, of course, on many occasions and as she would exclaim: "Jesus, Mary, and Joseph, Stanier! What have I told you about that!" Such was the pressure that some days everyone on the 30-bed ward would know about everyone else's bowel movements, as I shouted the full length of the ward to enquire who'd had their bowels open that morning so that I could record it before she arrived. If she caught me, she would be totally unimpressed, just as she'd be unimpressed if she spotted a urine bottle sitting on a locker.
She firmly believed that someone might mistake it for being that well-known health drink Lucozade, and

perhaps take a hefty swig of it (who knows, maybe it had happened to her in the past!). We didn't follow all of her or the hospital's rules completely, though, and she would often slide back onto the wards to catch us out doing something or other that we shouldn't have been. For

instance, on more than one occasion she caught me and the team eating food in the kitchen from the food trolley - which was an absolute no-no, despite the fact that it was going to be thrown away.

Other offences included calling each other by our fore-names, smoking in the changing rooms or wearing

inappropriate footwear. We'd be instructed that it "Must never happen again!" Even if the ward were perfect, she would inevitably find something amiss. No-one could match her eagle-eye, diligence, and professionalism as a nurse. We both feared and loved her in equal measure.

Within six months of qualifying, I was promoted to Charge Nurse on one of her Surgical Wards. At least a third of my classmates went on to work overseas once they'd

completed their training because the SRN qualification was transferable in so many countries around the world. But I continued to work happily for Miss. Kelly for several years after that.

She even offered me the opportunity to gain additional qualifications and study Intensive Care Nursing at another hospital which, once again, I grabbed with both hands. On my return, Kelly insisted that I be part of a clinical team that set up the hospital's first Intensive Care Unit (ICU).

Miss. Kelly was, and always will be, a legend to me as I never had to fight against a culture of low expectations as far as she was concerned.

She pushed me beyond my own expectations of what I could achieve. Eventually though, the time came for me to say goodbye to both her and my training hospital. -

My mission in life is not merely to survive, but thrive, and to do so with some passion, some compassion, some humour and some style.' *Maya Angelou.*

CHAPTER TWELVE

'Beyond the blue horizon'

"Our Graham will not be joining the family at Christmas because he will be wintering in Barbados!" my Dad announced to everyone listening in the Spotland Reform Club that day. He didn't mention that it was also my goal to visit all the gay capitals: Amsterdam, New York, and San Francisco – but then I didn't mention that bit either.

I had prepared myself psychologically for the conversation with Dad. In his opinion, I had a job for life with great prospects and a good pension at the end of it. He would definitely want me to stay at the local hospital and, in a meeting that went on for hours, he persistently tried to encourage me to rethink the whole Barbados idea. I emphasised that it would be an escape from the daily grind and an opportunity for me to meet like-minded people, make new friends and have new experiences that would last me a lifetime. I wasn't embarking on the journey to build confidence - or, for that matter, to gain independence and self-sufficiency, because I'd already achieved that. I was stepping outside my comfort zone and although it made me feel nervous, if not anxious, it also felt exciting and that it was something I had to do.

For his part, my Father expressed his concerns about me giving up my career, status, salary, benefits and accommodation, and of course he was quite right to be concerned. What won the day though was his realisation that I wasn't dropping out, I was just taking a working holiday because there was absolutely no way I could survive without an income for two years. It was to be a working holiday with lots of down time.

There were lots of uncomfortable moments during our discussion and lots of shuffling about in our chairs as we both fought our corner, Dad throwing in his usual clichés such as, "The grass is not always greener on the other side," which I countered with, "You can't please everyone either, Dad." Days passed without any communication between us but finally, after much soul-searching, he gave me his approval and also the confidence to go back to the hospital and resign, albeit with a few reservations that Dad had successfully planted in my brain.

I handed in my resignation to Kelly four weeks later and, just like my Dad, she asked me to reconsider my decision. But I had decided that the time was ripe for me to discover what the wider world had to offer and I was sticking with it.

The following month, I packed up all my belongings from the Nurses Home and stored them in Dad's cellar. I sold my car and most of my belongings to raise the money for the impending three-month sojourn in Barbados and made my travel plans. Before I knew it, Hendy and I were landing at Grantley Adams Airport in Barbados, bursting with excitement and with our suitcases crammed full of presents for all of his family. This had been our plan for some time and I could hardly believe that it was finally happening. We were not in Rochdale anymore - this was the Caribbean and I was overwhelmed by the whole experience.

Andy, a family friend, and neighbour, was waiting to meet us at the airport's Arrivals Hall, wearing the biggest smile on his face and clearly very thrilled to see Hendy. I stood by and watched as they spoke excitedly and embraced each other. Finally, Hendy introduced us and Andy proceeded to look me up and down slowly before announcing, "But wait, dat boy is white, white, white!" and pointing to the sun to advise me how it would burn me. Both he and Hendy just cackled with laughter as we walked to the car. I could barely believe I was there in Barbados, a place I'd only ever read about and known as a holiday destination for the rich and famous. They, however, stayed in their palatial homes and upscale resorts on the west coast. Although I was also heading out to that coast, it certainly was not as a platinum or gold-plated visitor, as I'm sure my Father alluded to when talking to his friends in the Reform Club. In actuality, I was headed out to St Michael on the south-west coast.

To get there we travelled through miles of lush green vegetation and rolling green hills planted with sugar cane, on narrow roads with no pavements, occasionally slowing right down to swerve around the pedestrian traffic, until finally arriving in St Michael. There we were met by many friends and family gathered outside the house waiting to welcome us and we just stood there for ages chatting excitedly and embracing everyone, including neighbours. Their Hendy had returned home and they were over the moon. I could barely understand a word anyone was saying as they spoke excitedly with each other in the Bajan dialect, and to me in more accented English.

The detached white and lime green house where we were staying had a corrugated tin roof and brick walls and was located off the main road to Bridgetown. It was to be my home for the next three months and I couldn't have been more excited. The house had a huge wooden porch at the front and on the gable end, a small shop had been incorporated for the locals. It was stocked with all manner of drinks, food, and household items, all neatly lined-up and dusted every morning by 'Grandma.' There were no supermarkets, mini-markets or convenience stores close by, so the shop was a focal point for everyone in the neighbourhood. Everyone would gather there in the evenings, often until late into the night and even when they weren't buying food supplies.

Grandma insisted that I address her as such. She was the shop owner and also head of the family. Ma Clinton – Hendy's Mother - was the nurturer and homemaker who said very little, but when she did speak it was profound. Hendy's sister, Coleen, was responsible for the housework and keeping the place clean and tidy. If you made a mess in Coleen's house, you could expect repercussions! In all, there were 10 of us living in the house and it was busy from early morning to late at night every day. It was a constant hive of activity and within weeks I felt like I was part of the family. I would sit with Grandma in the shop most mornings and just watch the world go by for hours on end. Sometimes she would be serving customers or busy preparing food for the evening meal, shredding dried salt fish or peeling vegetables, before handing it to Ma to make the meal.

Grandma was constantly observing everything and everyone and asking me if I could see 'yonder' - and would then proceed to tell me what was happening yonder. If anyone was misbehaving, you could guarantee they'd get cussed out by her. She would peer over the top of her glasses and bang her stick on the counter, hollering at them. If the dogs barked in the backyard then it was a sure sign that someone might be near her prized mango tree. She would be up and out into that yard quicker than Sir Usain Bolt hurtling off the starting blocks! Grandma guarded that mango tree with her life and did so better than any Neighbourhood Watch could.

I loved watching Grandma because she had a rounded character; she had a heart of gold but conversely she could be fiery and fierce. No-one one messed with her or her shop and they certainly didn't mess with her mango tree. Not even family were allowed to serve in the shop as that was her domain, unless it was late evening and Grandma was tired. Then, and only then, would Coleen be permitted to take over.

After only a relatively brief period of time, I'd settled into the slower pace of island life and began to form an understanding of the dialect and local sayings, which initially had seemed like a whole different language to me. That was entirely thanks to Grandma, who would laugh like a drain while teaching me Bajan.

Mornings were always hectic and Grandma's shop was a refuge as Ma would be busy getting children ready for school. None of the younger children were biologically related to the family, but they were still her pride and joy. Having raised four children herself, Ma had also fostered four more with ages ranging from three to fifteen and all of them were living with the Clinton family long-term. I didn't learn the reasons why the children were fostered, but they were certainly loved and cared for by the whole family.

Before leaving home each morning, Ma would inspect the children to ensure that their uniforms were immaculate and spotlessly clean. They would then depart clutching their lunchboxes and school bags to catch the bus at the bottom of the road. Sometimes I would accompany them to the road and wait at the bus stop with them. Not only did Ma's children wave as the bus departed but nearly every child on the bus did too. I think I'd become a bit of a novelty. I was always so impressed at how polite and generous everybody in the neighbourhood was towards me.

Most weekday evenings I would sit out on the porch after dinner, playing cards or dominoes and watching the girls braiding each other's hair, indulging myself with a Banks Beer and sipping Mount Gay rum while listening to the amazing stories told by the family and neighbours.
Neighbours passing by would often stop for a chat and you could also hear the others on their porches talking loudly, joking, playing dominoes — and sometimes
even arguing. The laughter was infectious and it
permeated the air, as did the arguments. If someone was quarrelling you could guarantee that the rest of their neighbours would be joining in and laughing at them.

That porch just got busier and busier as the night wore on and Coleen would be constantly vigilant for any 'rude boys' trying to set up a date with the beautiful Faye, one of the foster children. Faye was fifteen and once she'd finished her education she was going join her Mother in the United States. Coleen was just making doubly sure that would happen without any complications. If the rude boys were not initially afraid of Coleen, they soon would be when they saw the thermos of water she had ready to launch at them if they didn't heed her warnings.

I seemed to spend a lot of time just chilling and enjoying the island's slow pace. All the children had a scheduled time in the evenings when they had to be back on the porch. Coleen would be constantly checking her
wristwatch to make sure they were not late (they never were!) and that there was never any backchat from them. In essence, those evenings were really an excuse for big social get-togethers.

On Fridays we'd hop on the bus and head off into Bridgetown to do the week's food shopping, then return burdened with heavy shopping bags. Andy would drive Coleen to collect all the heavier shopping from town and to also get supplies for the house shop. Only then could the weekend begin. Most weekends we would be buzzing and getting ready to celebrate in Baxters Road in Bridgetown, which was only a 15-minute walk from the house and an area were the locals socialised. It was a fun place to be for everyone except Grandma and Ma, who encouraged us not to go because, according to them, it was dangerous.

That was never my experience though. It was littered with interesting people who would greet you every evening with a 'Good night.' I liked being among people who were interesting, especially when they were celebrating their differences, and I always felt totally safe in their presence.

We would hang around the street cafés and bars as loud music blasted out from every corner of the road, the whole area energised. People would stand around or sit on the café steps with plates of food in their hands, drinking until the early hours — you could buy food and drink at any hour of the night on Baxters Road. We would move around the cafés, buying a quarter bottle of rum and mixers (We didn't but drinks by the glass) before eventually ending up at Nick's Bar, where we'd catch up with David and his friends.

David was a pre-op transsexual living as a woman, as were two of his friends, and they all lived on the street behind Baxters Road. We would join them to hear all the local gossip and listen to their amazing stories and all about their goals of saving enough money to go to Brazil to have gender reassignment surgery. They were constantly saving money for the trip and such was their enthusiastic paucity that they once served us tinned sardines when we went to their house for lunch. Hendy was totally unimpressed, "Waaaaat, ya playin' de fool, ya does feed cats tinned sardines!" I ate them out of politeness but Hendy refused and, in typical style, referred to it non-stop for the whole time we were there, and then again to Coleen once we got home. She in turn mentioned it to Andy and so the local gossip went on. There was no malice in any of it, but it generated lots of joyous laughter. We socialised with David's crowd whenever we saw them in Baxters Road or Nick's Bar. They were very noticeable when they got dressed up and paraded around, and make no bones about it, they were fierce girls - (a term they gave themselves). They were certainly no shrinking violets.

The patrons of the bar we passed when we left Nick's would never disappointed us either as they sat there shouting abuse at everyone who passed by. Most times Hendy and the fierce girls just shrugged it all off, but the first time it happened I felt intimidated. However, once I witnessed the response from Hendy and the girls I had no qualms. They took no prisoners, hurtling a tirade of abuse back while offering to give their abusers "Sum licks." No one ever stepped forward to take up the offer.
Occasionally you would also come across foreign visitors from cruise liners docked close by, but they'd always do a quick about turn and disappear rapidly when they heard and saw the road in full party mode.

Sometimes we wouldn't get home until Sunday afternoon, having left Baxters Road and headed straight to Brandon Beach - especially if we could get a lift there. We'd sleep on the white sand still in the clothes we were wearing the night before and then swim in the sea when we woke up - that's if Coleen didn't wake us first! She'd sometimes arrive on the beach hurtling abuse at us because we hadn't told her we were going to be late, but she still brought sandwiches for everyone and we never got any 'Licks.'

When we arrived home from Brandon Beach, usually late morning, we always had to be on the lookout for Grandma as we turned the corner into Kew Road. She never missed church on a Sunday morning and there was always the distinct possibility that she'd see us. She wouldn't have approved of our partying ways. Whenever we did see her walking down the road wearing her finest outfit and one of her impressively large-brimmed hats, chatting and laughing with friends, we hid until she went inside the church. Nothing stopped Grandma from going to church on Sunday, not even the rain, which was unlike most Bajans in our neighbourhood who wouldn't dream of going out anywhere when it was raining. It made me smile recently when I read that the singer and Bajan girl Rihanna had visited the 'Power in the Blood' Assembly Church on Kew Road to attend a Christening, wondering what Grandma would have thought if she were alive today and had seen the Paparazzi jostling outside her church.

I was loving island life and living with Hendy's family. My heart was telling me to stay but we'd already signed contracts and were soon due to travel to Holland to work and, hopefully, party - or so we thought. Amsterdam was our first choice but as there were no jobs available at the time of applying, the recruiting company assured us that Nijmegen was the next best option and that we wouldn't be disappointed. Clearly, we would have been sensible to have done some homework about living and working in the city, but our expectations were that it would be a fast-paced, fun, and exciting place to be, just like Amsterdam. WRONG!

We travelled from the UK to Rotterdam by ferry with several other nurses who were heading off to other destinations in Holland, eventually splitting up at Rotterdam railway station and going our separate ways. Nijmegen itself was beautiful: the oldest city in Holland and just a few kilometres from the German border. But fast-paced it wasn't - nor did it have much buzz about it. We lived in one of the suburbs outside the city centre in a rural setting. It was green and spacious and surrounded by woodland, moors, and dykes. Countless outdoor activities were available to us - running, cycling, and walking - but little else. Disappointingly there were no clogs, tulip fields or windmills.

It was solitude on a grand scale and definitely not what we were expecting or looking for. However, since I hadn't taken the time to find out what to expect in Nijmegen, that was my bad luck. It was to be my home for the next six months. There was also a new language to be learned and so I enrolled in a Dutch language school full-time for six weeks before even starting work and continued to attend several times a week after that. I quickly discovered that not everyone in Holland spoke English as I had originally thought, particularly outside the cosmopolitan cities such as Amsterdam, and that learning the language was going to be a challenge.

Although Holland is just across the North Sea from the UK, the cultural changes could be somewhat surprising and, once again, prior research would have helped me considerably in my day-to-day life. Breakfast was provided for all the nurses and we would all congregate in the staff room in the mornings to eat it together. On my first day, introductions came thick and fast from the other nurses, but my main focus was on the food on the breakfast table and how it was being prepared. The Dutch love their dairy produce. To them it's not just a food group, it's a way of life. The breakfast table would be littered with cheeses, yoghurts, milk, butter, buttermilk, sliced bread and coffee - but most of them drank milk. Clearly, it would have been a struggle if I were lactose intolerant. That said, for those not partaking in the dairy option, there was always the sweet tooth option in the form of sprinklings of chocolate flakes, brightly coloured fruit flakes, or both, on toasted bread. It was more of an art form than breakfast and would have been perfect for a children's party. Most

mornings, however, it was a simple cheese butty for me. I'm sure that caused as much amusement to them as their choices did for me. Dutch cuisine did have its plus points though. In Holland, if you wanted good chips you couldn't go wrong, but probably not with mayonnaise - and you would need plenty of vinegar and salt sachets in your pocket to season them. Some of the healthier options were definitely a no-go area for me, especially the stomach-churning raw herring and onion butty, or the even healthier option of no bread and just raw herring. The brave souls opting for that particular delicacy would lift the herring in the air by its tail and simply drop it into their mouths, chewing furiously. I am dry retching just thinking about it!

There was also the dreaded purchase of a second-hand bike to get me to and from work. It had been years since I had been on a bike and I was never going to be enthusiastic about cycling to work in the mornings, particularly when I was still half asleep. I was mostly like a meerkat on wheels, remaining extra vigilant at all times and staying in the very slow lane of the cycling superhighway. The Dutch were expert cyclists who rode their bikes in all weathers and didn't take any prisoners, particularly if you were a bit of a slow coach blocking their way.

Surprisingly, though, after only six intensive weeks, I already had a basic understanding of Dutch and had become fluent enough to hold a reasonable conversation, even though locals would need to be patient with me and very good listeners. To be fair I suspect it was more a blend of English and Dutch language. Hendy, on the other hand, struggled: his accent just made him sound like a Bajan with a sore throat and resulted in no-one being able to understand him. Since he was working in a Surgical Theatre, conversational Dutch was not as important for him as it was for me working in ICU. Nonetheless, conversational Dutch became more and more frustrating for Hendy and, once we'd graduated from language school, it was apparent that he was as fluent as the day he enrolled and so he stopped trying to speak Dutch altogether. Still, we settled into suburban Dutch life as best we could and lived in a shared apartment with two other nurses, one from Germany and the other from Aruba.

My first day on the ward was a very daunting prospect as my Dutch was still quite basic and I certainly didn't want to make any mistakes. For the first couple of months, it was very stressful coping with the language barriers and work practices but Anja, my Nursing Supervisor and Mentor, helped me on both counts. I thought initially that she was a total battle-axe because she would frequently criticise my work and language skills. I soon learned though that she was just open and direct with everyone on the ward and didn't trim her sentences with any politeness. Her philosophy was that you learn by your mistakes and mustn't feel bad about making them - and I made many. Over time my mistakes became fewer, but she would still always let me know when I irritated her. I also let her know when she was irritating me, but she would shoot me down in flames saying, "Thank you for sharing that with me," glare at me, then laugh.

She was a great teacher though and, in many ways, very patient and quite determined to improve my Dutch
language skills. She refused to speak to me in English at work except when it was absolutely necessary, but over time we became inseparable and worked the same shift pattern throughout my contract. We socialised together in the evenings and some weekends too, when Anja would only speak in English until the Genever Dutch Gin kicked in, after which she was barely understandable in any language!

Nijmegen may not have been a hot-spot for socialising back in the day but it did have some good bars, and Anja was acquainted with them all. We had some great nights out but, in sightseeing terms, Nijmegen could be covered by foot quite easily over the course of just a couple of days. So, at any given opportunity, we travelled far and wide by train, often staying overnight in Belgium,
Germany, Luxembourg and other Dutch cities such as Eindhoven, Rotterdam, and Amsterdam. Dad came over to visit on one occasion but naturally he sailed because he never did trust airplanes.

Nijmegen was pleasant but we really wanted to live and work in Amsterdam and eventually would, but not for another three months. Before the ink had dried on the new Amsterdam contract, we'd already booked flights to San Francisco, via Barbados, New York, and
Washington. Why San Francisco? Well, it had always been the plan to visit but our plan gathered urgency when Hendy, the hopeless romantic, fell in love with a ballet dancer. His name was Robert and they had met one evening when we were out clubbing in Rotterdam and,

coincidently, San Francisco was where he lived. Me, I just thought that San Francisco was going to be a hip, cool and happening place - and it turned out to be just that.

******

CHAPTER THIRTEEN

'Travelling'

I was so excited about every aspect of staying in San Francisco, particularly as I'd read and heard so much about the city and, this time, I'd actually carried out some background research. We lived in an enormous, shared house in the Castro District where the first thing I noticed was just how popular my housemates were. There was constant pedestrian traffic leading up to the front door, people laughing and joking and generally very chilled. Visitors were entering the house at all times of the day and even when the door was closed the bell would ring constantly. It only took a couple of days, though, to work out why the house was much frequented: most of the rent money was being accrued through the retail marijuana service operating from the kitchen and conservatory.

It didn't bother me, it was just a new experience but certainly not one I would be writing to my Dad about any time soon. After all, I was just a visitor. It wasn't my house or my plants and the retail industry of growing and supplying marijuana would continue no matter what my thoughts were. Richard (the grower) did, however, reassure me that it - and I - was safe because he only distributed to friends in the neighbourhood - or the 'gaybourhood' as they called it - and that not just anybody could walk in off the street. I took his reassurances on board but kept my room door locked at all times, not least because the sampling room was directly opposite mine.

There were many occasions when I would leave my room when the sampling room door was open, only to be greeted with a lobby filled with plumes of thick, pungent marijuana smoke and buyers' exclamations of, "Man, this is great shit!" Still, the constant flow of people to the house meant that we were not strangers in the city for long. When socialising around Castro it felt like we knew everyone, or maybe they could just smell the incense and assumed that we were the residents from that house. The lingering smell of incense came from the joss sticks that would constantly be burned in the house to cover the smell of the cannabis. Seriously, though, I think anyone, even law enforcement, would have clicked that anyone smelling of Tibetan Musk incense probably had cannabis growing at home.

All of the customers I met, of which there were many, were always very pleasant. They varied from Marlene the ageing Hippie (who talked incessantly about the 'Summer of Love' in 1967), Jim and his dog (also called Jim), gay men in tight white t-shirts, and the beautiful Cassandra, who was transitioning and would, at the drop of a
hat, show her new tits to anyone - even those who hadn't asked!

We blended in perfectly and did all the 'touristy' stuff like visiting the Golden Gate Bridge, Alcatraz Island and Fisherman's Wharf. After only a short while I just felt like a native and most of my clothing had All American Boy emblazoned across it. We would always have a plan at the weekends. Usually it would involve spending time in the great outdoors by setting up camp at Russian River, but other times we would spend the most part of the weekend in the bars and clubs in the Castro district. Neither location ever disappointed.

While Russian River was quiet and sedate, the Castro District was completely the opposite - especially on Sundays, when hundreds if not thousands of people would congregate on the streets and in the bars and cafés. It was packed full of vibrant energy from lunchtime to whenever o'clock with street festivals, and a world away from anything I had ever experienced. Occasionally trucks would park up by the roadside and before you knew it, speakers and microphones were being set up, roads were being cordoned off and people would be on their feet cheering and dancing. A spontaneous gig would unfold out of nowhere before our very eyes and the camaraderie would continue long into the night.

Some Sundays, Sylvester – aka the 'Queen of Disco' - would turn up and give a surprise performance. When that happened the streets would go into turbo charge and high energy would extend the length of the Elephant Walk. Castro was always amazing and such a wonderful place to socialise at any time of the day, on any day of the week. You could meet liberated and like-minded people there anytime and obviously I had more people to talk to because of my frequent introductions in the hallway of the house.

On Sundays, Richard would leave his regular marijuana in small 10-dollar bags under a plant pot outside for his regulars to collect and leave their money. Each week when we returned home, however, it was always the same - no marijuana under the pot and little or no money either. But he still continued to put the bags out every week, preferring instead to believe that the wind had blown the money away, even on a wind-free day.

San Francisco was liberated, flamboyant and full of passion, yet there was also discontentment and anger within the community at the time I was there. Those people partying in Castro at the weekends were the same people who marched in their thousands to City Hall to

177

protest at the lenient conviction and sentencing of Dan White.

Dan White was the man responsible for killing Harvey Milk - the first openly gay person to be elected to public office in California, winning a seat on the San Francisco Board of Supervisors. White had been charged with his manslaughter rather than first-degree murder because his defence had argued that White had 'diminished capacity' at the time of the shooting, in part because of his addiction to sugary foods. The community deplored what they called the 'Twinkie Defence' and were outraged and angry about what they perceived to be grave injustice.

The night before we were due to leave San Francisco, Robert came to my room and I knew immediately from his face that it wasn't good news. He was very down and upset about us leaving and spoke about his uncertainty in being able to sustain a long-distance relationship with Hendy. He therefore thought it best to end their relationship and asked whether, once we were on our way home, I could give a letter to him that explained how he felt. With great hesitation and trepidation, I took the letter from him but insisted that I expected him to find the courage to speak to Hendy face-to-face that evening at their planned private 'farewell' dinner.

The morning arrived for us to leave San Francisco and Richard and all the guys from the house were up and about but, worryingly, there was no sign of Robert or Hendy and all efforts to trace them had been exhausted. No one in the house had a clue where they might be, other than that Robert's car was missing. Therefore the assumption was made that they'd already gone ahead to the airport. Richard dropped me off at the airport on my own and we said our goodbyes, then I walked straight to the check-in desk to look for Hendy and Robert - as Hendy had my ticket — but there was no sign of them anywhere. I made several enquiries at the desk but the staff assured me that Hendy hadn't checked in or left my ticket to Amsterdam with them either. Then came the announcement that the gate was closing and all I could do was sit there contemplating my fate because now I was stranded in San Francisco airport with no return ticket, a missing companion, little money, and resigned to the fact that I was now stranded in the USA.

The flight departed and there was still no sign of Hendy. I genuinely thought the worst and spoke to the check-in staff about the dilemma of my missing friend. They were in the middle of suggesting that I call the Police if he didn't turn up within the hour when suddenly, (a moment that is forever etched into my memory), Hendy came storming through the revolving door at breakneck speed in a blaze of drama, wearing a full-length maxi coat, shouting my name, and weeping hysterically. That precise moment was obviously not the time to ask him where he'd been or how he had acquired the maxi coat.

As he approached me, he fell to the floor at my feet sobbing, totally unintelligible other than the words "Robert's finished with me!" Within seconds he was hyperventilating, flailing his arms everywhere and undoubtedly drawing everyone's attention. I didn't know who to reassure first, the onlookers, the check-in staff or Hendy. I decided on the onlookers because from experience I knew that the Hendy drama could last a while and, of course, it did. There was no way I could get him to focus on the fact that we needed to be calm and speak to the airline about a flight to Amsterdam.

By that point, airport staff were bringing him cups of
water and reassuring him not to worry about missing the
flight as they would arrange another one for us without
charge. They were clearly of the opinion that the drama
unfolding before them was due to us missing our plane. I
thought it best not to enlighten them as to the real
reason. Travellers, on the other hand, were judiciously
avoiding the person slumped on the floor, sweeping past
him with their trolleys as they rushed to check in.
Eventually I managed to get him to sit up on a chair and
retrieve the airline tickets from his hand luggage while he
continued to sob lightly, but by the time I reached the
check-in desk he was once again wracked with increasingly
louder sobs.

Luckily, it was mission accomplished once I'd spoken with
the airline staff about our flight home, which would now
take two days via every US state known to man.
Meanwhile, the Hendy situation quickly escalated as I
sighted Robert approaching and the drama kicked off all
over again, only now I had two sobbing individuals to
contend with! They were hugging each other and crying
and I was beginning to experience compassion fatigue with
them both. But finally with new tickets clasped in my
hand, I ushered them away from the desk while expressly
thanking the check-in staff for all their help.

Hendy really was leaving his heart in San Francisco but he
and Robert had finally agreed to give a long-distance
relationship a chance. We now faced a 48-hour flight to
Amsterdam, with stopovers in Minneapolis and New York.
"Thank you, Robert – and all for nothing it would seem,"
came to mind as I ripped his letter up and binned it in the
men's toilet. Then the burning question, where did that
maxi coat come from and where the hell had Hendy
been? Seemingly they'd spent the night in the car, using

Robert's maxi coat to keep them warm. A stunned silence was all that I could muster!

By the time we reached New York I was totally exhausted. We weren't due to catch the flight to Amsterdam until the following morning but, not to worry, because Hendy's Dad, who lived in New York, would be at the airport to collect us and put us up for the night. As we entered the Arrivals Hall my eyes were barely open but my ears were immediately assaulted by an ear-piercing screech of "Guuuuurlfriend!" Then from behind me, a similarly ear-piercing screech of, "Lord Jesus, look at you!" Clearly Hendy was acquainted with the man wearing a brightly-coloured robe and turban - but it certainly wasn't his Father. All eyes were upon us as we walked through the Arrivals Hall, with other travellers intent on listening to the conversation being had between Hendy and the mystery man in the robe. They were communicating from a distance of 500 metres and the volume didn't reduce even as they embraced. They chatted, laughed, screamed, and generally behaved in an outrageously theatrical manner as I stood by silently, waiting to be called to the stage.

They were clearly pleased to see each other but it wasn't long before Lorelei (aka James) suddenly turned his attention to me. He didn't speak to me directly but, while looking me up and down, loudly asked, "Who's the white girl? She skinny, skinny, skinny, she needs to eat some food!" Once more, Hendy and Lorelei erupted into loud cackles of laughter and my bit part was over. They laughed and reminisced, loudly, for the entirety of our walk across the airport terminal, which seemed to take forever, before we finally reached Lorelei's car.

The car journey from the airport seemed to go on and on but a least gave me the chance to learn more about our current situation. Lorelei was an old friend of Hendy's from Barbados and he currently lived in the same apartment block as Hendy's Dad.
On learning of our stopover in NYC, he volunteered to provide a meet-and-greet service at the airport. It turned out to be more than just meet-and-greet though because it soon became clear that Lorelei had also planned out our whole evening. As the plans unfolded, it became increasingly evident we had a hectic schedule ahead of us. But first, we had to put our bags in the locker room at Penn Street Station, have a strip wash in the toilets and change our clothes. I enquired where we would be sleeping but was quickly dismissed with: "Guuuurl we ain't sleeping - this is NYC, Skinny!" I was to be forever known as Skinny to Lorelei – or, "Skineeeeeeeeeeeee," addressed at such a pitch that only myself and dogs with perfect hearing could detect.

I reminded Hendy that we had no money but it turned out that actually we did, because Hendy's Dad was aware of our financial situation and had given Lorelei some money to spend with us. By the early hours of the following morning, I must have had a drink in every bar in Greenwich Village, had been introduced as 'the skinny white girl from England' to more people than I can remember, refused entry into the Ramrod Club because Hendy was wearing white shoes, (strictly against the dress code), and had danced until I was drenched in sweat. It was almost dawn by the time we headed to 'Marks' to get some sleep. Its actual name was St Marks Bath House and, as Lorelei's friend worked the graveyard shift there, it was free entry and finally an opportunity to rest.

It was my first time in a bath house and the biggest dilemma was how to wear your bath towel. I had no idea because there were a number of ways. For many, bath towels were worn sarong-style, low on the hip and long in length or high on the waist and mid-calf. For the more daring, towels were folded in two and worn very short in length like a curtain pelmet; and for the very daring they were worn as a scarf or head dress. Personally, I favoured the sarong style. It was another world and a hive of activity, with hundreds of men draped in towels everywhere.

There was a Café, Swimming Pool, Steam Room, Jacuzzis, and people everywhere, either socialising or just walking around the seemingly miles of hallway and rooms, some with their doors left ajar by those looking for their 'Mr Right.'

We did not sleep. In fact, we only stayed an hour because there was absolutely no way we were going to miss another flight. Lorelei dropped us off at JFK and we staggered into the airport and checked in, continually pacing to stay awake until our flight was called. I don't even remember the flight itself, I just remember arriving in Amsterdam and seeing Eileen, our new flat mate, waiting to greet us at the airport.

Finally back in Holland, I started another six-month contract. Eileen was no stranger to us as we'd met on the journey out to Holland on our first contract, although at that time she had been posted to Utrecht. English was definitely spoken more in Amsterdam, both at work and when socialising. So, with the help of the ex-pat community, we settled in very easily and in no time at all felt comfortable in calling it home.

Amsterdam was an exciting city to be working and living in and I had lots of fun-loving people around me. But it was also very expensive. I worked as many hours as possible, but never at the weekends because that's when the city came alive, especially at night. I partied hard with Hendy and Eileen and most nights turned into early mornings but never once did I feel exhausted. I was too excited for exhaustion to kick in. During the day I would visit museums, explore squares, walk by the canals, and wander through the flower market and parks. It didn't take long until I was acquainted with the city - and it had been well worth the wait.

My only concern was that Dad didn't seem to be his usual self. During my 'phone calls home he was noticeably less animated, almost to the point where I could tell he was holding back and afraid of saying something to me. I couldn't quite comprehend what was going on but I knew that something was wrong. Then my brother enlightened me. Dad was feeling down and had been on sick leave for several weeks but didn't want to worry me. The bottom line being that he had been diagnosed with hypertension and occupational tinnitus and was finding it difficult to concentrate during conversations due to hearing loss and the constant ringing noise in his ears, all of which had been diagnosed following a fall from a ladder during a dizzy spell. Consequently, he had been put on sick leave because he needed time to rest until his blood pressure stabilised, with the help of prescribed medication, and his tinnitus had subsided.

He was right in that I did worry but not unduly because I called him regularly and over the next few months his condition improved. Within a month or so he was back to his old self and had returned to work. However, it was at that point that I knew I needed to go back to the UK once my current contract expired. I wasn't alone in my decision because Eileen was also planning to return to the UK at about the same time and Hendy just wanted to return to the US to live with Robert.

I on the other hand had plans to go back to factory work, but this time it would be different.

Within weeks of my return to the UK, I enrolled on a college course to study Occupational Health, while simultaneously working for a Nursing Agency to support myself during my studies. It was good to be home again and able to catch up with Dad more regularly.

Starting this new chapter of my life was exciting and I was genuinely looking forward to my new college course and my compulsory secondments to the factories.

Occupational Health was in its infancy and I wanted to be a part of it because maintaining the Health and Welfare of employees working in factories felt right for me, as did preventing work-related illness.

During my childhood on the estate I had witnessed first-hand how employees in the factories suffered ill-health that was directly associated with their workplace. Coughing, wheezing and shortness of breath was common among adults on the estate and Dad's cough was always especially evident first thing in the morning. There was no need for an alarm clock because once Dad was up, every-body was awake. Clearly, smoking didn't help but the main cause was his exposure to Asbestos dust and fibres in the workplace. Eventually many of my family would end up with a diagnosis of conditions such as Byssinosis, Silicosis, Asbestosis, Asthma and, sadly, some of their work colleagues would be diagnosed with the dreaded Mesothelioma (lung cancer) from working with Asbestos.

The best way to prevent these chronic and sometimes fatal lung diseases was to avoid inhalation of dust and fibres, but for many adults on my estate it was far too late because the damage to their health had already been done. For years they had worked in factories without adequate personal protection or ventilation. Our parents worked in there to provide a better future for us but unknowingly, in doing so, many were also limiting their life span. In some cases they wouldn't live long enough to see their children's achievements or, more so, to hold their precious grandchildren.

******

CHAPTER FOURTEEN

'Was his sister there as well?'

My brother called me at college one afternoon to tell me that Dad had been taken to North Manchester General Hospital and that I needed to get there as quickly as possible. Within 30 minutes I was in the A&E department, pacing the floor as I looked for Warran and Dad, eventually finding them behind a closed curtain in a cubicle. Whilst we waited for a Doctor to arrive, we tried our best to calm Dad down but he was confused, irritable and had difficulty both formulating his words and understanding us.

As I held his hand trying to reassure him that everything was going to be all right, it was obvious to me that he'd suffered a stroke, as he couldn't grip my hand in return. The Doctor eventually arrived and examined him, after which he was quickly whisked off to the ward. All we could do was sit and wait by his bedside while various tests were carried out and, after what seemed like hours, the Doctor returned and ominously took us aside to have a private word. He confirmed that Dad had suffered a massive stroke, but that it would be impossible to say exactly what to expect over the next couple of days. At that point they didn't know how much brain damage he had suffered or which areas of his brain had been affected. However, just looking at him in bed, the prognosis was not looking good.

Still, where there was life there was hope. Warran and I agreed without hesitation that over the next couple of days we would be with Dad 24/7. As it turned out, it proved to be more of a commitment than I had ever envisaged as Dad was to remain in the hospital for the next two months. But that didn't affect our determination to be by his side at all times. It was our duty to be with him no matter what. After all, he'd always been there for us throughout our lives.

Over the next few weeks, it became increasingly difficult to balance my commitments to Dad with my work and studying. However, as my primary commitment was to my Father, I decided that in the immediate future I needed to give up work. In terms of studying, the college agreed to accommodate any absences until the end of the course, as long as my assignments were submitted on time.

The Doctors and Nurses were amazing and nothing was too much trouble when it came to them caring for Dad. Every day I would bounce into the ward, give him a kiss, and then scrutinise him for the tiniest sign of improvement, but there never seemed to be any change other than that he'd now stabilised - and for me that was a good sign. I would lie to him every day, saying that I could see he was on the mend. His speech and level of understanding was impaired and limited, but most days we were able to communicate through gestures - the good old 'thumbs up, thumbs down' routine - and I bombarded him with conversation at every opportunity when he was awake. I would reminisce about good times we had enjoyed together and his many accomplishments, telling him how proud I was that he was my Dad. He was kind, humble, loving, and funny and I wanted with all my heart for him to know the positive difference he had made to our lives. He was the very heartbeat of our family, a saviour, and I was desperate for him to know that his life had such meaning and purpose and that he needed to get better.

I would sit by his bed day and night, moistening his lips, washing, shaving, and dressing him in clean pyjamas. I regularly had to hoist him up in the bed as he was effectively bedridden and, due to the paralysis, was constantly slipping down. On leaving, I would always give him a kiss and tell him to keep up the good work and that I'd see him in the morning.

Over the coming weeks, however, his deterioration was slow but obvious and eventually he was being fed by a nasogastric tube and hydrated by an IV drip, all the while drifting in and out of consciousness. It was at that point that the medical staff summoned Warran and I for the dreaded conversation. Dad would now be made as comfortable as possible as there was no hope of him recovering and, basically, we were helpless in preventing the inevitable. From that point onwards, Warran and I sat by his bedside, just waiting, watching, and remembering. Then one evening, behind closed curtains and as my brother and I were holding his hands and listening to his laboured breathing, Dad took his final breath and slipped away from us. My brother looked at me across the bed, I nodded to confirm his thoughts and then there was just peace and silence.

We sat with Dad for a while, not speaking, gave him a final kiss goodbye then informed the Nurse. As I stood in the Nursing Sister's office thanking the staff for everything they'd done for our Dad during his stay in hospital, I noticed that Warran had vanished. I assumed he'd gone to give the news of Dad's passing to all of our relatives gathered in the waiting area, which he had, but after doing so had left the hospital immediately. After a search, I eventually found him in the car park, crouched down at the side of my car sobbing his heart out. We just hugged and held on to each other for what seemed like forever. My big brother was hurting in a way that I'd never seen before and, frustratingly, there was nothing I could do to fix it. It was heartrending to watch.

It was a slow, quiet journey home in the car that evening and we eventually parted company in silence. There were no words of comfort I could offer him as I watched him walk dejectedly down the path to his front door.

The following day I felt a calmness come over me as Warran and I returned to the hospital to collect the necessary paperwork for the Funeral Director. Along with the documents were my Dad's personal belongings in a huge brown paper bag. It was deeply saddening – I was taking home his watch, ring, clothes, books and reading glasses, but I wasn't taking him.

Once again, we sat in the hospital car park, the silence being broken only by Warran's expression of anger at the unfairness and injustice of losing our Dad at the relatively early age of 56. My brother was, once again, inconsolable. He'd thrown the bag of personal effects into the back of the car and we just sat there for what seemed like an age. On the way to the Undertakers to make the necessary arrangements, Warran became more and more emotional each time he spoke about Dad and the impending funeral plans. I hadn't anticipated the depth and intensity of his grief, neither at the hospital or on the journey there, and when we eventually arrived at the funeral home, it became much worse. It was not even remotely possible for my brother to speak to anyone without feeling angry and upset, so he left the meeting rather hurriedly. I found him slumped over a wall on the High Street, sobbing his heart out, "I can't do this Graham, it's killing me."

I promised him there and then that I would take full responsibility for all of the funeral arrangements, with the provision that I would check everything with him first. From that point onwards, I switched into robot mode. I knew that I could and had to be strong for my brother, just like he and my Father had been strong for me on so many occasions. Now it was my turn.

Taking sole charge of the funeral arrangements took time and was physically draining. I needed to be strong to support my brother and, thankfully, I found that strength. This was the time for me to think, plan and organise and I had willingly accepted that responsibility. Dad had to be buried properly and with dignity. They say the risk of love is loss, but the pain of lost love felt immense to my brother and me. All I could think about was coping. I simply had to cope.

The day we had all dreaded finally arrived, bringing with it such intense grief but, as with many things in my family, nothing - even a funeral - was ever straightforward. Dad was 'laid out' in a coffin in his living room so that friends, neighbours, and relatives could come and pay their final respects before the cortège left for the church service. Inevitably, there was a constant flow of pedestrian traffic that morning.

Then came a knock on the door, a sudden and unexpected sharp rapping that startled everyone. Dad's coffin had already been sealed and we were just about to leave for the church. My brother and I went to the door, opened it, and saw two men stood on the doorstep, suited, and booted formally for a funeral and asking if they could pay their last respects to our Father. Neither one of us recognised them, but then Dad was very well known in the area and at work, so we couldn't possibly know everyone that he had come into contact with. They were very polite and, on hearing we were about to depart for the church service, wished us both well and repeated several times that they were sorry for our loss, which they appreciated would be huge, as Ernie was a good man. I thanked them then suggested that they get a move on if they were to make the church before our arrival. Again, they thanked me but, slightly confusingly, they didn't actually leave for the church, choosing instead to stand respectfully on the opposite side of the road until the coffin was placed into the hearse.

By this time, my family were slowly leaving Dad's house and getting into their assigned cars. The two men still watched from the pavement and, finally, once everyone was in their cars and I was locking up the house, they crossed the road to speak to me once again. "You're a Green, that's for sure," said one of the men, to which I didn't respond. He then followed up with, "We'll leave you in peace now to bury your Dad." It was very puzzling to say the least but something I didn't dwell on for very long as I had enough to contend with that day - and, fortunately, things took their course after that and Dad's funeral proceeded as expected.

After the committal service, Dad's brothers and his lads carried his coffin, with obvious love and pride, out of the church and over to the graveside. But throughout the service my entire focus was on my brother. Eventually, as I left the graveside and walked to the waiting cars, I glanced across the cemetery and there they were, the men who'd been at our front door earlier. They were standing near another open grave, alongside a man in Army uniform, and all three of them were supporting a grief-stricken woman with distinctive flame-red hair.

As the car from our cortège drove by the other funeral party, I had the opportunity to observe their grief closely and, at that point, the man wearing the military uniform and the two mystery men turned and looked directly at me.I felt a shiver run down my spine and had the strangest sensation. The mystery men looked like me and it was at that moment that the penny dropped and I realised that I needed to speak to my Uncle Frank urgently.

I finally caught up with him in the pub car park and pulled him to one side. He knew what I was about to ask him and he absolutely knew that he had to be honest with me. I didn't say anything at first, but then out it came. The men who knocked on the door that morning were, in fact, my Mother's relatives and one of them was definitely my Uncle whom I'd lost contact with the day my Mother abandoned us. They were burying my Maternal Uncle that same day and had decided to pay their respects to my Father on their way to the cemetery. I asked, "Was his sister there as well?" Uncle Frank stared back at me and replied, "Yes, the woman with bright-red hair at the graveside was your Mother!"

So, there it was. The man whose funeral had been taking place at the same time as Dad's was my Maternal Uncle, and my biological Mother had been standing just 200 yards away from me in the cemetery as I went by in the funeral car. I was emotionally numb and said nothing, other than making sure Frank knew that I would be the one to speak to my brother, because it was not the day to be having that particular conversation. I didn't want to know who in our funeral party was aware of what had just happened, but my Uncle Frank needed to make sure even the merest mention of the topic was shut down. I was later to discover that my Father and Maternal Uncle, aged 48, had also died on the same day, the 27th of July 1982, but under very different circumstances.

The subsequent newspaper articles reporting my Uncle's demise informed readers that he'd died from a drink and drugs overdose. An open verdict had been recorded because the Coroner could not be satisfied whether he'd intentionally taken his own life or had just been careless. His report stated that 'He treated the usage of drugs with a degree of contempt. He was extremely careless to the point of gross negligence.' The Consultant Pathologist also stated that the deceased had taken between five and seven times the normal dose of barbiturates which had been prescribed to treat his insomnia which, in combination with the alcohol, had killed him. His Doctor had prescribed the sleeping tablets for him at a time when he had "gone to pieces" because he had no work. Through unemployment, he had turned to drink as a coping mechanism and in the eight months prior to his death, he had on three separate occasions been admitted to the local hospital because of drink and drugs.

******

CHAPTER FIFTEEN

'That was our Ern'

It was a sad time for all involved but Stanier funerals are nothing if not unique. Once we'd all decamped to the pub, the time spent talking about what a lovely service it had been, the weather, and other such trivialities, was brief. Instead, we reminisced about my Dad and spun many yarns about him. When our family gets together, no matter what the occasion, we tell stories. At funerals, the stories are inevitably about the deceased person's life, always resulting in much laughter and tears. It's never dull and sombre but always respectful. When all is said and done, funerals are a celebration of someone's life and achievements. There's always plenty of food and drink available on such occasions, but more importantly, love and support for the family abounds in great quantities. It's what we do and the way we do it.

If my Auntie Mickey – who was married to Uncle John – was at a family gathering, even a funeral, then you could expect the total opposite of gloom. She was a party woman and inevitably caused total pandemonium. Mickey liked a whiskey, and over the years had caused many a disruption at family celebrations, particularly if there was a set of drums in the room. In fact, even if there wasn't, she would always 'drum' using a knife and fork on a tabletop, believing that she could easily compete with the likes of the late, legendary Keith Moon. Often you'd hear someone call out, "For fuck's sake Mickey, we're trying to have a conversation over here!" But it would never have any effect. She would only stop when she either fell off the drum stool or from a table. She was the only woman I know of who would have milk as a mixer with whiskey! She said she liked it that way but, in truth, had to take it with milk because of her acid reflux and gastric ulcers. Not drinking whiskey wasn't an option for her — she imbibed morning, noon, and night, as the occasion required.

Sadly, Mickey's drumming was missing after Dad's funeral because she'd had one too many whiskies and milk while boating on the Norfolk Broads. As a consequence, she'd fallen overboard into the water and drowned. To this day she is sadly missed at our family gatherings but is fondly remembered, not least because of the circumstances of her unfortunate demise.

It was also guaranteed at any funeral that my Auntie Gladys would have a story about how the deceased had contacted her on the day. She didn't disappoint on this occasion either, telling us all that Dad had communicated with her because, when she went to the bathroom, the lights flickered on and off - "That was our Ern," she insisted. It was her way of finding peace and comfort and we loved her for it. We would always encourage her to tell her stories at family gatherings, particularly the one about her seeing the image of Jesus on a piece of linoleum!
Auntie Gladys kept a piece of lino (linoleum) that she'd cut out of her floor covering after claiming to have seen the sacred image of the Lord in it. As children and even as adults, we would encourage her at every visit to show us her treasured piece of lino and she would proceed to painstakingly point out every detail of 'Jesus.' Sadly, - and to Auntie Glady's immense frustration, - no one else could ever see it. But she could and that's all that really mattered.

Unlike Mickey, though, Auntie Gladys was not a party woman, nor was her husband George. She was a very religious woman, her only wish in life being to one day visit the Vatican in Rome. My cousin, John, arranged just that for her and, true to form, went one step further and booked both of them on a private tour there, which allowed them to skip the lengthy queues. My Aunt was over the moon when told about the trip and for months could hardly contain her excitement knowing that she was finally going to visit the Holy See.

On arrival at the Vatican, John spoke to a Swiss Guard, who advised that they were a bit too early and to return in half an hour. When they returned, the same Guard ushered them through a gate and into a room where they were quickly seated along with around ten other people, all barely concealing their excitement as they waited for the tour to start. However, there seemed to be more people in the room than seats, with three people having to stand at the back. With careful 'Uching up' and expert guidance from Aunt Gladys, though, everyone was eventually seated, just in time for the entrance of His Holiness the Pope, who proceeded to give them all a Papal blessing. His Holiness was stood only a matter of feet away from Gladys, who just sat there in awe and stunned silence.

John also sat in stunned silence, having quickly realised that the Swiss guard had made an error and that a Papal Audience was definitely not included in the tour itinerary he'd booked. That also probably accounted for the three unfortunates who had initially been stood at the back of the gathering. Gladys, however, wasn't any the wiser and cherished every precious minute. She's the only woman I know that could drop her Papal Audience into any conversation. Naturally, the tale also received an airing at Dad's funeral, maybe more than once - and if she could have perceived the future, she would also have relayed my later 'lunch meeting' with His Holiness the 14th Dalai Lama of Tibet.

She would definitely have dined out on that story had she been alive to hear it. I didn't actually receive an invite to lunch with the Dalai Lama, nor did I sit at his table. I was, however, in the same room and we were both having lunch (I was eating a humble sandwich washed down by bottled water, whilst the Dalai Lama's lunch looked far more sumptuous)! I was also gazing at him in silence while he dined and conversed with several dignitaries and monks at his table. The dining room itself was very quiet with few other people and I'm guessing I shouldn't have been there, but no one stopped me either, not even the armed guards in uniform whose presence was evident everywhere and who looked slightly incongruous around that calm, serene and spiritual individual.

From the moment I saw him I was in awe and, yes, it did cross my mind to get closer to him, maybe even a selfie, but my ever sensible husband - who can read me like a book - put his hand calmly on my shoulder as I inched forward and said "No - whatever you're thinking - IT'S NO!" It was a surreal experience which we had stumbled upon quite by accident while visiting the main Tibetan temple in Dharamshala in India. Days later I would still be asking myself whether it had really happened, which it had. His presence at the temple was confirmed in the Indian press the following day, with a report revealing how the Dalai Lama had given a speech at a 'Thank You India' celebration held at the temple.

However, my Aunt Gladys was able to dine out on 'Did you know our Grahams been to dinner with the Queen Mother'. It wasn't actually dinner but more afternoon tea hosted by the Queen Mother at the Royal College of Music and I was a plus one. It was a very pleasant afternoon and fortunately no one enquired about my musical talents on triangle, tambourine, castanets and recorder or for that matter my lip synching skills whilst performing 'All things bright and beautiful'. I can only but imagine the embellishment my Aunt Gladys added to this event.

On the day of Dad's funeral, his Brothers, Frank, and John, were both 'bladdered' and spent the whole time fluctuating between tears and laughter, as is often the case on such occasions. Leaning on the bar, they grabbed me at every opportunity to hug and kiss me, telling me that I was, "A good lad," and that Dad was so proud of me and Warran.

I didn't have the heart to tell Uncle Frank that his well-worn toupee was by that stage perched at a jaunty angle on his head and essentially looked more like a fascinator. That was, however, par for the course whenever Uncle Frank got hammered. He was a real 'ladies' man' and never did come to terms with male pattern baldness. I remember the first time he wore his hair piece was at my cousin's wedding, where he'd walked into the church with a full head of hair - and the entire Stanier side of the family just fell about laughing. To say that he stole the show from the Bride and Groom is an understatement and he was ribbed mercilessly about it at the wedding reception afterwards. That didn't stop him wearing it though and, similarly, it didn't stop us from talking about it. The toupee genuinely looked like a lump of brown felt perched on his head and certainly didn't resemble anything like real hair. But Uncle Frank thought it looked great and knocked years off him, and that's all that mattered really.

Uncle George, being the eldest of all Dad's brothers, was his usual sober self all that day, wandering around the room, nervously rubbing his hands together, Silas Marner like - and always in protective mode. He scanned the room like a hawk, giving various people mostly unsolicited sage advice, such as telling them that they'd "Had enough!" His wife, Auntie Connie, often received a nudge from him regarding her behaviour after having consumed a fair share of the grape, but it never stopped her from ordering more of her favourite 'Rum and Black' tipple. The usual sign that Connie had had enough was the sound of her piercing, high-pitched laughter, which could even be heard above Mickey's drumming and possibly in the next town! Uncle Frank's wife, on the other hand, just sat in a corner of the pub, gossiping about all and sundry and blatantly ordering drinks from anyone who had the misfortune to be stood at the bar. Occasionally, my other Aunts would dip in and out of her conversations for an update on the gossip and scandals of the day.

All my cousins made merry that day with the exception of my cousin Philip, who sat alone for long periods of time, desolate and drowning his sorrows, despite his normal rule of not touching alcohol. Philip had not just lost his Uncle but also a very good friend. They'd often met up to socialise and play snooker together so his loss was palpable. With all my heart I wish that I could write that my Dad's sister, Auntie Winnie, along with Uncle Tom and their family, were at Dad's funeral, but sadly she'd also passed away at an early age, leaving behind her husband and my 4 cousins – Gerard, John, Michael, and Angela.

I never got the opportunity to meet Winnie or Tom because Grandad Stanier's strict Victorian values had forbidden any family member to speak to her after she had committed the ultimate sin - in his eyes - of marrying a Roman Catholic. Grandad Stanier imposed his will on all of us almost like a mafia don whose every instruction had to be obeyed, or else you would suffer the consequences. However, unbeknownst to the 'Don,' his wishes were not always obeyed and over time we would reunite with all our first cousins from Winnie and Toms marriage. Had he been alive, the 'Don' would have been furious about the reunion, but that would be his problem, not ours.

My cousins, Aunts and Uncles gave my Dad a good send-off that day and I was very proud of them all, as I still am today. I am privileged to have them as my family and honoured to be a part of theirs. As 'last orders' were called at the bar and taxis summoned, however, I knew in my heart of hearts that the loss of my Dad was the worst thing that could ever happen to me and that any challenge from that point onwards in my life was just going to be a lesser hardship. He was my life and a giant of a man whose unconditional love I would miss every day for the rest of my life.

******

CHAPTER SIXTEEN

'The time after the funeral'

I remained on autopilot for several weeks after Dad's funeral, particularly as there were still so many things to sort out. I just threw myself into it all, despite suffering a permanent headache-from-hell and feeling physically exhausted. The plan at the time was for me to have a few weeks off after sorting everything but things just started to slide away from me.

I couldn't find the motivation to even look for work and spent most of my days doing absolutely nothing. I couldn't be bothered with anything and felt tired constantly; it was like someone had switched me off. I just put it down to physical exhaustion because I wasn't sleeping very well, either. That feeling continued for weeks and, eventually, I was convinced I had a serious physical illness. I would fret about it constantly but couldn't bring myself to visit my GP. Then I started to worry that I had cancer because I was losing so much weight. Had I thought about it logically, it was because all I was eating was toast and, even then, only when I felt really hungry.

My days continued to be empty and I had a total absence of any feelings, other than an awareness that my anxiety was getting worse. When I wasn't worrying about my health, I was worrying about work and managing my money without an income. I was constantly trying to regulate my breathing and my sleep pattern was getting worse. I was spending most nights awake just worrying and I was exhausted. I would try and catch up during the day by sleeping on the sofa but even then I would wake abruptly, struggling to breathe and overwhelmed with fear.

It was a vicious cycle. I did eventually speak to my GP but only to discuss my insomnia. I genuinely thought that if only I could get a good night's sleep I would be fine. He subsequently prescribed a night sedative for two weeks but even though I slept better during that period, I wasn't improving nor was I repairing - and I was still worrying.

Without work to provide me with a daily routine, my lethargy persisted and I continued to spend all my days doing and feeling nothing, other than what seemed like constant waves of anxiety consuming me for hours on end. I would regularly stand at the kitchen window, just looking out and observing life passing me by. I didn't want to be any part of it and just wanted to be left alone. Eventually, even the 'phone became problematic. I dreaded it ringing and most times just ignored it because I knew it would either be Warran, another family member, or a friend.

I had no interest in anything or anyone. I didn't want people calling me anymore and I didn't want anyone visiting me, including my brother. He was obviously concerned about me but I didn't want his concern, and his endless prompting about me needing some help was wearing pretty thin. It was during one of those conversations that I exploded with anger and told him not to bother calling me or contacting me ever again, then slammed the 'phone down. The calls dried up after that, except for the agreed odd 'coded' message from my friend Janet. She would give three rings on my phone to inform me that she would be calling by my flat in about 10 minutes' time with my shopping. She would do that a couple of days a week, bringing my godson, Adrian, along with her.

I'd known Janet for years. She was so easy to be around and, to be fair, when she visited we didn't talk much as she was always busy with Adrian, who was a toddler at the time. After so many refusals, she'd stopped asking me to socialise with our mutual friends. But she continued to drop my shopping off and clean the flat, with me continually apologising about it being in such a mess and asking her not to do it. She always did it anyway.

Mornings merged into afternoons which then became evenings, and I'd done nothing with my life. Most days I hadn't even bothered showering or shaving because - well, what was the point? I'd arrived at a stage in my life, a point of acceptance, that on the day my Father died, joy and happiness had left my life forever and were unlikely to return. I was in a downward spiral. What with having no income and dwindling savings but still with rent to pay, crisis was not far away. I needed a job and wanted a job but I hadn't the motivation, self-confidence, or energy to seek one. I had previously wanted so much from my life but now I no longer had any ambition and felt like a failure. I was lost somewhere but didn't know where - and I'd alienated those who'd wanted to find and help me.

I would wake each morning with nothing to look forward to and felt I had no meaning in life. I wanted to talk with Warran but wouldn't because he wanted to talk about Dad and I couldn't face that. I just didn't want to talk to anyone and the world had suddenly turned a darker shade of grey. The only asset I had left now was my car, which hadn't been used for months. I decided to sell it because that way at least I would have enough money to last me until Christmas. Ominously, I had no plans beyond that.

Janet gave her usual three rings and 10 minutes later came a knock on the door. I opened it to find Janet with the shopping, only this time she wasn't alone and I vaguely recognised the man with her. It was my GP. I looked accusingly at Janet and she immediately burst into tears and started apologising profusely, saying how scared she was for me because I wasn't getting better and how she'd spoken to her husband, who was also a GP. Alarm bells for my safety were apparently ringing everywhere and Janet felt she had no option but to get my own GP involved.

They both walked straight past me without invitation and sat down at the kitchen table, where I then joined them and started chatting with the Doctor. Thinking about it in retrospect, he was cleverly assessing my condition and I cooperated fully, answering his searching questions and subsequent relevant suggestions. I continually interrupted him, insisting I wouldn't go into a Psychiatric Unit, no matter what the outcome of his assessment. He was of the opinion that I was experiencing a mental health crisis and my admission to hospital might be the best way forward to keep me safe, particularly as I was living alone and becoming socially isolated.

The Doctor did his best to reassure me that hospitalisation might not be necessary if I cooperated fully, then went on to diagnose me with having major depression. He prescribed an antidepressant but with strict conditions attached. One of these was that I was to call the Surgery every morning at a specific time to check in with him and provide a progress report. My not contacting him would set the alarm bells ringing and so wasn't an option - not if I wanted to avoid the Psychiatric Ward and stay at home. Consumption of alcohol was not allowed and Janet was burdened with the responsibility of daily visits to take me out for short walks around the neighbourhood.
I felt huge relief that day knowing that, yes, I was broken but like Humpty Dumpty, there was a possibility I could

also be put back together again. My antidepressants, which I took in the evenings, helped me sleep better but they also made me feel very drowsy and I struggled to wake up in the mornings. Over the next two weeks, with the invaluable help of an alarm clock, I was able to meet the commitment of calling my GP every morning at the scheduled time.

******

CHAPTER SEVENTEEN

'The floodgates open'

After a fortnight of taking the antidepressants, I felt that my focus was shifting marginally to the point of me wanting to get better, as opposed to being completely apathetic. My anxiety, although less consuming, was still present. I was sleeping better, which helped, but the depression was still there, sapping my energy and making even the simplest task very difficult. More importantly, it had stolen my voice and interests. I needed to find my voice very quickly though, as I had a forthcoming appointment with Lawrence, a Psychologist.

I considered cancelling my appointment with Lawrence several times because I didn't much relish the idea of talking about myself and I certainly wasn't comfortable talking about my feelings with a complete stranger, even if he was a Psychologist. However, I did attend my first appointment in the end and, after much form-filling, followed by a 15-minute chat to which I didn't attach any real importance, it was over. Looking back that was more than likely due to my constant monosyllabic responses to Lawrence's questions, which he probably interpreted as me not wanting to engage in conversation. If he did, then he was probably right. I also didn't need him to confirm that I was in the throes of overwhelming and intense grief and that I needed to share my pain with him, nor that I was running away from my grief to avoid that pain. To be honest, I actually left that first session feeling quite irritated.

Our second session, however, was totally different,

probably because I was still annoyed with him. Lawrence opened the session with general chit-chat before saying he understood that I was upset about the passing of my Father and started using language along the lines of needing to "embrace my grief." I cut him off in mid-sentence and proceeded to rail at him for the next 15 minutes, telling him in no uncertain terms that he had "No fucking idea," what it felt like losing my Dad because even I didn't know what I felt like anymore, other than feeling totally empty most of the time and an anxious wreck the remainder of it. I didn't end my rant there:

"How is it possible to talk about my Dad when every time I think of him, all I see is him lying in bed in distress and dying at the age of 56? That, and the sheer injustice of him dying so young? How is it even possible that this beautiful, caring and kind man could be taken from me in the most hideous and punishing way? He was deserving of better and I have every right to feel angry, so talking about it won't make it any better.
And how could I have failed Dad in such a massive way? I could have saved him and I'm to blame. I was too selfish and should have come home from travelling as soon as I'd heard that he'd been unwell. I should have taken him for a second opinion and then things could have turned out so differently, so talking about what I should have done won't help. What would help however would be the opportunity to relive everything once again, do things differently, have a better outcome and you can't do that Lawrence - you just can't do that for me!"

The floodgates opened and, for the first time in months, I cried out so loud to the point my body was shuddering and my feelings finally surfaced. It was painful but also very cathartic. Lawrence was not in the least bit overwhelmed by what I'd said and remained silent and composed throughout my rant, only gesticulating with his hands to validate that it was OK to let my feelings out. My depression to that point had seen me cocooned in a quiet, lethargic state but suddenly the noisy active state of pain I'd held on the inside - and that was consuming my entire body - just erupted.

I apologised profusely to Lawrence. I knew I had behaved badly towards him but once I'd composed myself, he booked another appointment for me and made it clear that this was my safe place to say anything and to express exactly how I felt. I hesitated before I left the room and told Lawrence I probably wouldn't visit him again as I just couldn't talk about my Dad, but I would certainly let him know. Lawrence rose quietly from his chair and stood between me and the door. His words were profound. He said that he wanted to remove my pain but he couldn't and that I had to accept my life would never be the same again because my Father was irreplaceable. He also said that I had to accept that my meetings with him would not be easy but would instead take me on a very painful and unavoidable emotional journey, which in his opinion I could cope with. He then grabbed both of my shoulders and told me that by the end of this journey I would be able to remember all the love and joy my Father brought to my life and be able to open the treasure trove of beautiful memories he had given to me.

As he said the last part, the flood gates opened once again and I felt so alone and unable to cope. But that afternoon, as I walked home in floods of tears, zig-zagging the road from pavement to pavement and avoiding all eye contact, I pondered Lawrence's final words and they suddenly made sense. I didn't want to lose my Dad forever, so I kept my next appointment - and the ones after that. Over the next three months, I saw Lawrence regularly and we painstakingly worked through my past and present problems. Then, once I was coping better emotionally, he discharged me with a whole raft of homework exercises, including how to monitor my mood.

For several months Lawrence had been a trusted support for me and I knew that I'd miss him terribly, but now it was time for me to go it alone, although this time with the support of my family and friends. Warran was also back in my life - not that he'd ever left it really because I subsequently learned he'd been speaking to Janet regularly and monitoring my every move.

Christmas came and went and, although I spent it alone in my flat, I didn't feel lonely because it was my choice to be alone and not the 'demon depression' dictating my every move; I now knew the difference. I just wanted peace and quiet because I still felt extremely tired and needed to enjoy the simple things in life such as watching TV, reading, listening to music, and occasionally talking on the 'phone to my friends and family again, which no longer felt intrusive. I could also think about my Father without becoming emotionally overwhelmed. There were still many tearful days, but they felt less painful.

While reminiscing about my Father over Christmas, I never once thought about the material presents he had given me or the money he had put in birthday cards. Those gifts paled into insignificance compared to the life experiences - both good and bad - that we'd shared. Dad himself was a gift to me that just kept on giving and which was priceless. The wisdom, love, compassion, support, and security he had given me were qualities for life and would never end up in a landfill. More importantly, they were qualities I could share with others throughout my life, and I do.

Yes, his death had left me broken-hearted but he had left behind a beautiful legacy to be treasured and I thank him every day for this. Of course, I still miss him terribly but I was also able to forgive myself and the only way I could do that was to accept his demise was inevitable and, importantly, that Dad would forgive me anything.

However, processing my grief without my usual escape of work was proving to be a challenge. Work can be a good and necessary distraction sometimes, and I hadn't worked in almost a year.

******

CHAPTER EIGHTEEN

'Saudi Arabia – Sun, Sand and Siddique

It seemed that things were picking up and that my life was gradually improving. I felt stronger and, despite the recurring moments of sadness, they were no longer as intense and I found that I could finally cope with them. There were still remnants of guilt but I had the benefit of having a more rational mind to help me confront and deal with it.

With my sights set on a fresh start, I gave notice on my accommodation in the Spring, moved in with a friend and eventually boarded a flight to Saudi Arabia, not least because all my savings were gone and I was stony broke. Saudi Arabia was definitely going to be a good earner and an ideal opportunity for me to make that fresh start.

When I called Lawrence to tell him, however, he didn't entirely agree with my plans and had reservations about me being alone and without support. I also had the same concerns, but sometimes you have to do something that you're not totally comfortable with. My Dad had been my world and my love for him was immeasurable. His loss had broken me but I wouldn't have had my life any other way. While I finally knew and accepted that I would never stop grieving for him, I had to make sure my grief didn't run or ruin my life. I had to learn to live without his physical presence.

Arriving in Jeddah in the late evening was a bit of a culture shock. I was giddy with excitement and also a little anxious as I'd absolutely no idea of what life was going to be like once I'd passed the first hurdle, which was getting through the airport's Immigration and Customs check unscathed. Despite the fact I'd been meticulous in my packing, I was still worried that I might have inadvertently packed an item that was banned and would have to spend my contract time in a prison cell. To my relief there was no cause for concern and I quickly passed through into the Arrivals Lounge. Once my luggage had been checked thoroughly and with my favourite book – Harper Lee's 'To Kill a Mockingbird' - in hand, I heaved a sigh of relief and was through to the other side of the airport in no time.

It felt like I was the only Westerner in the Arrivals Lounge. There were women everywhere, draped in black abayas with their faces covered, and men in long-sleeved white robes wearing head coverings, mainly in red and white check. It felt slightly scary but at the same time very exciting to be in the midst of such a different culture. My imagination ran riot; perhaps I would be met at the airport by Peter O'Toole dressed as Lawrence of Arabia, offering me a lift to my destination on the back of his camel. Reality kicked in when I spotted a guy holding a sign above his head with my name written on it. Before you could say 'Graham Stanier' I was whisked away from the crowds, placed into a car and - after having to sit patiently in one of the multiple traffic jams around the outskirts of the airport - was heading off towards my ultimate destination, Ta'if. It is the summer capital of the Kingdom and known for being very traditional in its views and way of life.

I couldn't see much of the landscape out of the car window, but I could see and hear the brightly illuminated trucks hurtling towards us on the opposite side of the road, always at breakneck speed. Occasionally there would be other distractions such as the aftermath of several car accidents, which my driver reassuringly told me would be dealt with the following morning. I saw a sign for Mecca above the road and then we reached a checkpoint where an inquisitive guard peered at the car to see what or who was inside. Having been given the all clear, we quickly left the tarmac road in the opposite direction to Mecca to take the largely unmade road signposted for Ta'if.

I was quite relieved it was dark because the road wound its way through the mountains and I just knew there were sheer drops on either side of us. Cars and trucks were still speeding past us, tyres squealing as they attacked the hairpin bends. I recall thinking, "please make this journey end and quickly." Finally, and after what seemed like a lifetime of holding my breath, we reached the top of the escarpment and entered Ta'if in the early hours of the morning.

Arriving at the entrance to the compound, we were greeted by another serious-looking security guard. He was fully armed with an automatic weapon and he peered into our vehicle suspiciously before thoroughly checking the boot and then the rest of the car. It was an unnerving and menacing experience but eventually we were given clearance to proceed into the compound - only to be met by yet another security guard who also scrutinised our documents closely.

Once inside the compound, the driver took me to a small group of houses and pointed to the one that I'd be living in, handing me an envelope containing the door keys. As it was by then very late, I let myself in, dropped my cases inside the room, showered and went straight to bed. I woke early the next morning and proceeded to check out my accommodation. It was certainly not particularly spacious, but it was adequate for one person and had everything that I would need, such as a kitchen, bathroom and living room, etc. I then walked outside to check my new surroundings.

The first thing I noticed was that the whole compound was encompassed by high concrete walls, with functional wood and brick buildings dotted around everywhere. It felt like the place was deserted as there was no sign of life and the only landscape I could see outside the compound walls was the dry, arid hills covered in dry vegetation. There was no evidence of the agricultural area of Ta'if that I had read about before departing the UK – producing grapes, pomegranates, figs, roses, and honey, but hey, at least the sun was shining!

At 8 am there was a knock on my door. I opened it to find a man stood looking bleary-eyed and slightly worse for wear. He introduced himself as my neighbour, saying that he'd been tasked with showing me around the compound before I reported to the site office to go through all the necessary formalities of being registered in the Kingdom of Saudi Arabia (KSA) and to have my all-important ID issued. We wandered around for half an hour as he showed me what resembled a small village but which had the distinct feel of a prison camp.

The compound itself was brand new but unfinished and was made up of diverse types of accommodation, large and small houses and two huge housing units of dormitories. There was a communal dining room, a small swimming pool, a social club (which did not sell alcohol as it was illegal and banned in the compound) and interestingly, an empty medical clinic. The compound was also only partially occupied, hence the lack of people walking around, although there were plans to have it at full capacity within the next few weeks.

The whole compound housed about 150 men, 20 of whom were a mix of American and British, but the vast majority being from the Philippines, Thailand, Sri Lanka, India, Pakistan, or Bangladesh. Anyone on the compound who was not a westerner was collectively referred to as being a TCN (Third Country National). It was a term commonly used for a person whose nationality was different from that of the company they worked for, and of the country in which the firm was operating. By their definition, people like me were also TCNs but also token Americans and therefore segregated from the other TCN employees in terms of accommodation, dining, and recreational facilities.

Westerners, who primarily occupied the managerial jobs, were accommodated in the houses. The remaining employees were housed in the dormitories which, although new, were already looking overcrowded. Most of the TCNs were employed in skilled and semi-skilled jobs such as cooks, food handlers, clerks, electricians, carpenters, drivers, construction workers and general maintenance operatives. To be honest, it felt like I was back working on a building site and for a split second I asked myself what I'd done, However, since I had no money to my name, it remained only a passing thought.

We then walked to a much larger compound, about ten minutes away, which housed approximately 200 -300 employees, some with their families and It then became apparent that the staff living in the smaller compound were effectively providing services and support for the facilities on the larger compound, which was also brand new.

The housing on the larger complex was closer to western standards with two, three and four-bedroom houses — all fully furnished and carpeted — and a swimming pool, soft-ball field, and bowling alley. This compound also had its own medical clinic for the residents and families living there, which was staffed by a Doctor and several female Nurses who were also wives of employees. They were all very friendly and pleased to see me because up until that point, the TCNs had been using the clinic's medical facilities and the staff there were becoming overwhelmed with appointments.

The prevalence of intestinal parasitic infections was high in the TCN community and the emphasis was on treating those conditions, but more importantly to concentrate on prevention. My job was to set up a Treatment Clinic and Occupational Health Service for the employees, including Health Screening and Health Education, particularly for the Food Handlers. That in itself was going to be a huge undertaking but, in addition, I was also required to set up and staff a General Treatment Clinic for those employees on the smaller compound were I was living.

After my tour of both camps, my neighbour left me with a chilling warning to be on the lookout for camel spiders, because apparently if one were to get into my room, it could eat my flesh while I was sleeping!

At lunchtime I had an appointment with the guy who managed the small compound where I would be living and working. He was an elderly ex-US Military serviceman who had clearly learned an awful lot during his time in the Services because, according to him, he could do everybody's job on the compound much better than they could - including mine - with less resources and expenditure. His disdain towards the TCN population, including myself, was evident from the outset and, to be honest, I hardly spoke as he was more interested in trying to impress me with his military record and achievements generally. I think the military phraseology is that he was continually on 'send' and didn't 'receive.'

I wandered around the compound with him for a second time as he surveyed his empire. He was wearing a Stetson hat, puffing on a huge cigar, and throwing all his substantial weight around. It was clear that I was destined to have a very difficult relationship with him.

Fortunately, I was spared his presence in the evenings and at weekends as his self-importance and grandiosity meant that, in his eyes, we minions were not worthy of socialising with. He would only mix with the population in the larger compound. By comparison, I was more than comfortable with the people in my community. He may have had some impressive military title, but to the residents he was just 'Commander Arsehole' - or, if he were in earshot, he would just be referred to as 'CA' - and it would become increasingly clear that he was most deserving of that title. Regrettably, I had to meet up with him frequently during my first month, as there was a lot of expenditure he needed to sign off during the setting up of the clinic. Fortunately, after that we met only once a week at the Managers Meeting.

During the initial stages of my one-year contract it was non-stop work and I didn't have time to socialise very much. I didn't leave the compound for at least two months, other than to drive the car to the local hospital to set up services with them. I was totally focused on establishing the clinic, ordering equipment and stock, and recruiting and training Nurses. In the evenings, I would stay in my room and read or occasionally watch a film. There was a constant feed of films but frustratingly no TV channels, so I couldn't even watch the news.

From the very beginning, I had accepted that my time in KSA was a temporary measure and that I had to make the most of it, but that didn't stop me waking up every morning expecting the unexpected. And there were many occasions when I was not disappointed. Living on the compound was boring and bleak at times but, fortunately, I didn't experience any homesickness, nor did I feel lonely or isolated. I continued to maintain contact with my family and friends through letters and the occasional phone calls to friends, particularly Janet, Hendy and Warran. Hendy had now settled into his new life in the USA and, as his relationship with Robert had come to an end, he was living with his Father, in New York. I couldn't wait to visit him once my contract was over.

My work routine was basically dictating my lifestyle, particularly as I was also on call most evenings for medical and welfare emergencies. But then again, how else was I going to pass my time? Some days I was able to think rationally about my grief and put some meaning to what I was feeling, telling myself that I needed to adjust to a life without my Dad, but I knew I would never stop loving him or missing him. There were days when I would unexpectedly feel weak and despairing, believing that my emotional pain would last forever and never pass. On other days, I would remember happy times with him and feel joy. It was an emotional rollercoaster but most days, in public, I could put on a brave face. Privately I faced my grief full-on, alone (which I wouldn't recommend to anyone). I just needed to be patient with myself and cope as best I could because this was my reality - and I wasn't about to catch a plane home.

"Life can be good, then you lie down, and stare up at the ceiling, and the sadness falls on you. Things move on, time passes, people go away, and sometimes they don't come back."

Robert Frank

During free time, we Westerners tended to socialise together in the smaller compound, particularly in the evenings and at weekends. Although the demands of our jobs meant that we didn't leave the compound for prolonged periods of time either, other than for work-related matters, we did get visitors from other compounds at the weekends and sometimes also from women who were in relationships with the single guys.

Getting girlfriends in and out of the compound, however, was something akin to a chapter from one of the adventures in Enid Blyton's 'Famous Five' series. If anyone knocked on my door asking for the Chevy Suburban keys, I knew without asking that a stealth operation was i
n progress to get someone's girlfriend onto the compound. To get past security, which was often more relaxed at the weekends, the woman concerned would be smuggled in on the floor of the Suburban, covered by a blanket, and later back out of the compound again, using the same covert method. It wasn't unknown for them to travel in the boot of the car either. Love, or lust, will always find a way.

After a few months, things had settled down a bit. The demands of the job got lighter and there were more opportunities for me to leave the compound after work in the evenings. I always felt the need to be vigilant when out shopping in Ta'if and in the marketplace, or souq, because I didn't want to violate the rules of Saudi culture or break its laws unknowingly. I always felt there was a risk of me doing so and then having to suffer the consequences - something I definitely wanted to avoid. That feeling especially wasn't helped when encountering or hearing the Mutawa - the Islamic Religious Police - who roamed freely around the souq, supposedly promoting virtue, and preventing vice but in general appearing to just shout at people.

I always presumed it was me they were shouting at but fortunately it never was. It was probably just my conditioning from living on the council estate because then when people were shouting near me on the street, it probably was me they were shouting at. Part of the adventure was that you had to survive the car journey down to Ta'if on the roads, which many locals treated like racetracks. Nobody used their indicators, overtaking was from both the left and right and cutting across lanes in front of you was the norm. It was a memorable experience and, more often than not, a 'near-miss' one.

Back in the compound, we would normally socialise either in the dining room/social club or gather around the small swimming pool area. When the sun went down, the socialising would continue at someone's house.
The conversations were certainly more joyful at these gatherings than during work time, when everybody seemed to be complaining about life and work in Saudi Arabia and, of course, our arch-enemy - the bellicose, bullying, and obnoxious 'CA.' Socialising for the ex-pats was certainly important because the work could be very challenging at times. Homesickness was a problem for many, particularly for those who'd left their loved ones back home. Let's face it, the only reason they were in Saudi was to earn enough money to provide a better future for themselves and their families.

Despite alcohol being illegal on the compound, the home-brewed variety was freely available; indeed, it was a small cottage industry on the compound itself. Siddique was 90% proof and can only be described as a brain explosion. It was the drink of choice for many but could be extremely powerful, if not dangerous. Most people would drink it with mixers, but there were also those who took it neat as a shot. If you saw someone with what looked like a litre bottle of water walking around the compound during the evening, you could safely assume that it was more likely to be Siddique, or 'Sid' to give it its code name.

The ingredients to make Sid were grape juice, sugar, and yeast, all freely obtainable in all the local supermarkets. Many of the men made their own variation of Sid in their homes, safe in the knowledge that the Saudis couldn't just walk onto the compound to socialise with us. However, the drink was also being distributed outside the compounds by TCNs and several were caught in possession, resulting in them being arrested and spending time in jail, with the possibility of deportation. While imprisoned, it was paramount that they ate decent food, so I would go cap in hand to the Catering Manager to organise food parcels for them, handing the food over to their colleagues to be delivered to the jail. This was obviously outside 'CA's' awareness because compassion was definitely not one of his strong points, especially considering most of our weekly meetings ended with him telling me to, "Get the fuck out of [his] office!"

Daytime shopping could also be an opportunity to experience the unexpected, such as the time I found myself on a visit to Ta'if with one of the Clinic Nurses. We'd set off to carry out welfare visits to the hospitals, where several of the employees were in-patients, followed by a visit to the Souq to do some shopping.

Arriving in the Ta'if, we were distracted by a large group of people dressed in traditional costume, accompanied by a heavy Police presence, gathering in the town square. My initial instinct was to get out of there but curiosity got the better of me. My colleague suggested they were all probably celebrating a festival of some kind, either that, or someone from the Saudi Royal Family might be visiting. So we headed discreetly towards the crowd, who by now were jostling for position and cheering loudly. Although we tried to maintain a low profile, it was very difficult being discreet when dressed in Western clothing, particularly when everyone around you was wearing traditional dress.

Suddenly the crowd started dispersing and gaps were appearing in their ranks. Whatever the occasion had been, it was now over and everyone was leaving. I assumed we'd missed a ceremonial sword dance or something like that because there in full view was a man dressed all in white, wearing a mask and walking away from a podium carrying a huge, fearsome sword. It was then that I saw a kneeling, headless corpse slumped forward on the ground with its head just feet away from the body. I just froze in fear at this horrific reality of life in KSA and stared at everyone around me to see whether they had noticed the look of horror on my face. It was one of those occasions when you didn't quite know how you were expected to behave. Should I, as a Westerner, have been seeing this sort of thing and in doing so, had I violated a law?
More importantly, could I be punished for witnessing the scene of the execution?

But everyone around me seemed totally unconcerned by our presence and sauntered away, smiling, chatting, and continuing on with their day. I slowly turned on my heels and had no other thought than to get away from that square and back to the safety of the Suburban as quickly as possible. Once I reached the car, I locked the doors and just sat there for 10 minutes, letting the anxiety wash over me. The Nurse on the other hand was not in the least shocked by the events, but then he'd already lived in the KSA for several years. He continued his shopping trip alone, while I - discretion being the better part of valour - waited in the car. There was no way I was going to risk bumping into the man in white!

Our weekly meetings with 'CA' and the other Managers from Site Services were scheduled to take place on Mondays and always in his office. Before each meeting, 'CA' would have closely scrutinised all invoices and schedules and then, one-by-one, would start challenging us regarding their content, hoping and praying that he'd find something wrong. He rarely did, but he tried his best. Predictably in my case, he would go through my invoices with a fine-tooth comb and disagree with all of them, right down to last bottle of Tylenol. He would then proceed to tell us all, with great relish, just how incompetent we all were, how we were not reaching our targets and that, if we wanted to keep our jobs, things would need to improve.

Then would come the dynamite moment that everyone waited for each Monday, the handing over of the Sickness Absence List. This was composed of any individual who I'd signed off as being unfit for work (in the majority of cases Food Handlers because their stool samples indicated the presence of an intestinal parasite infection) with the anticipated amount of time they needed to be absent in order to fully recover. Always, at that precise moment, the rest of my colleagues would start moving their chairs backward to avoid being drenched with spittle as 'CA' inevitably erupted in fury, thumping the table and branding everyone on the list as, "Lazy fucking bastards!" This would usually be followed with thirty minutes of 'CA's' absolute volcanic rage, his face turning puce and eyes bulging. It was a joy to behold, even though the majority of 'CA's' bile was directed towards me and the unfortunate Catering Manager.

Both of us would be dismissed from the meeting with the usual departing message, "Now get the fuck out of my office!" Afterwards, all the Managers, with much merriment, would gather around the swimming pool to debrief. There would be even more hilarity and issuing of brownie points if we'd managed to get 'CA' to mutter the self-important phrase, "Yes, I am the Camp Commander!" That response was usually prompted by one of us telling him: "I'm only bringing this to your attention because you're the Camp Commander." It was our goal to get him to use the phrase at least once a day because the personal fall-out for 'CA' was the stark realisation that he was not omnipotent and in control of everything, particularly sickness absence and of course him referring to himself as a camp commander was a bonus for me.

For him, it was all about control and power because, in reality, the impact absent employees had on Catering Services was relatively minimal. The worst-case scenario might be that someone on the larger compound had to wait a couple of minutes extra for their pizza or, God forbid, having to get their own drinks from the soda machine.

To rescue his ego, 'CA' would walk around the compound to abuse the TCNs, even though the number of his victims became fewer as everyone grew wise to this deeply flawed and insecure individual who could only cope with his insecurity by bullying and verbally abusing others.

He would then inevitably vanish across to the large compound to lick his wounds and no doubt complain bitterly about us all.

Homesickness was a problem in the compound, particularly with those guys who were away from their homes for lengthy periods and who didn't cope well with long separations from their family and friends. They would experience difficulty trying to adjust to the unfamiliar environment and the added culture shock. Adjusting to KSA and compound life did not happen overnight and while the majority had good coping strategies, others didn't.

Managers were always vigilant about spotting staff who they thought were struggling and would refer them to the clinic, hoping they'd confide in someone, usually me, to help ease their burden. Even if they didn't, I could always offer them some guidance on how to cope better or try to find a solution to their problems. It's not easy getting men to share their feelings but once they'd started talking and realised that they could trust you, many would confide in you. Unfortunately though, some of them were coping with the help of Sid, which was a whole different ballgame.

Some Managers would call me up in clinic looking for their staff if they hadn't shown up for work, thinking they had an appointment with me. It was often the case that they were with me, but on one particular occasion a Manager called to say that the member of staff he was looking for hadn't been to work for a couple of days. We arranged to visit the absentee employee's room where, after knocking several times without any response, we eventually had to get someone to let us in with a master key. As we walked into the darkened room, we saw a man sat on the side of his bed crying, his head clasped in both hands. I could hardly make out a word he was saying because he was sobbing so loudly. He was also sweating profusely, unable to keep his hands still and became highly irritable each time I asked him a question.

On first impression, he looked like he had a fever and the only way we could establish the cause was to get him to the hospital as quickly as possible. But each time I suggested that course of action, his irritability increased. He just wanted us to leave him alone, saying that he was going to be all right. Clearly, that wasn't going to happen, so I left it with his Manager to talk some sense into him while I opened the front door, curtains, and some windows just to get rid of the acrid stench of stale vomit. At the same time, my neighbour appeared at the door with a bottle of water and entered the room, encouraging the stricken man to have a drink. I instinctively knew from the worried look on his face, along with his and the Manager's suspicious behaviour, that something was clearly not right.

I stood back, observing the whole scenario and it didn't take long for me to establish that something wasn't adding up. What was obvious, however, was that the glass of water, which had now been flavoured with orange juice, couldn't be grasped properly by the patient and my neighbour had to hold it for him as he gulped it down. The penny suddenly dropped - it was all to do with the demon drink. I closed the door and insisted they told me the truth because if they didn't, I would be calling an ambulance, even without consent. With the patient still crying and a second glass of orange juice being prepared by his Manager, my neighbour took me outside for a chat. He confirmed my suspicions that the patient had a history of alcohol addiction and had relapsed badly on Sid since arriving in Saudi. This had been his attempt at going cold turkey, which he'd tried on several other occasions, each attempt ending in failure.

Back in the room, the look on the patient's face told me he was fully aware of what I'd just been told. He pleaded with me not to say anything, becoming more and more tearful and distressed. He had every right to be worried and upset because not only could this result in him losing his job and ruining any future plans he might have, more importantly, his life was at stake. After about an hour he became much calmer and I reassured him that I would help him as much as I could but that we all needed to meet that evening at his Manager's house. My neighbour would have to monitor him and his alcohol consumption until then.As I left, his Manager confessed to having known about this problem for six months and that he'd been covering up for his employee.

When we met up that evening, there was to be yet another serious disclosure. My neighbour was also an alcoholic and both he and the patient were boozing buddies. The two of them had tried several times to go cold turkey but without any success; both had struggled with acute withdrawal symptoms and would always start drinking again within hours. I genuinely feared about how all this was going to pan out because a treatment programme for someone in a country where alcohol was illegal wasn't an option.

Discretion was my primary concern; nothing could be shared with anyone outside the room and definitely not with 'CA.' We sat there until the early hours of the morning as they shared stories of their past issues with alcohol addiction and rehab attempts while back in the UK, and how they'd both been in recovery when they'd accepted contracts to work in Saudi. The priority for them when they arrived in KSA had been to use the opportunity to rebuild their lives after years of addiction. They thought that Saudi was an excellent choice because it was a 'dry' country and so the temptation to drink alcohol would not be there. However, they'd not foreseen the easy availability of Siddique and both had relapsed very quickly after their arrival.

Their families and friends back in the UK were totally unaware that they'd relapsed, especially as they continued to send their salaries home each month. Supporting their families financially was hugely important to them because after years of addiction, which had brought financial hardship and emotional turmoil to them and their families, Saudi was the opportunity for them to make amends. Sadly, and predictably, it had backfired spectacularly on both of them.

I had no substantial plan for either of them other than insisting they both start gradually reducing the amount of alcohol they consumed and ruling out any attempt to go cold turkey again. I didn't want to run the risk of them having a seizure during their alcohol withdrawal, a distinct possibility that would result in a hospital admission and even more problems by extension. Worryingly, they were both still driving around Ta'if, which also had to stop immediately. One accident was all it would take for catastrophic consequences, particularly if a Saudi were involved. So, they were grounded in the compound for the foreseeable future and would be monitored at work by their Manager until we could all come up with a long-term treatment plan.

Over the next days there were few encouraging signs that they were actually reducing their alcohol consumption, even though their behaviour socially didn't suggest they were physically dependent on it. However, every time they spoke to me their distress was obvious and so, with no other option available, I decided to talk to the Doctor working on the other compound. I'd established a really good relationship with him but had no idea how he might react once I told him about the situation. The night before my meeting with him, I laid awake pondering every scenario and by morning, I concluded that I would just have to tell him the truth, but not share the names of the two workers involved.

My conversation with him began as a hypothetical scenario but quickly moved to the real situation and, as I expected, he strongly advised they leave the country to get help. He would not budge, reiterating time and time again that repatriation was their only option. I knew, however, that neither of them would be prepared to go back to the UK, not least because they feared how their families would react to the news of their relapse, but also because of the distinct possibility they'd lose their jobs, jeopardising the fresh start they'd planned for themselves and their families.

The Doctor's rather simplistic solution was that the men could just leave Saudi and walk into a Rehab Unit for several months and then everything would be fine. In reality, they would be put on a long waiting list for a place and they certainly hadn't earned enough money in their first year to pay for private treatment. Equally, if he thought that 'CA' would keep the men's jobs open for the amount of time Rehab would take, he was sorely mistaken. What I needed - and what they wanted - was an on-site 'home detox' which I could then monitor and supervise.

But for that to happen, I needed the Doctor to first examine them and prescribe medication.

230

Following much pleading, begging and promises that I would take responsibility for the pair if he agreed to prescribe a home detox, he finally said he would consider the option and after a game of tenpin bowling, which he won, he eventually agreed to prescribe the appropriate medication. He made it very clear though that it would be a one-off and only on the condition that he examined them beforehand and that he visited them daily during their detox. He would take full responsibility for their care plan and I would be responsible for observing them 24/7 and ensuring they stayed safe during their recovery.

I was so relieved at the outcome because the guys had shown such motivation attempting to abstain on several previous occasions, even if it had always ended in failure. This time, the medication the Doctor prescribed would be enormously helpful in relieving the acute withdrawal symptoms they'd experience. Even better, the Doctor agreed to order the medication on his pharmacy order. There was no way I could include it on mine because 'CA' would inevitably question the need for it and that would then let the cat out of the bag.

Armed with the good news, I called a meeting and told them about the home treatment plan. They couldn't believe their luck and gave me permission to disclose their names to the Doctor. The following day I organised their appointments with him and within a couple of days, all the arrangements for the home detox were in place. They both took a week's break from work and took up temporary residence at their Manager's house.

The first three days was a struggle as the medication didn't completely relieve them of their withdrawal symptoms. But they were able to cope and, by the end of the week, were both coming off their medication slowly. Having taken that first big step towards recovery, both of them could return to work under the supervision of their Manager, who had been a heroic supporter throughout. The most important objective now was preventing a relapse and, in the absence of any Alcoholics Anonymous meetings in Ta'if, the guys both agreed to support each other and kept their daily appointments with me in clinic.

Crisis had been averted in the short-term but they had to continue to work hard at staying sober. Eventually, they gradually shared their story with others on the compound, including the fact that they were in recovery, although no one knew about the detox programme other than those who needed to.

Towards the end of my contract, we had the opportunity of leaving the compound for the weekends and so, on Saturday mornings, a whole group of us would travel in convoy down the scary escarpment to Jeddah and we would pitch up on a beach for the weekend, sleeping on sun loungers under the moonlight. It was a truly amazing adventure and a fantastic opportunity to relax and de-stress. Several of our group would go diving, whilst the rest of us spent hours snorkelling in the Red Sea, then sunbathing until sundown. Once it got dark, we'd light a fire and cook dinner, chatting until the early hours. Living the dream!

Snorkelling was an amazing experience because I'd never done anything like it in my life. The Red Sea was like an underwater paradise and an unknown world to me. I'd never seen colours like it and was in awe at the sight of clownfish in among clusters of anemones, and huge manta rays gliding effortlessly along. There were hundreds of species of fish and coral and it truly resembled a tropical rainforest below water. My closest proximity to fish up till then had been at the fish and chip shop in Rochdale, goldfish at the Fairground and sticklebacks in the Little Dell.

I was so fortunate to have met such a great bunch of people through working in KSA and having that truly memorable experience. I was sad to leave because I knew that I would miss the new friends I'd made. We had built up a special bond with each other over the year, not least because most of us had arrived there alone and were initially isolated behind a huge wall. The network of friendship we'd built together was the closest thing we could get to family and it became very important to us all, especially in times of need. On the evening of my departure, everyone waved me off in style - including the two recovering alcoholics, who I'm pleased to say were still sober. It was all quite emotional.

Incidentally, I never did encounter the dreaded Camel Spider while in Saudi Arabia, despite checking my room every night just in case there was one lurking there. Camel Spiders had been given a bad press, depicting them as being large, venomous predators, as fast as a running human and with a voracious appetite for large mammals. Those myths are untrue. Camel Spiders don't actually eat camels' stomachs or sleeping soldiers and they are not particularly large. Nevertheless, they are still amazing predators and should be avoided at all costs. You've been warned!

—

Once again, it was time for me to make another fresh start and so I returned to the UK and the Camel Spider-free zone of Salford, to continue working in Occupational Health.

Before starting work, though, it was off to Australia to visit Barbara, obviously via New York for a catchup with Hendy and Lorelei. I arrived in Brisbane feeling totally exhausted but Barbara and Dave were at the airport to meet me, with their now four children all shouting "Uncle Graham!" from the roped-off area in the Arrivals lounge. I was immediately energised as soon as I saw them and tears of joy flowed as we hugged each other for the first time in many years - and continued for some time afterwards as we travelled to their home in Goombungee, in the Toowoomba region of Queensland. It was an absolute tonic to see Barbara again and to know that she was settled in the very small town she called home. She was working part-time as well as raising her family and had friends and great neighbours. Without doubt, Toowoomba was spectacularly beautiful.

We spent many happy days over the next six weeks, travelling around Queensland with the kids, just enjoying the outdoors and occasionally travelling into Brisbane to visit her in-laws, who'd subsequently emigrated to Australia once Barbara and Dave had settled there.

She was the best Mum and interestingly had adopted a parenting style similar to Dad's. I would often hear her use the 'W' interrogation method with her own children and she told me she probably knew what the boys were up to long before they ever did anything. She put that down to being raised with Warran and me.

On my final day, all the family accompanied me to the airport to bid Uncle Graham farewell, but the tears shared

234

between Barbara and I were ones of true sorrow rather than happiness. As the plane took off, I wondered when I would see her again.

Back in the UK, my rented flat felt soulless on those grey Salford days. I liked the area because it had a great sense of community and I had good neighbours, but inside the flat was a different story. It just felt barren, sterile, and cold, not least because of its bare white walls and cold floorboards. I couldn't be bothered improving it because I didn't know how long I'd be staying there.

Work was easy to find through an Agency, which meant I wasn't spending too much time indoors and I'd been able to reconnect with some of my friends in Manchester.
Meeting up with Ken, Derek, Alan, and Tommy again was a real boost as they always brought joy to my life and we'd shared several good holidays together in Spain. We booked through the same Travel Agency every year, paid our deposits, and made monthly payments until it was paid off. With every monthly payment our excitement grew.

Sitges was always our preferred destination when we went on holiday together and we would reminisce about our times there at every opportunity. Sitges was a glorious place and most years a group of us would holiday there for at least a week, sometimes two if we could afford it. We would always opt for B&B at a hotel rather than full board because money was always in short supply. What little money we had left over after paying for the holiday was spent on buying new outfits and socialising in Sitges, which meant that, effectively, our daily holiday budgets went on booze, cigarettes, and sun loungers, with just the occasional meal out.
Breakfast at the hotel was always a stealth operation as, shark-like, we would circumnavigate the buffet table

235

collecting as much food as possible to last us the entire day.

We lived off tinned tuna and tinned peaches, which we ate in our room straight out of the tins. Either that or we'd become lavish and buy a whole chicken and chips from the vendor on the main street. That was always a welcome relief because there are only so many boiled eggs, ham sandwiches and crisps you can eat within a two-week period, in whatever combination - and believe me, we tried them all. Our suitcases were also crammed with dried food, such as packet soups, so that we could supplement our diets.

On one memorable occasion as we sunbathed around the pool, one of our group shouted from the hotel's 10th floor - in full earshot of everybody - "Soup's ready!" Obviously, we didn't answer or respond and just smiled at those around the pool, who by now were sneering at the shouting and questioning what lunatic would drink soup when the outside temperature was easily at 100-degrees. We joined in with the condemnation and started to turn our heads to look for the people he was screaming at, just to confirm to everyone around the pool that it wasn't us. That, however, just prompted more vociferous yelling as he started calling us all by name, "Tommy, Alan, Graham, Ken, Derek, soup's going cold!" Hunger finally got the better of us and, one-by-one, we peeled off back to our room, trying very hard not to be noticed and pretending we were just going inside to get some shade.

Food didn't really matter to us that much but we realised it was a schoolboy error to go out drinking on an empty stomach. The holiday was all about socialising and we'd spend the whole time living a hedonistic lifestyle and making every attempt to look fabulous each evening, preparing ourselves for the walk along 'Sin Street.' Sin Street was lined on both sides with outdoor bars, clubs, and restaurants and only the brave dared walk along there because it was the classic people-watching alley. No one held back with their observations or comments but, equally, it was THE place both to see who was around and to be seen. You'd have no option but to run the gauntlet of criticism or applause and only then could you take a seat at one of the countless bars to join everyone else watching the endless parade of mainly gay men and women and a plethora of drag queens struggling to walk on the cobblestones, hurtling the odd juicy profanity as they fell off their heels.

Later, everyone would move inside en masse to the clubs, which would be packed to the rafters until the early hours of the morning, much like the beach was during the day. A varied mix of nationalities from Europe, Australia and America would gather in Sitges during the summer.

Everyone was there to have a great time but no matter how late a night you'd had, it was compulsory to be on the beach for sunbathing the next day. The beach was also the perfect place to catch up on missed sleep, waking only for the daily gossip, to reapply sun lotion or admire the view of the queens preening themselves.

And then there was the compulsory synchronised movement of sun beds several times a day to get the full benefit of the sun's rays. It was an art form and, had it been an Olympic sport, we would have won Gold. As the sun went down, everyone would head back to their hotel for a siesta and to grab something to eat before regrouping for 'party central' once more.

Most nights, queens staying at our hotel would stagger through reception at dawn glistening with foam from the clubs' foam parties, sometimes clutching at their last bottle of beer and sometimes eating a 'dick baguette' from the late-night tapas bar. It was chicken, actually, but the similarities between the Spanish words 'pollo', which means chicken, and 'polla', which means dick, got lost in translation during the ordering process. The regulars in the tapas bar would howl with laughter as drunk queens queued up and one-by-one and deliberately ordered a 'polla sandwich.'

The hotel's reception staff also enjoyed hours of entertainment as they observed the once immaculate queens tottering through the hotel foyer, just shadows of their former selves. Drag queens with wigs askew - that's if they still had them - clutching stilettos, handbags, and broken heels; leather queens rattling like chain link fences, drenched in sweat, and half-undressed queens, having shed various items of clothing during their partying. There were queens trying to smuggle their latest beau past vigilant reception staff and unaccompanied queens screaming for their beds.

But no matter what state they'd been in the night before, nor the hour they finally got to bed, they were always up and about by breakfast the following morning, ready, willing, and able to give a blow-by-blow account of the previous evening's escapades. That was the time when you either held your head in shock and disbelief, bowed your head in shame or rewarded them with a beaming smile, envying their successful night out.

It was also in Sitges that I met Steve, my husband-to-be.

CHAPTER NINETEEN

'Things begin to fall into place'

In my wildest dreams I never thought that in my lifetime I would ever legally refer to another man as my husband. Steve, my very own 'Cockney Rebel' – although I have no idea why, after 35 years, I refer to him in that way
because he was certainly not born within the sound of Bow Bells and he certainly isn't a rebel.

Maybe it was because he was from the South of England and called Steve and bore a vague resemblance to Steve Harley, the lead singer of the pop group 'Cockney
Rebel.' Interestingly, Steve looked slightly more like Steve Harley once his much-used hair lightening product kicked in. He couldn't resist the temptation of spraying his hair daily with it, when just one application would easily have been sufficient. As a result, his hair was more 'dirty blond' than sun-kissed highlights, but nevertheless he was very tall, blond, and strikingly handsome.

I found him much more interesting than most people I'd normally meet while on holiday and I was immediately attracted to his personality. Back then, I would have described him as being a 'posh lad,' mainly because of the way he spoke. He also had an aura of amazing calmness about him that made me look positively manic by
comparison. Steve had - and still has for that matter - such a great sense of humour, almost childlike, and was the sort of person who was caring and considerate enough to ensure that all of the late-night revellers got home safely.

He is a non-drinker and given that these holidays were loud and boisterous by nature and more often than not fuelled by alcohol, anyone not drinking automatically faded into the background. Maybe he chose not to drink because he didn't need to in order to enjoy a good night out. He is the quiet one of any group, not because he is shy or lacks confidence but because he has no desire to be the centre of attention. I'm sure he loved watching and observing our ridiculous drunken antics though and was thankful it wasn't him, especially when he saw our fragile state in the mornings, slaughtered from the night's shenanigans.

Like me, Steve was with a group of friends on holiday when we met, and fortunately everyone gelled. We socialised most days and continued on until the early hours of each morning. The two of us got on really well, even when it became apparent that we didn't share any mutual interests. He was a complete petrol head, while what I knew about cars could be written on the back of a postage stamp. We came from very different social backgrounds but I didn't feel there were any major stumbling blocks in the way of us getting on. It was such a contrast meeting someone that was not a mirror version of myself, someone who was comfortable in his own skin - and I also liked the fact that he'd paid for dinner when we went to eat out on my final night of the holiday. We connected quite easily and for most of the holiday we ditched our friends and went out without them, regrouping with them in the early hours of the morning.

When it was time for me to leave and face the trauma of an early morning flight home after a very late night of socialising, I discovered I'd lost Steve's 'phone number in the hurried chaos of packing. I searched my luggage several times once I got home but it was nowhere to be found. I cursed myself because his two-week holiday had only just started when I'd left and now I was back in the UK, desperately bored and missing some of my friends who were still out there partying with him. The best I could hope for was that he had also shared his 'phone number with them but when I checked in with them on their return, they didn't have it and I remonstrated with myself for not having given him mine. He was, after all, the sensible one and would not have lost it.

Several weeks had passed when Tommy and I met up for our usual Saturday night out in Manchester when we happened to bump into Sue, who'd also been on holiday with us in Sitges. Immediately on seeing me she produced from her bag a scrap of paper with Steve's 'phone number on it. Sue was the last person I'd thought would have it but she told me, "He knew you would lose it!" That Sunday night, while nursing the hangover from hell, I called Steve. He sounded genuinely surprised to hear from me but invited me to visit him in London.

I didn't really want a long-distance relationship but there followed many months of commuting between Salford and London to spend the weekends with each other. It became more apparent with each visit that, despite our differences, there was also compatibility. Steve loved spending time in the North-West just as much as I loved spending time in the South. That said, he found my accommodation quite challenging. It was a very cold winter that year and my rented flat in Salford didn't have any central heating, just static electric wall heaters in the living room and bathroom, leaving every other room in the flat freezing cold. Even in one's wildest imagination, the place couldn't have been described as being cosy.

The following summer, and after much deliberation, Steve asked me to move in with him and I agreed. I had no regrets about giving notice on my flat and, having secured a job in Occupational Health down South, I loaded up my car with all my possessions and headed off to London. Moving in was effortless really because I didn't have much in the way of household items, but I did have money in the bank from my sojourn in Saudi Arabia.

"OH ALAN!"

One Sunday morning, Steve's brother and sister-in-law arrived unannounced at his house. News had filtered down to them that me and Steve were now living together and no doubt they were curious, as were his parents, to see who Steve's new 'friend' was. They came armed with an invitation for us to attend a Sunday lunch at Steve's parents.

At that point I knew very little about his parents, other than that they lived several miles away in Middlesex, in a small farm cottage on land they'd farmed for most of their lives. They were now semi-retired and spent most of their days tending to the kitchen garden, growing vegetables and flowers. Steve's Father also worked part-time as an Airline Courier and his Mother worked as a volunteer at the local hospice. I knew it was going to be a challenge and, the night before the planned lunch, I hardly slept a wink worrying about what searching questions they might ask or what food they might serve. - Avocado, asparagus, peppers, mange tout, petit pois - I'd only just acquainted myself with stuffed courgettes!

Thankfully it turned out that my fears were totally groundless because they couldn't have been more welcoming - once we finally got through their front door.

242

That part proved eventful as Steve's Father, Alan, couldn't open it and so we were left standing on the doorstep for ages. The front door never did open as Alan had pulled the front door handle off during his struggle to open it. We eventually entered through the garage, surprising Steve's Mother, Rita, who was busy preparing lunch in the kitchen. She seemed totally unfazed by Alan placing the front door handle on the draining board and announced with great excitement that lunch would be served soon and that she'd bought a bottle of wine to mark the very special occasion.

We all settled into the living room and Alan sat struggling unsuccessfully with the TV remote-control, which he eventually handed to Steve, then his brother and finally to me. I'd never seen a remote control like it, not because it was complicated but because it was just a melted, mangled piece of plastic with several buttons missing. Steve explained that his Dad had mistakenly thrown it onto the fire several months ago while topping up the grate with wood.
Apparently, it was working fine when he recovered it so there'd been no need to replace it! I was already getting the impression that Alan was, shall we say, slightly clumsy, and both his sons confirmed as much. While we were waiting for lunch they each told endless stories of his previous mishaps.

Steve grew up on a farm and, when it came to haymaking time, everyone mucked in to get the hay from the fields to the barn. Those were the days before Health & Safety and Risk Assessments and Steve and his cousins, whose ages ranged from 3 to 12-years old, rode backwards and forwards to the fields on a trailer towed behind the Ferguson tractor. All the kids sat on the top of the full load of hay bales on the trip down the rough unmade track back to the farm and then bounced along on the empty trailer back to the fields to collect another load.

Unfortunately, like quite a few things on a working farm, the trailer had seen better days and had a large hole in its floor through which the road could be clearly seen.

On one particular trip back to the field, tractor driver Alan decided to put his foot down - although, to be more accurate, in the case of the Ferguson it was a case of pulling the accelerator handle back. All the kids were hanging on to whatever was at hand as the tractor and trailer thrashed down the lane at speed. On arrival at the field, the kids noticed that one of their number was 'absent without leave.' Their cousin Charlie, who was just three years old at the time, had somehow fallen through the hole in the trailer during the journey. Alan quickly retraced his steps and there, sitting in the middle of the field was the bold Charlie, seemingly unconcerned and fortunately none the worse for wear.

My favourite story, however, will always be the one about Billy the horse. When Steve was a toddler, his Father operated a milk round from their farm in Iver, Buckinghamshire. Those were the days before electric milk floats and Alan had a milk cart which was hauled around the Iver streets by the carthorse, Billy. It was quite a load for the horse to pull, as the milk was delivered in glass bottles, with cardboard discs sealing the milk in.

Billy was a fine horse, but one of his least endearing qualities was his ability to get a bit bored part-way through the milk round. Many a time Alan had emerged from a front garden, having delivered a couple of pints to the front doorstep, only to find that Billy and the milk cart had disappeared. On those occasions, Alan had no option other than to catch the bus back to the farm with only half his milk round completed, where he would find Billy wedged in the stable door with the milk cart still attached. It was a regular occurrence and on each occasion Billy had navigated the journey back to the farm by himself without ever having an accident. Despite his wandering ways, Alan never parted with Billy and in his old age Billy was put out to pasture.

On another occasion, Rita decided that the large weeping willow tree in the garden could do with a trim, known officially as pollarding. Not daring to let Alan loose with a chainsaw, she seized the opportunity to ask Steve's brother, Bruce, to carry out the task while he was there on a visit from New Zealand. Bruce duly climbed to the top of the tree with the fearsome electric saw, while Alan was given the important job of holding the stepladder steady. Partway through the pruning, however, Alan got distracted and set off across the lawn - and in doing so managed to trip over the chainsaw's power cable. Poor Bruce was jerked violently backwards and only just managed to avoid falling from the tree and probably doing himself irreparable damage with the chainsaw.

We all remained seated in front of the blazing wood fire listening to the many 'Oh Alan' stories while Rita prepared lunch. She suddenly appeared, proudly pushing her teak-effect hostess trolley into the dining area, announcing that the gravy would be ready soon and we could all be seated. As we sat waiting for her to return, Alan started helping himself from the trolley and, by the time she came in, he'd already eaten his entire lunch, minus the gravy.

As such, my first meeting with Steve's family was certainly memorable - but for all the right reasons. They were kind and welcoming and Alan's clumsiness was endearing. It was very clear that his sons loved him and they howled with laughter as he entertained them with his antics and clumsiness. And Rita - well, she was just conditioned to

Alan's ways and accepted that he wasn't going to change any day soon.

There would be many more 'Oh Alan' moments over the years, such as the time we were staying in a very old hotel in the Dordogne. Arriving late in the afternoon, we retired to our rooms to take a shower before dinner. Shortly afterwards, we heard an almighty crash from Steve's parent's room next door and the floor literally shook. Hardly daring to leave our room, but knowing we had to find out what had happened, we discovered that, on exiting the shower, Alan had slipped, grabbed the shower frame to try to stop himself falling and had managed to end up on the floor in an ungainly heap with the complete shower cubicle on top of him. It wasn't a pretty sight. Fortunately, Alan was unhurt, the only thing bruised being his dignity. Luckily the hotel owners were very forgiving about the whole episode. It could easily have been curtains for Alan, though!

Rita and Alan also loved travelling and visited destinations all over the world. But once they were in their 80's, they needed a bit of help and guidance, so Steve and I would chaperone them on their trips to Europe. On one such trip to Annecy we had stopped to eat in a restaurant. However, because we'd been unable to park the car nearby, we'd left Alan and Rita sitting in the eatery whilst we went to collect it, intending to return to pick them up. In the meantime, while exiting the restaurant, Alan had found a very convenient 'shiny drum' to sit on. When we returned a few minutes later, we found Alan laid on his back in the road, floundering turtle-like, with Rita laughing so much that she couldn't help him up onto his feet. A passing Frenchman, unable to disguise his disgust, walked over, helped Alan to his feet then walked away muttering about how the English couldn't hold their drink. Unfortunately, Alan had chosen to sit on a traffic barrier which had withdrawn into the ground when a bus approached.

Steve's family were indeed very different to mine and were very accepting of us being together. As an innocent, Alan had no filter between his brain and mouth and I would have known if he'd disapproved of either me or our relationship. I felt truly happy with Steve, and the fact he had such a loving family made me even happier.

Once we had settled in Middlesex, my 'petrol head' wanted to buy a new red BMW Estate, which he did. Steve's pride and joy were clearly evident as we drove North to meet up with some of my family on Boxing Day. The time had come for Steve to meet them face-to-face and we'd arranged to have festive lunch with Warran, his wife, Jean, and their family.

When we arrived at their house however, we were greeted at the door by a frantic Jean who informed us that Warran, accompanied by his dog, was stuck in the snow out on the moors. We were quickly despatched off to the moors on a mercy mission to find him, armed with a shovel and rope. Sure enough, there he was with his dog, Buster, shivering beside his car, the bonnet of which was embedded in a deep snow drift. I knew very little about the technicalities of freeing a car from a big pile of snow but I did know that this particular challenge was going to be time-consuming and that it would require something more than a little push to resolve things.

There followed many valiant attempts at rocking the car, turning the steering wheel, and putting the car into reverse and then forward, but all to no avail. The car was most definitely stuck fast and by now we were all freezing. So it was time for 'Plan B,' which was to break out the shovels and clear the snow from around the tyres, with a view to then putting something underneath them to help gain a grip. Unfortunately, the only things that we could find to use were Steve's brand-new car mats.

Naturally, Steve was a tad reluctant to donate them, but needs must on such occasions and, despite the fact the new mats got completely shredded during the ferocious wheel spins, it did the trick and we got the car out of the drift. Once freed, my brother kept driving for fear of getting stuck again, while we got into Steve's car and slowly headed back.

We arrived to the familiar greeting of Jean's voice from behind a closed front door, asking loudly and repeatedly, "Is that the front door, Warran?" Eventually, he appeared at the window, gesticulating, and pointing for us to go around to the back door. We carefully negotiated the path down the side of the house while at the same time trying to fend off Buster, their huge German Shepherd, who just wanted to jump up and lick you to death but in so doing could easily floor you.

Arriving at the kitchen, we were greeted effusively by Jean. Normal conversation by that point was largely dependent on lip reading skills as the noise level was the equivalent of a Jumbo Jet taking off. The house was full of children, grandchildren and friends who were literally shouting at each other in order to be heard above the combined noise of someone singing Karaoke, Warran watching football on TV and the numerous buzzers and bell sounds coming from the various electronic games that were being played.

Steve had clearly made a friend in Buster, who'd decided that he wanted to sit on his lap and use him as a launchpad to play with Elvis the budgie, who was sat out of harm's way up on the curtain rail listening intently to Buster's barking. It's not easy removing an 80 lb dog from your lap, as Steve found out, but maybe Buster was just showing his gratitude for being rescued from the moors.
The noise level increased throughout the day and only abated when we sat down to lunch, with Buster's eyes firmly and longingly focussed on Steve's plate throughout. Even though our families were essentially different, Steve was blending into mine as I blended into his. It has been said frequently that Steve and I are different in many ways and maybe it's those profound differences that have kept us together for 35 years, with the inevitable compromises along the way.

One classic example was when Steve opened his picture framing shop in Twickenham shortly after we met. He was struggling to make any profit in the first year and, despite working long hours and weekends, we were barely surviving on our savings and my wage. In light of his need to make money, Steve asking me to work in his shop on Saturdays was probably not the best Business Plan. I enjoyed working there, meeting people and being creative, but I was losing money hand over fist when I introduced a discount for the OAPs' tapestries. Pensioners had lovingly worked on their tapestries for months but would quickly realise when they brought them to the shop that they couldn't afford to have them framed. Rather than deal with their disappointment, I introduced a Discount Scheme.

Predictably, word quickly got around that there was a nice man at the framing shop on Saturdays who gave OAPs a 50% discount on their tapestry framing and poor Steve was inundated. He would calmly try and explain that it was not cost effective but, once word got out, there was no turning back. There was a constant stream of elderly ladies, smelling of lavender water, clutching their tapestries, queuing patiently outside the shop on Saturday mornings waiting for it to open. To be fair, I think Steve made more compromises than me on that one and I had to accept I was not the best person for him to employ. It was obvious that retail was not my forté but I still continued to work in the shop on Saturdays, but under strict instructions not to operate my Discount System for anyone else other than those who had already been promised it.

I loved my varied work and social life. Friends and family from the North visited us often, I had accumulated all of Steve's friends, as he had mine and, through socialising, we made many more. It sometimes felt as if I was living in a gay metropolis, not least because my GP, Dentist, Car Mechanic, Accountant, Hairdresser and even the local Police Sergeant were gay, as were many of the tradesmen we employed to modernise our new home in Twickenham. However, I was not living in a 'gaybourhood' and our friendship group was not exclusively gay; it was eclectic and packed with fabulous people from diverse backgrounds and cultures. Many, like myself, had migrated to London from the four corners of the UK and overseas and, in the absence of our families, we somehow created a substitute family.

During the week, we socialised in smaller groups that catered to everyone's different interests. I joined the theatre group and went to the theatre often, but never attended the petrol-head gatherings or their car cruises for that matter. That was probably because I still had vivid memories of my childhood when my Father uttered those immortal words, "Let's go out for a run in the car."

Steve did, however, go on all the car cruises and briefly joined the theatre group. I say 'briefly' because it didn't last long. He absented himself pretty quickly after committing the ultimate sin of snoring in the stalls during a performance of 'Lettice and Lovage,' the comical and satirical play by Peter Shaffer. The audience members sat behind us could be heard protesting loudly mid-performance because of the racket he was making – I'm sure even Dame Maggie Smith heard the kerfuffle from onstage. Steve was never a massive fan of the theatre, nor did he display much interest in being a member of the skiing or tennis groups either. I on the other hand joined both and I didn't feel like a novice either. Perhaps slamming a tennis ball against our gable end, bogies and ice slides prepared me for both.

Socialising at the weekends was certainly different to weekdays and it was often the case that we would all meet up in Earl's Court on Friday night to do a grand circuit of the gay pubs and clubs. The initial meeting place was always 'Brompton's' and once everyone was accounted for, we moved on to the 'Copacabana' or the 'Catacombs' via the blacked-out windows of the 'Coleherne Bar.' Most nights, the bars would be heaving with people stood so close together you couldn't get a Rizla cigarette paper between them.
When someone moved everybody else had to move with them. Drinks were frequently spilled as people jostled for space and negotiating your way to the bar could take at least half an hour. Returning from the bar with several drinks - well, that was something else!

It was fraught with danger as you negotiated limited space to get back to your group while balancing drinks in both hands. Saying "Excuse me," had no effect because no one shifted - and to be fair there was nowhere they could shift to. Shouted apologies could be heard all around as drinks were inevitably spilled; most of them loudly accepted with a cheery "No problem."

Occasionally though, some vociferous queen would entertain the room by responding to a spillage with a volley of abuse especially if a new checked blouse had been soaked. Every bar was loud, fun, sometimes chaotic, and it seemed we all loved being packed like sardines inside these places.

The pavements outside the bars in Earl's Court were just as busy with gay pedestrian traffic as everyone wandered with eagerness to complete the bar/club circuit. At closing time, they'd be busier still as people stood around soaking up the gossip before heading off home. Had Princess Diana ever written a book about her late-night observations while living in Earl's Court, it would have undoubtedly been a bestseller. She practically lived on the doorstep of most of the gay venues in the area and she described that time as being her happiest. We certainly enjoyed ourselves.

Saturday afternoons were a more sedate affair, when the designated meeting place would be the 'Markham Arms' on the King's Road, or the 'Queen's Head' just around the corner. Once again, the pubs would be packed to the rafters with gay men socialising and in good weather, and to avoid drink spillage, it was actually possible to stand outside on the pavement and be heard.

Closing time was the cue for shopping the entire length of the King's Road before regrouping for coffee in 'Habitat' and the chance to have a quick rummage through each other's shopping bags. Sunday nights were also less hectic, our preferred meeting place being The 'Dog and Fox Ballroom' in Wimbledon.

Hundreds descended on the venue on Sunday nights to

enjoy the final weekend hours before work on Monday. The place never disappointed and despite drag queens and constant music providing the entertainment, it also had the luxury of having inside quiet areas where we could actually have audible conversations.

My Dentist was often in attendance, sometimes wearing roller skates and a pink tutu while speed skating the perimeter of the dance floor, occasionally pausing in quiet areas to remind people of their forthcoming appointments. He always met with everyone's approval as he joined others in hurtling around the periphery of the dance floor on their skates, bouncing along to a sound-track. Not my GP though, who, far from giving him his approval, instead just admonished him for his lack of decorum.

Collisions between roller skaters and fan dancers - think aggressive Flamenco and not Burlesque - were commonplace as they all vied for space on the dance floor. Roller skaters would weave in and out of suitably attired fan dancers, some in full clone mode (my Plumber), projecting masculinity for an evening of flailing their arms about while holding a fan, occasionally launching them in the air. They would only pause when a drag act (My Hairdresser) or male stripper took to the stage and suddenly, to their dismay, the music stopped.

People were definitely at risk of being mown down by a drunk roller skater or sustaining superficial lacerations from a wayward fan, as not all of them had perfected the art of fan dancing while on holiday in Sitges that Summer. The organiser of the event frequently banned roller skates and fans in the Ballroom but to no avail. Should anyone sustain an injury, of course, my GP was always on call throughout the evening. He loved it.

The quieter areas may have been much safer but were just as busy as the dance floor as they were the places to catch up on gossip and discover who was with who and who was no longer with who; or to brag about a sighting of Freddie Mercury in the 'Coleherne' or Kenny Everett in 'Brompton's.' It was also a good place if you required the services of a Handyman or Tradesman. You could barely get the words, "I'm looking for..." out of your mouth before someone recommended the best Plumber, Carpenter, Electrician, Curtain Maker, Kitchen Fitter, etc, to work on your particular project.

"Graham, I don't want to alarm you but the Kitchen Fitter has just turned up and he's dressed from head to toe in women's clothes and is wearing stilettos!" That was the call I received one day from my cousin, Freda, who was staying at our house at the time. Her disbelief didn't last for too long though as the very next day I got another call from her, this time to inform me that she and my cousin Barbara were off to Marks & Spencer's to buy the Workman some flat shoes. Apparently, it's bloody dangerous working in stilettos! Well I never.

If it was going to be a full-on Sunday, then we would usually start drinking early afternoon in the 'Vauxhall Tavern' as we watched Lily Savage – Paul O'Grady's alter ego. She and her fellow drag artists would bring the house down, especially when they performed their interpretation of the Death Row Tango, or when Lily compered her Amateur Drag Competition.
The judging panel on those occasions were the heavily inebriated audience and, to put it mildly, they were harsh, with most of the amateur drag artists being awarded their P45's. On those Sundays, we definitely needed to pace ourselves.

Saturday nights were often designated recovery nights in our house, not least because we had to recover from Friday and, more importantly, prepare for Sunday. But we didn't necessarily stay home. Often we'd venture out to the house of a friend who was unable to socialise because they had young children, or sometimes we had friends round who just didn't do the gay scene. I loved my life, my friends and my family and I definitely loved difference.

I felt blessed and so nothing could have prepared me for the dark times ahead as 15 of my close friends became sick and died.

Most were in their late 20's and 30's, people who should not have been dying and many of them in circumstances you wouldn't wish on anyone. Our beautiful friends were dying of Aids. This hideous disease was taking their lives and, as if that wasn't heartbreaking enough, homophobia was once again raising its ugly head as a result, primarily fuelled by misinformation in the tabloids. The red-tops were having a field day with headlines such as 'Britain threatened by Gay Virus Plague,' and 'My doomed son's Gay Plague Agony," and 'I'd shoot my son if he had Aids,' started to appear everywhere and, once again, gay and bisexual men were being demonised.

Sadly, our friends who had been diagnosed with HIV/Aids were only too aware of the hideous stories, as were their friends and families. It was cruel and ignorant victimisation of the worst kind. As a consequence of gay shaming being back on the agenda, some of our friends chose not to share their diagnosis outside their circle of family and close friends. Had they done so, they feared

255

that they would almost certainly leave behind a legacy of shame for their loved ones to endure.

In some cases they even chose not to inform their families about their diagnosis, particularly if their relatives lived hundreds of miles away or, in some cases, thousands of miles away in countries such as Australia, New Zealand, South Africa or the Caribbean. Some of our friends had concealed their sexuality from their families for years and their dilemma seemed insurmountable once they were diagnosed HIV/Aids. Not only did they carry the burden of speaking to their families about their sexuality for the first time, they also had to explain their diagnosis and its poor prognosis.

Over time it became a given that each month we would receive news of friends diagnosed with HIV/AIDS or a friend who had died. The calendar just kept filling up with more and more funerals and some weeks I just dreaded receiving the news. But denial was not an option -it was real, it was happening. More importantly, our friends needed us more than ever and for those friends whose families were thousands of miles away our support was even more vital.

The disease slowly took the lives of our young, beautiful, handsome, and fun-loving friends and all we could do was provide them with comfort and emotional and practical support. We cared deeply and watched over them as they succumbed to the disease, losing their eyesight and memory, struggling to breathe and swallow and, in some cases, becoming slowly disfigured by cancerous purple patches of Kaposi's Sarcoma on their body and face. It was emotionally and physically draining but we ensured they would never feel alone and would always know that they were loved.

My one abiding memory of this time will always be their bravery and courage. I witnessed it first-hand, just as I witnessed their tears, fear, sadness, depression, and anger. Their suffering triggered within me a depth of empathy I never realised possible and it also pushed the reset button to change my career path.

The sense of injustice and unfairness many of us felt was present most days, as was our anger at watching the suffering of our friends and their loved ones who were caring for them. It was difficult to know how to channel that anger and my only answer was to be more proactive and become a volunteer for the Terrence Higgins Trust (THT). At least that way I could provide practical help and emotional support for those either in hospital or feeling isolated in the community.

Other friends channelled their energy into raising money for the THT by organising a plethora of events, ranging from the dignified to the outrageous. Each was memorable and always in honour of our absent friends, who we missed desperately. We celebrated their lives, their joy, their fun, their friendship, and the love they brought to the world and our lives. We grieved publicly, supported each other and, most importantly, we vowed to remember them, as we still do today.

Today HIV-positive individuals can lead full and healthy lives if they are diagnosed early enough and receive treatment, but sadly times were very different back then. The suffering of our friends is forever etched into my memory. Their names are still in the address book, they will never be erased because each Christmas as I write my cards their names trigger wonderful memories for me and I am able to spend time with them once again.

The Reset

The work commute into London each morning was taking its toll on me and my career reset button had been well and truly activated. It was time for me to start considering my career options, either a complete change or even a sideways move within Nursing that didn't require me giving up my Nursing Registration.

Counselling was also an option as I'd already completed a course on Introductory Counselling Skills. While the course hadn't equipped me with sufficient knowledge to provide a full Counselling Service to anyone, it had certainly given me an insight.

So, finally I decided on a career move that did not require me to give up my Nursing Registration or income. It would, however, be a gradual process evolving from Nurse to Psychotherapist, although at the time I was totally unaware exactly how long that process would be. I would discover eventually that my academic studies and vocational training would take me 10 years to complete before finally achieving a Master's degree.

The early years of my studies were challenging to say the least and at times it proved to be a difficult balancing act between work, study, and home life. Some days I was returning home after a 15-hour day of work and study, which is not something I would recommend to anyone. Despite that, I loved my new career choice and studying Psychology, Psychotherapy, Counselling and Supervision at college and university. But the long hours took their toll and I had to accept I no longer had a work-life balance. It was just work, work, work and eventually, to avoid burn out, I decided I had to sacrifice my income and resigned from my full-time job to work once again as an Agency Nurse. That certainly helped because now I had much more flexibility in the hours I worked and my shift choices were much more compatible with my studies and home life.

One week the Agency called and asked if I would go to the ITV Studios in London to cover an evening shift in their Occupational Health Department and from that day onwards, I became their Preferred Agency Nurse whenever they needed cover. The workload was slightly unpredictable and varied; some days I could be working in the recording studios, while on others I could be on location providing a treatment service for minor ailments, illnesses and injuries to the cast and crew. On other days, I might be working in the Occupational Health Department alongside a Doctor, Occupational Health Nurses, Counsellors, and Physiotherapists.

The days could be long but it was always a very happy workplace and I looked forward to getting the call from the Agency each week with my ITV shifts, not least because I needed the money to survive, as studying was financially demanding. On the weeks I wasn't needed, I would have to seek out other Agency work around the Central London and Middlesex areas.

Over my ten-year study period, I'd taken so many courses and learned so much about Psychological Theory, the various approaches to Counselling and Psychotherapy, Supervision, Mental Health and Risk Assessments. I had participated in practical courses, role-played, worked on several help and advice telephone lines and in GP practices. I had spent hour upon hour sitting in sessions with Counsellors and Psychotherapists and even worked alongside the counsellor in ITV's Occupational Health Department. Nevertheless, the thought of going it alone as a Psychotherapist was daunting. The transition, however, from Nurse to Psychotherapist proved seamless in many ways because, coincidently, the ITV Staff Counsellor — A Mentor and Supervisor whom I had worked alongside as a colleague for many years while studying — was retiring and I was to become her replacement. I learned a great deal from her during the time that we worked together.

People often self-referred to the Counselling Service with work-related issues such as stress, overwork, difficult colleagues etc, whilst others presented with more personal issues that were having a negative impact on their mental health. Some were going through a life-crisis such as bereavement and loss, relationship and family difficulties, substance misuse or stresses at home. Occasionally, I would also have to make home visits to someone who was absent from work due to mental health issues.

The Counselling Service was available to all ITV employees and it was their safe and confidential place to talk. The appointment diary was always full and, when I wasn't working in the clinic, I would be working closely with the rest of the OH and Health & Safety teams.

It had been a long haul combining studying with working and, at times, emotionally and physically draining, but I had no regrets about the new career path I'd taken. I also had no regrets about devoting 50% of my private practice to clients at low cost, which effectively meant the vast majority of them didn't have to pay. As a consequence however, I needed to keep my paying day job.

I attended numerous personal therapy sessions throughout my training because, like everyone else, I also encountered difficulties in my life. Over the years, however, I'd also learned to put some things on the back burner. One thing in particular was still simmering away and it was time to acknowledge and face up to it; I needed to track down and speak to my Birth Mother. But first I would have to find her — and once I had, what exactly was I going to find out?

CHAPTER TWENTY

'The woman with the flame-red hair and the man in Army uniform'

As a child I never did see myself through the lens of abandonment and I really didn't feel the emotional impact of my Mother's departure unless it was triggered by external events. Of course, there were times when I perceived myself as being different to other children living with their Birth Mothers but, in general, it wasn't something I would dwell on. I certainly didn't feel emotionally scarred by her sudden departure because I had my Father's nurturing and love. My Aunts, Mrs. Dawson, Warran, and other members of my family also loved and supported me throughout my childhood and had collectively encouraged me to feel self-love.

That's not to say there weren't occasions when, as a child and even as an adult, I would think about why she'd left and what had happened to her. But to address those questions with any member of my family would have been futile. Their sworn silence about my Mother would always prevail, even though by the same token they didn't bad-mouth her either. In their eyes she just didn't exist and we never anticipated her coming back. I had never previously felt the need to have contact with her either. Then, in my 30s, curiosity began to get the better of me and I started to ponder whether or not to seek answers.

I eventually decided to place an advert in the local newspaper. It didn't particularly fill me with dread, nor did I have any anxieties thinking about what I might do if she didn't respond. After all, I'd never felt a persistent longing to have her in my life, but at the same time I was fascinated by the mystery of who she was and where she'd been for most of my life. More importantly, I was intrigued to know the circumstances that had led to her abandoning me and Warran. I was also keen to learn more about my maternal ancestry as the void caused by not knowing had existed for so long.

I did get slight palpitations when a reporter from Rochdale's local newspaper, where I'd placed the advert, contacted me, and asked if they could document the reunion, should it ever happen. My answer to that question was a resounding no. Much to my surprise, though, my advert was successful and, within seven days of placing it, my Mother contacted me by telephone. I was at home doing some chores when the phone rang and I answered it just as I would any other call without caller ID. Once she had established who I was, she introduced herself as Dorothy.

There followed a very long pause because I had absolutely no idea what to say. I certainly had not anticipated tracking her down in such a short space of time. I don't know how I felt to be honest, other than recalling the shock at hearing her voice, but I did at least stop ironing! I was totally unprepared for the conversation because I didn't really believe she'd ever respond to my advert, let alone so quickly.

We shared pleasantries, discussing the weather and other minor details about our lives, but there were no intrusive questions on either side. No mention was made of why she had walked out on us, nor our brief chance encounter on the day my Father was buried. I was grateful for that because I didn't want to have that particular conversation over the 'phone. I just kept the conversation very light-hearted and made sure I didn't say anything I might regret. The call lasted all of 10 minutes but now, at the very least, we each had the other's number and further contact was possible. I was hopeful that this initial conversation would give me an opportunity to have all my burning questions answered and I was determined to do that face-to-face.

Several weeks passed before I finally made the call to arrange a meeting with her but she was very hesitant to commit. Instead, she suggested that we remain in contact by 'phone for a while longer, which I agreed to. However, she rang again the following day to agree a face-to face-meeting, implying that this change of heart had been triggered after discussing things with her sister, Hazel, in whom she confided.

The meeting was scheduled for two weeks later, on a Sunday afternoon, at Hazel's house in Manchester. I was very calm about the whole reunion but then I was neither seeking her love nor approval and didn't need her support either. I didn't even expect or want an apology. I felt no anger towards her for abandoning me; all I wanted were answers. If she was prepared to do that for me then I would be thankful. I did, though, also want to make my own mind up about her rather than listen to anyone else's narrative.

Warran wanted no part of what I was doing but accepted my reasoning for meeting up with Dorothy and didn't have a problem with my doing so. He wasn't shocked or disappointed but, in his view, I should let sleeping dogs lie. He did, however, want to know the outcome of the meeting. Warran didn't harbour any animosity towards Dorothy, he just wanted a quiet life with his family without any disruption.

On the day of our scheduled meeting, though, he called me and I could detect the concern in his voice as he attempted to persuade me not to go through with it, simply because he believed I would only end up getting hurt. But I was equally determined to go.

I felt neither excited nor anxious as I drove North in studied silence. After a four-hour journey, I finally arrived at the house. There was nobody standing on the path or waiting at the door to greet me, but I did notice a net curtain twitching as I knocked on the door. I knew instantly that the woman who answered it was not my Mother. She introduced herself to me as my Aunt Hazel, Dorothy's sister. She quickly became tearful and gave me the most enormous hug. We were joined in the lobby by her husband, who introduced himself as Uncle Barry and who also gave me an enormous hug while welcoming me into their home. We walked together into the living room and there was my Mother, sitting in a large armchair opposite the TV, still wearing her coat as if she had been uncertain about staying after she had arrived.

I knew instantly that it was her because, for the first time in my whole life, I was looking at someone who really looked like me. It was a surreal moment because we had the same facial features – I simply couldn't believe it. Throughout my entire life no-one in my family had ever looked like me, but now they did. It wasn't just a physical resemblance but was almost like seeing myself being reflected in another person's face - and suddenly from nowhere, I was emotionally overwhelmed. With my heart racing, I walked over to the chair where she sat and introduced myself, realising very quickly that I wasn't the only person feeling emotional. As I approached her I could read the fear on her face and, as I gave her a hug, I could actually feel her whole body trembling from head to toe.

Aunt Hazel started taking tea and coffee orders from everyone and busied herself setting up food on a buffet table, while I took a seat opposite my Birth Mother. Her face was full of fear and trepidation, then she asked me why I was looking for her. My response was unprepared: "I wanted to know if you looked like me," at which she laughed before immediately bursting into tears. Despite my many reassurances that I was not there to seek revenge or retribution, just answers, her tears continued to flow and she buried her face in her hands before walking into the kitchen to speak with Hazel. She returned a few minutes later, now composed but clutching some kitchen roll with which to wipe her tears away and then retook her seat opposite me.

It was a one-sided conversation as she spoke at length about her shame, guilt, and remorse at leaving me at such an early age and repeated the same words over and over again, "I'm sorry, I'm sorry." The constant theme was how she felt she wasn't deserving of Dad or her children when she was younger because she was not a good person. It was extremely hard to listen to because most of her narrative was self-deprecating. She took responsibility for everything and never once blamed my Father. It felt like she was focussed on beating herself up for being a bad Mum and her distress was plain to see. She asked for my forgiveness and said that she would understand if I couldn't, but the question foremost in my mind was whether Dorothy could forgive herself.

Our meeting lasted only a couple of hours, so emotionally overwhelmed was she by the whole situation. During that time, however, I did learn that after she left Dad, Dorothy had married for a second time, had given birth to another two sons and that she and her family were happy. In many ways it sounded like history repeating itself but clearly on

266

this occasion she hadn't deserted them. It made me happy to know that she was settled and had joy in her life.

I left that day with many questions still unanswered, particularly in relation to my maternal ancestry, but I now had another Aunt and Uncle and I left them knowing they had another Nephew. Although, such was the intensity of the occasion that the buffet they had so kindly provided hadn't been touched.

After several weeks of no further contact, I telephoned my Mother to arrange a second meeting.

She readily agreed on the condition that the venue would again be at Aunt Hazel and Uncle Barry's home and not hers. I accepted without hesitation as it would also be nice to see Hazel and Barry again. What I didn't appreciate immediately was her reason for attaching that condition.

She then nervously explained that while her husband and two sons were aware of her first marriage to my Father, they did not know about me or Warran and she feared that, should they find out, her whole life would be turned upside down. She revealed that when she first met her husband, she had not been upfront with him about having two children from her previous marriage as she foolishly thought he wouldn't want her if he'd known.

She acknowledged this had been a huge mistake but, as time progressed within her second marriage, it became increasingly impossible to tell him the truth. Instead, she had just tried to forget about us and be happy in the new life she had created for herself.

I definitely needed time to process this information because it opened a 'Pandora's Box,' not only for me but for Dorothy and her family too. Our conversation ended with us deciding to hold off agreeing a date for our next meeting until we'd both had more time to reflect.

For weeks, I pondered my options. Should I end our relationship before it had even started or continue to pursue my original plan of finding out who I was through the simpler route of family tree research? I had only had a few telephone conversations with my Birth Mother and had met her only once, but I knew already that she was a very complex character. It really was unfathomable to me how she'd been able to maintain such a high level of deception for so many years. What made it even more intriguing was that all her siblings were obviously aware of the children from her first marriage and yet her new family were not. Maybe us Stanier's weren't the only family to maintain a strict silence on certain family issues.

It was never my intention to simply satisfy my own needs and leave a heap of emotional wreckage behind me - and certainly not to leave Dorothy's life in ruins - but I still wanted answers. So I called her several days later and agreed to her meeting request. As I arrived at my Aunt's house, both Hazel and Barry were once again kindness itself, greeting me warmly and walking me into their front room. Dorothy was sat in the same chair and remained seated as I gave her a hug. As such, our second meeting started much like the previous one, although much less emotional. This time, however, there were more people in the house and I was introduced to my first cousins - Aunt Hazel's and Uncle Barry's children.

The one thing that had not changed was the fear in Dorothy's face. I wasn't sure if she was trying to communicate her vulnerability to me or signal impending danger, but it turned out to be both. I knew that our second meeting was not going to be a discussion about mutual interests or browsing through family photo albums, but I wasn't prepared for the turn of events that was about to unfold.

Within minutes of my arrival the door bell rang and from the expression on Hazel's face as she peered through the window, it was apparent that the unexpected danger had arrived. There was a flurry of conversations going on all around me, none of which I understood. I did, however, establish that it was someone called Geoff outside, but no-one seemed willing to answer the door to him.

Chaos seemed to be raining down; people started heading for the kitchen and I overheard someone say that the back door had also been locked. Whoever this Geoff was, he was obviously not going to be let in.
Then, seconds later, there was a loud banging coming from the window and suddenly everyone in the house started scattering everywhere, most of them joining those already hiding in the kitchen. It left just me and Dorothy sitting alone in the living room and, as the pounding on the window continued, I could clearly see the face of the man asking to be let in.

Eventually Hazel came into the front room to tell Dorothy that, sorry as she was, she had no choice but to open the door, before announcing Geoff's arrival. To say I was confused would be an understatement, especially seconds later when Geoff walked in the room. His first question to my Mother, while looking at me, was, "Who's this?" Silent and visibly shaken, she didn't answer. Then Geoff suddenly embraced her and addressed her as Mum, and my immediate assumption was that one of her sons from her second marriage had found out about our meetings.

At that point Dorothy just stood up, ran from the room and straight upstairs to lock herself in a bedroom. Everyone in the room looked bewildered and nervous before finally I broke the silence by apologising because, from my perspective, I was responsible for this situation. There followed several minutes of tense, uncomfortable silence, broken only by me repeating my apologies. Geoff slowly walked towards me, sat down in the chair Dorothy had previously occupied only minutes earlier and then politely repeated his question, but this time to me directly, "Who are you?"

It was a question I didn't want to answer because Dorothy had already voiced her concerns of how her life might be ruined should her children find out about my existence. Fortunately, Hazel came to the rescue and answered for me, simply introducing me as Graham. "And who, exactly, would Graham be?" asked Geoff. My hesitancy in answering must have been apparent and I was rescued for a second time, but this time by Geoff himself, "I know who you are and I know you have a brother called Warran." I nodded to acknowledge he was correct. He continued: "I also know that your Dad is called Ernest, because he's my Father as well."
As I sat trying to rationalise what I had just been told, I could see Hazel now gently nodding as if to confirm what Geoff had just said. It suddenly felt like my safe world had taken a direct hit. I stood up and paced around the living room while everyone else, sensing impending disaster, all at once retreated back to the kitchen, leaving just Hazel, Geoff, and I alone in the living room.

Hazel explained that Geoff was indeed my full Biological Brother. Then the dark secret slowly unfolded. My Mother had been pregnant with him when she left my Father and Geoff was in fact his third son. My Dad had even been to the maternity ward following Geoff's birth but had disputed paternity because, subsequent to Dorothy leaving us so suddenly, he'd learned that she had been cheating on him with another man. I was in total shock and disbelief. I asked Hazel to fetch my Mother back but it had all

270

become too much for Dorothy and she'd managed to slip out of the house without anyone noticing. It didn't matter, I didn't need my Mother present to confirm what I'd been told   because I could tell that I was indeed looking at my Father's son. He was the spitting image of his
Dad and could easily be mistaken for being Warran's twin.
Geoff went on to say that he'd always known that Ernest Stanier was his Father but knew little else about him, me or my elder brother. Over the years, however, he'd worked out that he was not an only child but had no evidence to support his suspicions.
To my horror, he then went on to tell me about his many years in and out of the Care System and about how he'd eventually settled into Dorothy's new family.

He'd been introduced to them as the only child from her first marriage. I was devastated, tearful and just broken by all that he had to say that day and my feelings were amplified tenfold when I had to inform him that our
Father had died. Geoff and I really connected and I immediately loved him unconditionally as my own brother. My sadness for him was profound and I couldn't bear the thought of him being in the Care System.
I don't know whether our meeting on that day was purely coincidental or if strange forces were at work, but I was truly grateful either way. Geoff and I spoke together for hours that day and, the more we chatted, the more we realised that, in essence, we were destined to eventually meet.

On the day of Dad's funeral, Geoff had also been there at the cemetery, not at his Father's graveside but at his Uncle's. He was the man in the Army uniform that I'd seen. The distressed and distraught woman he was holding up was our Mother. Aunt Hazel clarified everything that had happened on the day my Father was buried, even down to the two men knocking on Dad's door on the morning of the funeral, one of whom it transpired was Uncle Barry.

On the journey home that evening, I indirectly vented my spleen at everyone and everything, with poor Steve having to listen to my every word but maintaining a largely stoical silence. I couldn't bear the thought of Geoff having been in Care. I desperately wanted his past to be so different and for him to have been raised with his brothers, but there was nothing that I could have done about it.

Days went by and my mind was totally consumed with thoughts of Geoff and my impending 'phone call to Warran, who I would obviously have to tell. I had no idea how I was going to explain to him that we had another brother but, when it came to the conversation, it was immediately a good sign that he just listened without interrupting me as I went over every detail. Then came his solemn words of wisdom, "You've opened a can of worms here." Little did I know at the time just how big that 'can' would turn out to be!

Most importantly, Warran was on board with me and that's what really mattered. I needed my big brother with me and shortly afterwards we both met up with our little brother Geoff together - and then we were three – and it was brilliant! We were all adult enough to understand that none of this was our fault and that we were just going to make the best of it. I can remember looking at them from one to the other as they both sat side by side laughing together, looking just like twins, and I felt so proud.

I knew Dad would have approved. Geoff and I kept in contact regularly and eventually we met with his wife and daughters. Neither one of us wanted to dwell on the past and, to be fair, Geoff's recollection of the past was vague at best, so we simply focussed on a new beginning and the future. I felt responsible for him, just as my big brother had felt responsible for me in Dad's absence. I worried each time he was posted to a military war zone and always hoped for his safe return.

He did, however, still have to negotiate a very difficult situation because Dorothy's second family remained blissfully unaware of Warran and I, with the upshot being that he could never mention us during his time socialising with them. There was so much unfinished business to deal with regarding my Mother, but I genuinely didn't know if I could, with Warran's phrase 'sleeping dogs' constantly rolling round in a repetitive loop in my brain. Aunt Hazel and Geoffrey were helpful in enlightening me as much as they could about my Mother's past, but Geoff's time in care and Hazel's adoption and separation from her family represented significant gaps in their knowledge. I had to consider that perhaps it was time for me to call it a day. Then, a month later, Dorothy rang me again.

Our conversation seemed to take up my entire evening but there was so much to discuss - and she had been busy since our last meeting. Her second family was now aware of all three of us brothers. How and when that happened she didn't say but she seemed pleased that finally the truth was out in the open. She wanted only one thing, that her five sons would one day meet and be there for each other. It was certainly something I also hoped would happen in the future.

She was one hundred percent certain that Ernest Stanier was Geoff's father and went on to apologise profusely for leaving Hazel's home on the day of the 'confrontation.' She explained that Geoff was only in Care because at the time she was a single Mother and couldn't cope financially or emotionally. When she met her second husband, she just wanted a fresh start in life. She also confessed that she'd left Dad for another man, which she acknowledged was a bad decision on her part. The relationship never worked out, not least because he quickly found out she was pregnant with my Father's third child.

It took a lot of courage for Dorothy to call me that day and to finally be open and honest with me about her past, and I respected her for that. She had attempted but failed in her quest to bury parts of her past but I assumed that shame and guilt had something to do with it. It must have been very difficult and painful for her to revisit her past and, on this occasion, her apologies seemed sincere. By comparison, her previous ones now seemed premature and less heartfelt.
Nevertheless, I didn't feel the need to forgive her and, while her regrets were appreciated and accepted, I feared that it would be a much longer process for Dorothy to forgive herself.

After that conversation, I had to make a tough decision about whether or not I wanted to continue my relationship with my Mother. If I was to have a relationship with all my brothers — and I genuinely wanted that to happen - then it would prove difficult if I didn't. She had shown remorse about her past behaviour and on that basis I was willing to give it a go. Importantly, she had also assured me she'd told me everything and there were no more skeletons in her closet. I concluded that her actions had not been borne of malice towards Warran and I, but that her decision-making at the time she left us had simply been reckless and lacking consideration of the consequences.

Also, by this time Geoff had fully integrated with the Stanier family and I absolutely loved presenting him to everyone as my 'little brother,' not that the title lasted for long. He lost that status the day I met my mother's youngest son - now we were four brothers! There was no fanfare or party as he breezed into the front room and just sat down with his Mum, Dad and myself to have a chat. Within weeks I'd also met up with her first son from her second marriage - and now we were five brothers!

On subsequent occasions that I met up with them, I was always happy to hear her husband and my youngest brothers speak fondly of Dorothy and remark on what a good wife and Mum she had been to them. Warran, on the other hand, was becoming increasingly overwhelmed by the number of siblings he now had, but he adapted well despite his goal of only wanting a quiet life. All five brothers slowly forged ahead developing relationships with each other, remaining mindful not to speak badly about our Mother. We all acknowledged that that period of Dorothy's life had been somewhat chaotic but, as the past couldn't be altered or erased, why bother talking about it? We had been afforded the opportunity to make a future together so we couldn't allow ourselves to be trapped by the past. Not one of us harboured feelings of anger or resentment towards her.

My Mother and I contacted each other regularly, arranging to meet up in Manchester every couple of months, but over time it was impossible not to notice her underlying anxiety. She told me anxiety was a constant in her life, even when she had no reason to worry about anything. Unfortunately, she'd been affected by it since early adulthood and felt that it had worsened as she got older.

Eating lunch was a particularly challenging experience for her as she'd scan the room assuming that people were looking at her and judging her, which resulted in her developing hand tremors. She found it very difficult to control, so much so that she had difficulty holding a knife and fork properly. On most occasions when we met, I would ask for a table that was not in full view of other people or position her chair so that she had her back to most of the other diners. Despite her anxieties though, she struggled through and I felt that we both really enjoyed our times together.

I still remember the first time I received a birthday card with 'Mum' written on it and how a relatively simple object like that could be so emotional for me. Our relationship worked because I never set out to find her with revenge and retribution in mind, nor with anger in my heart. I didn't want or need to burden myself with such negative emotions.

Some six years later, shortly before Christmas, she called me with the dreadful news that she'd been diagnosed with terminal cancer and that she wanted to see me at her home that weekend. I cancelled my plans and drove up North. When I arrived, her husband and my two youngest brothers were sat with her in the living room. She'd clearly deteriorated quickly since my last visit a few months earlier and was just sat crying at looking at me from the chair, fear etched into her face. She said she didn't want to die but knew that the end was imminent. When the room emptied and my brothers and her husband had left, she spoke only about how important it had been to have all her sons in her life and to know that all five of us would now remain friends and support each other in the future. On that day, I gave her my promise that

I would put every effort into ensuring that continued. She reached down by the side of the chair and gave me my Christmas present, but with strict instructions it could only be opened on Christmas Day. My brothers returned and we all resumed talking.
The conversations were about anything and everything, except for the very short time that my Mother had left to live.

As I left that day I gave her the biggest, gentlest hug imaginable, kissed her and told her that I loved her. I left in tears but with a promise that I would see her again before Christmas. Sadly, it was not to be as, shortly afterwards, my youngest brother called to say that she had passed away. Her funeral took place just before Christmas and all her boys were in attendance. Tears were shed and my younger brothers were inconsolable with grief over their loss. My Aunt Hazel brought some humour to the whole occasion, mumbling something behind me in the church. She later explained she'd just learned that my Mother had knocked five years off her age - and my Aunt wasn't impressed!

On Christmas morning I looked under the tree and two presents stood out. The one my Mother had given me and the one I had intended to give to her. Her present to me was a table lamp that I'd admired in a shop months earlier. It was surrounded by family photographs, of her, her brothers and sister, her friends, and even my Grandfather, all with her handwritten comments to identify the people in the photos. I was heartbroken because I really was going to miss her. I didn't grieve my Mother's passing in the same way I had my Father's, but she left a significant void in my life because, over those six years, we had built a good relationship with each other.

I respected the fact she'd been open and honest with me from the start of our relationship and had taken full responsibility for her actions in leaving us all those years ago. She never once criticised my Father but praised him on numerous occasions. I respected her courage in answering my ad in the local newspaper, her courage to face me and my questioning, but even more so, her courage in revealing her secret two sons from her first marriage. It took a lot of bravery to do that and it demonstrated to me that she definitely cared and wanted a future relationship with her forgotten sons.

It was high stakes on the day she revealed all, but she was prepared to press ahead and do it, despite her fears that her secret might have a lasting impact on her relationship with her husband and sons, not to mention the risk of their rejection, judgement, and reprisals. Her fears, however, were totally unfounded because they loved her unconditionally and never showed the anger she had feared, only acceptance and understanding.

I'd waited all those years and now she was gone, as was my beautiful friend Henderson Western Karloff Clinton, who'd died a year earlier.

He'd called me late one evening and was his usual chatty self, updating me on his exploits since we'd last spoken. Our conversation, however, was constantly interrupted by his bouts of fierce coughing which at times brought him to the point of breathlessness. He put the coughing down to the change in climate, having recently returned to New York City from Monterey in California. The climate was not his only problem as he'd also undergone a change in personal circumstances, was flat broke, unemployed and was now living with his brother. When we finally got into a conversation about Barbados and his family, his tone suddenly changed from joy to sadness because he desperately wanted to go home and visit them. Unfortunately, his current abysmal financial situation wouldn't allow that.

It was very clear to me that, for Hendy, it was more of a need than a simple desire and so I offered to send him the money for the 'plane ticket, which he could always pay me back at a later date. With fingers crossed, I posted the cash and then worried for a whole week about it getting there without anyone intercepting it. Finally, he called to say he'd received the money, had bought a ticket, and was leaving the following day to spend four weeks at home. I was happy for him and thought that it would be the perfect opportunity for him to recuperate as well as experience the joy of being with his family.

Two weeks into his visit, I called him in Barbados to see how things were going and was really looking forward to speaking to him and the family, but it was not good news. His sister Coleen answered the phone and informed me that Hendy had flown back to New York City for medical treatment - that's when the alarm bells started to ring. Coleen became inconsolable and kept repeating that Hendy was dying.
After several minutes of trying to compose herself, she handed the phone over to her brother who then gave me the heartrending news that Hendy had told him he was terminally ill. While visiting them in Barbados, his condition had deteriorated, forcing him to return to New York City for more treatment.

I had no idea what to believe and hoped there'd been some misunderstanding because I felt certain that Hendy would have told me if he was dying. I tried to call him that evening and again over the next week. His 'phone just rang out each time and, ominously, there wasn't even a voicemail instructing callers to leave a message. I was frantic with worry and knew instinctively that something was seriously wrong. After a further two weeks of deafening silence, Hendy surprised me by answering the 'phone and acting like his normal self, telling me about his time in Barbados with his family and about his life in general. I could still hear his laboured breathing and frequent pauses to gain his breath, all of which was very disconcerting.

Despite not wanting to, I knew I couldn't end the conversation that evening without telling him about my talk with Coleen so, without hesitation, I came straight out with it and asked him how ill he really was. Apart from his laboured breathing there was only silence from the other end of the phone. When he did eventually say something, it was only to say that he was OK and that he'd call me the following day to explain everything. In my heart of hearts I knew that it was true, he was terminally ill.

Hendy called the next evening and told me the news I hadn't wanted to hear. He didn't explicitly say he was dying but said quite openly that his prognosis was very poor, hence the urgency to see his family in Barbados. Effectively, he'd made the trip to say goodbye to them. We spoke at length that evening but I was ever mindful of not upsetting him as I didn't want our conversation to end the same way it had the previous evening when he'd become obviously distressed. We spoke on the 'phone more often after his disclosure, but with the proviso that I never talk about his illness, never visit him in New York, even as a surprise, or tell any of our mutual friends of his prognosis.

I came to accept that that was how our friendship was going to continue for many years. However, just a month later, the ominous silence descended again and, of course, I feared the worst. I called Barbados only to be told the shocking news that Hendy had died peacefully at home in New York with one of his brothers supporting him. I never did get around to asking Hendy why he hadn't confided in me about his illness in the early days, but he did say he only wanted his family to know. Although heartbroken, I took immense pride and solace in knowing that he'd regarded me as being a member of his family.

Each time I visit Barbados now and the aircraft approaches the island, I feel an overwhelming sadness at the thought of not seeing my great and vibrant friend again. No more sitting on the veranda with him chatting and reminiscing about our life experiences together, or just going down Baxters Road for a drink. I truly miss the man but these days I never dwell on that, even though he's always stored away in a little compartment at the back of my mind. Instead, I try to put the sadness to one side and fondly recall the memories I have of all the good times we shared together. I am still able to sit on the veranda with his family — my Bajan family — drinking rum and celebrating Hendy's life, remembering the much-needed joy and laughter he brought to all of our worlds. I try not to think about how Hendy died, but more about how he'd lived his life to the full.

******

CHAPTER TWENTY ONE

'Introducing The Jeremy Kyle Show'

I wasn't expecting the call from ITV's Head of Daytime TV as I sat in the Occupational Health Department, ploughing my way through a very busy clinic day. But it sounded urgent so we scheduled a lunchtime meeting in the studio café.

As I ate my sandwich, she revealed the reason she'd summoned me. She asked whether I could take time away from my busy clinics to work at the iconic Granada Studios in Manchester for the next two weeks. She wanted me to join a team that were looking at the existing Guest Welfare Services on two conflict resolution shows being recorded there – *'The Jerry Springer Show'* and *'The Jeremy Kyle Show.'* The latter had already been filmed in both Norwich and London and both a Guest Welfare Service and an experienced Mental Health Assessor were already in place.

I didn't give her an outright refusal but told her I'd think about it. My initial thoughts were a resounding 'No.' because I already had a full workload and packed schedule. Over the weekend, however, I weighed up the pros and cons and concluded that maybe it wasn't such a big ask after all, especially since the pre-show services for the two shows were already set up and running. That meant most of my focus could be on the post filming and broadcasting phases.

On Monday morning I met up with my Manager, Jane, to discuss the logistics of my being absent from my ITV

Counselling Clinic for a two-week period should I accept the assignment. We agreed a plan and, from that point onwards, it was all systems go. I was back working in Manchester, my home city and - while I might be biased - the city I still regarded as being the best in the UK.
In the words of Sir Ian McKellen "Manchester - Where grown men call strangers 'Love' and I think if we all did that [the world] would be a better place wouldn't it?. And when people have got problems with gender and pronouns Love covers everything-Just call everyone Love".

I was born, raised and nurtured in this Northern culture and it's values, beliefs and attitudes will always resonate strongly with me. It just feels genuine and authentic, and Manchester and the North will always feel like home when I visit.

The first morning I arrived at Granada Studios, the Executive Producer and Production Manager were waiting for me in the car park, greeting me in true media 'luvvie' fashion with air kisses and open arms. My first impression of the office provided for us was that there were too many people and too little space - and I wasn't wrong.
To all intents and purposes, it sounded and felt like I had walked into a call centre. It certainly didn't compare to the workspace I was used to in London.

The noise level in the open-plan office was deafening as Researchers, Assistant Producers and Producers talked busily on their phones to potential guests, clearly competing with each other and trying to raise the decibel level above that of the person sat next to them. Most didn't have chairs, so were standing and shuffling about while making their calls, and there also weren't enough desks, computers or telephones for the 40-plus people working there. It was very clear that I wouldn't be the only one who'd be under pressure for the next two weeks.

I had to accept it was going to be a 'make do' situation until such time as the additional office furniture and equipment arrived. Then came a moment of respite as I walked into the oasis of calm that was the Executive Producer's office and received the welcome news that we'd both be sharing it. The two of us happily settled in, grateful for the luxury of a door that could temporarily shut out the noise coming from the open-plan space. In no time at all I had completed my assignment, Job done, albeit two weeks later than planned and without me having had the opportunity of meeting the show's Presenter himself, Jeremy Kyle.

On Friday, as I packed my things away in the office, I could hear the Production Team eagerly preparing for the last recording of the day, punctuated by a Producer's voice steadily increasing in volume. It was clear she was upset on learning that the expert she'd booked to appear on the show was currently stuck in traffic on the M62. But eventually, peace reigned once more as she and her team left for the studios.

I continued to mooch about, still packing my boxes and with mixed emotions of joy and sadness about leaving. I headed over to the studios to say a quick goodbye to everyone on the set before leaving for home ahead of the rush-hour traffic. From a distance I waved to the Editor and Producer who were in deep conversation, but I couldn't find the Executive Producer anywhere.

I was reliably informed, however, that she could be found in the car park, which was ideal as I'd be able to say my goodbyes before hitting the road. I found her nervously pacing the car park, wearing her headset as she awaited the arrival of the expert who'd been stuck on the M62 for hours. We said our goodbyes but then, as I was getting into my car, she began frantically waving at me, summoning my return. It had now become clear the expert was never going to make it on time and, short of airlifting her from the motorway, they had a huge problem -except, apparently, I was about to become the solution!

It was suggested I join the Producer to provide Jeremy with any advice he might need, via his earpiece, whilst he was recording the show. I could certainly give them 10 more minutes and, within a very short time, it was showtime. We all huddled inside the very small 'Talk Back' booth to discuss the story, which in itself was not particularly complicated. During a break in the interviews, Jeremy walked off-stage for further guidance.

I provided very little, but when I did, Jeremy addressed me for the first time, asking "Who are you?" Having introduced myself, he hurried back onstage to continue with the second segment of the interview. If Jeremy was bewildered by my presence, it became even more apparent when he was told I was coming to join him onstage to provide the guest with some advice.

It followed several seconds of persuasion by the Producer - and I mean seconds - during which she encouraged me to deliver my advice directly on stage rather than via Jeremy's earpiece. With her immortal reassurance of, "Don't worry you'll be fine," ringing in my ears, I was inched slowly towards the stage while someone fitted a microphone to my lapel. I walked out onto the stage, sat with Jeremy on the stage step, and once again from behind a bullet card he whispered, "Who are you again?" That was our very first meeting, after which I finally headed for home and back to my day job at ITV London. There was, however, still one big job outstanding.

I wanted the show's participants to have a comprehensive Aftercare Service and include longer-term post-show interventions. This was a big ask because it would require more money being allocated to the show's budget.
After presenting my proposal however the extra funding was approved and with additional staff recruited, the Guest Aftercare Service was finally born. Then came an offer I couldn't refuse!

Who wouldn't love a job where your employer gave you a budget to spend on improving someone's life, along with an amazing team to help you deliver that service? That was now the attractive proposition being offered to me under the title of Director of Aftercare on *'The Jeremy Kyle Show.'* Logistically, it was possible to divide my working week between Manchester and London – and so it was a resounding "Yes!" from me. And so my initial four-week stint working on *'The Jeremy Kyle Show'* eventually became a 14-year commitment. It was definitely a whole new unexpected, but welcome, chapter in my life.

In the early days, many of us working on *'Kyle'* would stay in rooms above a pub in Liverpool Street, Manchester just a 10-minute walk from Granada Studios. We shared many social nights together, but it was the same story every morning as we walked to work feeling absolutely knackered due to lack of sleep, complaining about the noise levels after closing time, which disturbed our slumbers. Most nights we'd wait in dread for the Bar Manager and his mates to start blasting out heavy rock numbers until the early hours of the morning. The music was relentless and, despite the band's compromise of rehearsing without using speakers, it failed to reduce the noise level to any appreciable extent.
There were brief moments of respite because the

members of the band often fell out with each other. We prayed for those nights when they had artistic
differences and refused to play as a group. A bit selfish, I know, but that's what sleep deprivation does to you. Over time, most of us checked out of the pub rooms and
between us built up quite a long list of budget hotels that we shared with each other.

Each morning from 7 am onwards, the *'Jeremy Kyle'* team would be the first to gather in the Granada Studios
canteen, where we were greeted by 'The Boys.' One would be sat by the till with perfectly coiffed hair, greeting everyone with, "Morning love," while occasionally filing his nails. The other would be stood behind the breakfast bar, less coiffed but still with pristine nails as he busily
prepared anything that could be fried or grilled, greeting everyone with a cheery, "Morning girlfriend!" The same welcome was afforded to everyone on the show,
irrespective of gender, and was quickly followed by their early morning entertainment routine as they bickered loudly with each other to a packed and appreciative canteen audience.

Most of us would opt for a 'Full English' breakfast, bacon butty, sausage butty or all manner of exotic combinations, as long as it was fried. Few of us opted for the healthier options on offer. Anyone putting more than the allocated rashers of bacon on their plate could expect another announcement from the server to the cashier along the lines of:
"She's got extra bacon on her plate so don't
forget to charge her," the terms 'she' or 'her' used irrespective of gender. The banter between the two of them could best be described as unscripted genius most mornings and it

certainly helped us to forget the sleep deprivation and miseries of economy accommodation. We all looked
forward to breakfast and break times in the canteen as it was the place the whole team bonded and prepared for the trials and tribulations that lay ahead - but the early morning canteen staff were definitely the stars of the show.

Jeremy would join us most mornings for breakfast and it wasn't unknown for him to escalate the banter further by ordering 100 cups of tea for the audience queuing outside, especially on a rainy day when he would sometimes open the security doors early without permission. Chaos would inevitably ensue as the Head of Security demanded to know who had opened the door, while the Production
Manager would want to know why she'd had a bill handed to her from the Canteen Manager for 100 cups of tea. A full investigation was conducted, with all roads leading back to Jeremy. Later, we would learn that he'd promised not to do it again - but of course sometimes he did.
Early breakfast time at Granada Studios was a tonic for the soul and a great start to our busy day.

CHAPTER TWENTY TWO

'Room Mates'

Within a few months, my friendship with Jeremy Kyle started to develop, but then that was always going to be a given because most weeks we were practically spending more time with each other than we were with our partners. It was early on in our working relationship that we discovered we only lived 10-miles from each other, so from the outset we started to travel together, work together, and live together when working away from home.

The first time we shared a room, however, was a warning sign to me that boundaries needed to be set about sharing accommodation generally, because we really were different animals. As we travelled together by car en-route to Manchester one day, we stopped over for the night so that JK could play in a golf tournament in Birmingham. I don't play golf myself but the offer of being a guest at this prestigious event - with an evening buffet and a full English breakfast the following morning thrown in - was all the persuasion I needed.

We arrived at the venue early evening and checked in to our twin room, but the signs were ominous from the start. Obviously, I'd anticipated the buffet to start immediately and eagerly anticipated the sight of silver tureens crammed with mouthwatering food. But I was wrong - there was to be a delay while JK carefully unpacked his many golf outfits, all folded in perfect symmetry, and laid them out on the bed while gazing at them lovingly.
I could cope with that, but then out came the ironing board and iron and he proceeded to iron out every crease

before carefully placing them on hangers. I could only think, "How many outfits do you need for a game of golf?" - and more importantly, "Are you not aware that the buffet has started?"

Then, while still focused on his ironing, JK began asking my opinion as to which outfit he should wear the next day. To be honest, they all looked the same except for the colour, but we eventually reached a mutual agreement as to which outfit was most appropriate. Then it was time for him to carefully arrange his toiletries in the bathroom, by which time we were well over an hour late in heading for the dining room - and my bag was still unpacked. By the time we arrived for dinner, the contents of most of the tureens had been well and truly decimated and it was clear they wouldn't be replenished anytime soon. JK mingled as I desperately scraped the bottom of most of the tureens. To add to my misery, there was no socialising in the bar to look forward to either because it was an early start for everyone. My bedtime thoughts were dominated by visions of a 'Full English' breakfast and, as I drifted off to sleep eagerly awaiting my 7 am wake-up call, I was reasonably content.

Those closest to me will know only too well that I'm definitely not a morning person. Even when I do get enough sleep, I'm still never at my best first thing. I need to wake up very slowly in the mornings and my sleepiness does not vanish for at least an hour, by which time I've hopefully had lashings of coffee and silence.
The early birds can have the worms but I need to wake up naturally - and certainly not to the sound of someone moving around the room.

I could definitely hear doors opening and closing and someone trying to walk quietly around the bedroom in the dark, occasionally stumbling, and mumbling profanities with each stub of a toe. Believe me when I tell you that that is not a happy morning wake-up call for me and, as I pulled the sheets over my head, the noise continued unabated. How was I to know that JK was so fresh and energetic in the mornings? Just listening to the racket he was making made me feel more tired and exhausted. My plan was to lie there quietly, not make a sound and just hope the noise would go away, but no such luck. Doors were still being opened with increasing regularity and, to add to the misery, a bedside light had now been switched on.

Pondering whether to ignore the sounds and play dead or enquire what was happening was a mistake, because I chose the latter. The very sound of my enquiring voice was a cue for JK to become even more energised and, suddenly, a sound and light show erupted in the room as he put the big light on and began his incessant chatter.

Through squinting eyes I could make out a shadowy figure holding something in both hands and asking me which outfit I preferred, even though I thought we'd already agreed on that - and anyway, what did I really care? I wasn't wearing any of them and, to be perfectly honest, the choices were limited; black and white, blue and cream, black and cream, or blue and white. In my monosyllabic state, I just agreed to all of them and pleaded to go back to sleep.

Sleep, however, was to elude me for quite some time because there were still the shoe options to go through. I again agreed to all of them in the hope that the sooner the choice was made, the sooner the lights would be turned off and I could return to blessed sleep. It was now 5.30 am. I am definitely not at my best at that time but there I was, suddenly and without warning placed in the role of fashion advisor to the star. Within seconds he was like a dynamo working his way around the room, turning the bathroom light on, and opening curtains to let yet more light into the room. It was then that the stark realisation hit me; I'd be starting my day suffering from sleep deprivation. AGAIN!

There was still a glimmer of hope that I could maybe get back to sleep once JK left the room for breakfast, but it wasn't to be. From the safety of the bathroom he announced: "G, you need to get up and get dressed because we have to check out of the room before breakfast." I was stunned into silence. It was only 6.30 am, but there was clearly no room for compromise. I had to be showered, out of the room with luggage and in the breakfast room within the hour. That was not a great start to the day and while he chatted on and on relentlessly, I remained monosyllabic with my responses - it was for the best!

My patent lack of enthusiasm for the day ahead was also evident as JK tried to impress me with pointing out the many professional golfers around the room, using only eye movement in an effort to be discreet. There was a bloke smoking a cigar, several wearing Argyle knitwear, a few wearing baseball caps and, apparently, I should have been mightily impressed by all that. Well, I wasn't. I just wanted to go back to the room and sleep, but of course that was not going to happen. With breakfast out of the way, I was allocated the job of ball-spotter, and the day went rapidly downhill from there. No explanation needed, but why would you give someone with failing eyesight the job of finding wayward golf balls?

That afternoon our journey north to Manchester took place in complete silence, particularly once I'd told JK I'd never share a room with him again. Well, that promise didn't last very long because, on our forthcoming work assignment in Kenya, I was once again doomed to share a room with JK.

I was so excited when I heard that we were travelling to Mombassa to film at an Orphanage that provided care for children who either had HIV/AIDS or were affected by the disease in some way. It was such a great opportunity to spread the word about the love and medical care the children were receiving in the Orphanage, as well as raise awareness of the wonderful work an amazing British woman was doing. Not only was she the founder of the Orphanage but she was running it solely on donations.

It was a baking hot day when we landed at the airport and the journey by road to the hotel seemed to take forever. When we finally arrived, we discovered the hotel was certainly not situated in a beautiful setting, nor surrounded by frangipani and bougainvillea. Neither did it have breathtaking views of the ocean. Nevertheless, it was going to be our home for the next week.

I hadn't even finished unpacking before the Assistant Cameraman knocked on the door, doubled up in pain and seeking medication for stomach cramps. I rooted through the first aid kit and medical bag, but there was literally nothing to give him, other than an unhelpful, "I told you so." He was the only one of our party who had ignored the advice not to eat anything bought from the street vendors during our journey from the airport to the hotel.

Fortunately for the Cameraman, the local fixer was able to find a Doctor quite quickly and, following treatment, he was fit again for work the next day.

I met up with the crew later that day and we all opted for an early dinner so that we would be ready to travel to the Orphanage early the next morning to start filming. An early night was music to my ears after the long plane journey but, within minutes of settling down for sleep, the Sound Man knocked on the door, looking for headache tablets. I was already regretting being custodian of the medical bag. Then, at about 1 am, came another tap on the door. By the time I opened it, having almost strangled myself on the mosquito net in the process, there was no-one there. Just as I settled into bed once more and tucked the mosquito net back in, there was yet another knock and the sound of a voice whispering, "It's me!"

I knew immediately who 'me' was. When I opened the door, there stood JK adorned in a dressing gown and looking terrified. Without being invited in, he just rushed straight past me and entered the room shouting something inaudible then proceeded to perch himself on the arm of the chair. Something was clearly wrong but when I asked him what it was, his answer came as surprise.

"There's a lizard in my room!" he said. After careful questioning, I ascertained that we weren't talking a Komodo dragon or a Monitor lizard. This one sounded more like the little Gecko variety, but it was in his room and he made it abundantly clear he was not sharing his space with it. I made it equally clear I was not swapping rooms with him either. I was also not prepared to go lizard hunting at 1 am or provide therapy for a possible past traumatic event with a lizard.

The compromise was that he could either sleep in Reception, where there was the risk of him encountering more lizards, or sleep in the spare bed in my room. He obviously chose the latter and, within seconds he was in bed, insisting I tuck-in the mosquito net to prevent possible mosquito and lizard attacks during the night.

Before lights out, however, came the house rules. Do not wake me up in the morning. Do not talk to me in the morning - and do not turn lights on or open the blinds. Just simple house rules, which of course JK did not observe. At 6 am, he asked if I was awake, kept repeating the question until I responded and, once again, I was starting the day deprived of sleep. Anyone could have read my angry face, but not Jeremy. He just continued chatting away about 'our' dilemma, because now apparently it was a shared dilemma!

The issue, according to JK, was how would I get him out of my room, escort him past all the other crew rooms on the same landing, then return to my room without being noticed by anyone. I explained to him that I had a better idea, i.e. how about he leave my room and if anyone from the crew sees him, just explain that he's afraid of the Gecko in his room and that I heroically saved him by allowing him to stay in mine. JK explained that he couldn't do that because it sounded so ridiculous - and he didn't want anyone to know he was afraid of small lizards. That was to be our little secret.

What followed was a stealth operation that even MI5 would have been proud of. After chasing several Geckos around his room, I arrived at breakfast looking dishevelled from having less than six hours sleep and sat silently glaring at him across the table. JK beckoned me to the hotel lobby for a discussion, using subtle eye movements and nods of his head. Apparently it was obvious that I was pissed-off with him and I needed to check my attitude. As tactfully as I could, I reassured him that it was definitely not going to change because sleep deprivation does that to me, but there was a distinct possibility that by lunchtime I might have recovered.

That evening during dinner with the crew, and with an equal measure of both joy and sadness in our hearts, we reflected on our experiences at the Orphanage. Once again, I noticed JK staring at me and nodding his head in a manner that indicated my presence was once again required in the lobby. He told me he needed to sleep in my room again that night because the Gecko was back and this time had his family with him. I shook my head, told him definitely not and advised him to speak to reception about the rogue lizards, then wished him goodnight.
The thought of a good night's sleep overwhelmed me with joy and, feeling energised for the next day's filming, I bade everyone a cheery goodnight.

There was no knocking on the door that night from the Presenter because, when I got to my room, he was already tucked up in the spare bed and, I suspect, pretending to be asleep. Just in case he wasn't, I issued a cautionary warning that I either get eight hours sleep or he gets out of my room! The following night it was fait accompli because when I got back to my room he had literally moved in, lock stock and barrel. The house rules were breached on many occasions after that but at least I did finally manage to get eight hours sleep most nights!

Each morning, however, we still had to go through the same stealth and surveillance operation and creep along the landing to his room to check for marauding Geckos, a couple of minutes after which he would appear outside his allocated room shouting a cheery "Morning!" to everyone.

On our return from Mombasa, we were summoned to see our boss in her office. She had viewed the Orphanage footage and was in tears throughout the meeting, having witnessed the plight of so many young children. Then came the offer of her finding us an apartment in Manchester which we could share when filming. Both of us declined her kind offer. It was never going to work. What we did settle for was sharing the same hotel. It became a great meeting place for everyone after work because it was literally a stone's throw away from the Granada Studios.

Most evenings, the lounge would be littered with TV people socialising or having post-studio production meetings but, alas, it was not to last. That's because the news was about to break that JK and I were having an affair!

Back at home, my partner Steve answered the door on Saturday morning to find a woman asking if I was in. I was but was also still sleeping after arriving home from Manchester in the early hours. I sensed it was urgent though because why else would Steve be telling me to "Get up now and speak to this lady." I stood there at the door, bleary-eyed, wearing my dressing gown and listening to her introduction but was jerked into instant alertness when I heard her claim I was having an affair with Jeremy Kyle and that this would all be disclosed in the Sunday newspapers the following day.

My mind went completely blank from that point onwards and I just remember her giving me her business card and saying that I could get in touch with her any time before the publication deadline. I was so confused that I genuinely sought clarification from Steve about what had just been said to me at the front door. I was not mistaken, I had heard her correctly saying I was having an affair with

Jeremy and that 'they' had the evidence to prove it.

Try as I might, Jeremy wasn't answering his mobile phone or responding to my texts. Then it dawned on me that he wasn't at home. He'd remained in Manchester for a social event. Eventually, and after consuming gallons of tea, he finally contacted me. He was totally oblivious of the allegations and, like me, was confused and bewildered about what evidence the newspaper could possibly have.

The whole day was consumed by 'phone calls from all and sundry and by now the Press were outside Jeremy's gate even though, fortunately, he still hadn't arrived back home. Eventually, the news came through that the story was being held back for a week so that all parties could seek clarification on the story about Jeremy and I.

That Sunday was not the best day of my life and I wasn't looking forward to Monday because that's when I had to be prepared for a conference call with the bosses at ITV. It took place early in the morning and, from the noise and chatter on the other end of the 'phone, the room sounded full as one by one everyone introduced themselves, my boss, people from the Legal Department and Press and Publicity. Finally, I became aware of the evidence which, I might say, was substantial and incriminating.

I had, in fact, slept in the same hotel room as Jeremy on Thursday night, despite the fact I had a room of my own. I did open JK's bedroom door on Friday morning to collect tea for two from room service, dressed in a towelling dressing gown - and yes, we did both leave his room on Friday morning to go to work. All of that was supported by photographs and CCTV footage. What else were people supposed to think? After several attempts at trying to explain why, everyone on the call at last fell silent and I took my opportunity.

I explained that the evening had started with us having a couple of drinks and dinner at the hotel with Patricia Cutts, who played Blanche in *'Coronation Street'* and Jeremy's PA. We all had a lovely time but, by the end of dinner, JK's PA was no longer fit to drive himself home and therefore decided to check into the hotel. Unfortunately, there were no rooms available.

We decided that he could have my room and that I would sleep on JK's sofa bed in his room, not least because we both had a 5 'am call the next morning. The accuracy of the story was checked with the hotel and the newspaper decided not to run their story. But our boss insisted we must never share a room again which, given our previous experiences, was music to my ears. We never stayed at that particular hotel again. Instead, we were offered accommodation within the Granada estate, in the Chairman's penthouse no less. Situated on the top floor of the iconic Granada Studios building, it could only be accessed by its own lift!

On the first night after filming, we quickly settled in and found our bedrooms, which were separated by a shared bathroom. Luxury indeed, especially as the 'fridge was stocked with all manner of goodies. However, it had been a long day and there was no celebration to be had, just a takeaway and a glass of wine before bedtime. We just watched TV and at bedtime retired to our separate rooms.

I was asleep in no time but, once again, someone or something woke me in the early hours. At first I thought it was JK playing some ridiculous game but it wasn't. From the comfort of my bed I could see a light flashing on and off, although I couldn't see exactly where it was coming from because of the pitch-darkness.

As I lay there for several minutes, my eyes became accustomed to the darkness and I could make out a shadowy figure crawling through the window. The flashing light was a cigarette lighter being used to navigate the intruder's way into my bedroom. Surely it wasn't Jeremy because, if so, he should have known better. As my eyes became even more accustomed to the darkness, I knew instinctively the shadowy figure wasn't him. "What the fuck's going on!" I shouted, whereupon the intruder retreated at speed back through the window and I could hear someone running along a walkway.

I just lay there for several minutes with my heart racing, checking I was not dreaming and managing my breathing. Then, I tried to rationalise the whole strange experience. How was it possible for someone to climb through a window on the top floor of the Granada building? Was it Spiderman by any chance? In fact, it turned out to be an opportunistic burglar who had taken advantage of the fact that the building had scaffolding erected on it, so he'd decided to check out the penthouse.

My boss despaired when I called later that day and immediately arrangements were made to transfer us both to another hotel. So it was bye-bye penthouse and hello (another) new hotel.

We were happy at that hotel for several months until the night we arrived and there were no rooms available. I'm sure that's because someone had forgotten to book them. Manchester was full that night and there were no rooms to be had anywhere. However, during JK's discussion with whoever was responsible for not booking the room, the Receptionist reliably informed me that one had suddenly become available. "By those two people that just left?" I enquired. The answer was, "Yes, should I make up a twin room?" — and "NO!" was the resounding response from me.

You see, I'd met those two departing hotel guests only weeks earlier. On that occasion, JK and I had noticed a frail, old man sat at the bar drinking alone, only to be joined later by a very heavy-set lady, wearing a large overcoat. He was dwarfed by her but as the night gathered momentum, it was clear they were having a great time chatting and laughing and eventually they both retired for the night.

The following morning, as we both stood at Reception, JK asked if anyone had heard any screaming and shouting during the night. I certainly hadn't and the Receptionist didn't answer as she was checking someone out. She did, however, give a knowing stare and, once the guests had departed, she enlightened us. The couple we'd seen at the bar regularly used the hotel for their secret 'S and M' assignations, the old man being frequently thrashed by the Dominatrix. On this particular occasion, the Night Manager had reported seeing the frail, old man limp out of the hotel in the early hours, followed by the Dominatrix clutching her bag of tricks! I offered the couple's room to JK that night - obviously without an explanation as to why it had suddenly become available - and just prayed they would not return. After all, they had paid for the whole night. I took a room at a neighbouring hotel.

The following week we moved, once again, to another hotel. In the following years we were like wandering nomads, but, finally, we settled into a great hotel in

Manchester which became a mainstay for many years.

Despite me telling our boss that we were never going to share an apartment together, it did eventually happen in New York, when an American network commissioned a US version of the show to be filmed there. It wasn't for long periods of time though and only when his family had returned to the UK and I was visiting. It had the cleanest kitchen surfaces and floors in Manhattan, not because we had a great cleaner but purely because JK loves cleaning and being tidy. Which was a perfect result as I don't see it as a fun activity.

******

CHAPTER TWENTY THREE

'The Show'

'The Jeremy Kyle Show' was not to everyone's taste. It was Marmite – you either loved it or you hated it. The strong feelings expressed about the show felt strangely similar to the divisions created by Brexit but, no matter what side you were on, people certainly felt passionately about the programme, not least the millions of dedicated viewers, hardcore fans and participants who chose to appear. The conflict resolution show was a huge ratings success for ITV, watched daily by millions and with approximately 20,000 participants appearing during its entire 14-year run. The participants were also part of the viewing demographic and probably watched the show daily, all 3,000-plus episodes.

Many probably watched every episode too, perhaps even more than once on repeat - and some probably saw the show as their only outlet to listen and understand problems that were present in their own lives. Importantly, they could also consider the many solutions for the problems being discussed on the show.

During the Production Team's selection and vetting process, it was a rarity for a guest to answer 'never' when asked how many times they had watched the show. Most confessed to watching either every day or most days and, when asked if they were aware of the presenter's style, 'yes' was the usual response. But conflict resolution was not the only content on *'The Jeremy Kyle Show.'*

The platform was also used to promote equality, condemn prejudice, raise public awareness on many issues, facilitate help, and provide valuable support and treatment services.

Comprehensive background checks, mental health appraisals and risk assessments were carried out on participants by the Production and Guest Welfare Assessment Teams, and, in some cases, recommendations put in place to ensure they were able to cope with the show content and their role in it.
As a result of the screening procedures, the number of declined cases far exceeded the 20,000 participants who actually appeared on the show.

Even when their appearance on the show was declined, those considered in need of support were not abandoned or ignored. Instead, both the Production and Guest Welfare Teams did their level best to provide ongoing help and solutions for them. Sometimes it was necessary to speak with them more than once, especially those experiencing a mental health crisis. In most cases this approach paid off, as the Team were able to re-engage many individuals with services they had long since abandoned or point them towards appropriate statutory or voluntary services. Numerous times callers told how they no longer engaged with their local Mental Health Services, Social Services or even their GP because they felt let down by them or that no one cared about their problems.

There were even people who contacted the Production Team with no desire to appear on the show but simply because they were struggling to cope, viewing the show as a kind of helpline. Sometimes these individuals would be sobbing and in desperate need of help and support. Some days it was just skilful negotiation by the 'JK' teams that saved the day and possibly even a life, especially when the caller was threatening to take their own. They listened and cared and on those days especially, it was all about skilful communication, listening, gaining the individual's trust, and paying attention to the details, because details mattered.

Sometimes it was just about providing practical assistance and emotional support or connecting people with the right support agencies. Whatever the circumstances, it was always busy and frequently stressful. The 'JK' Guest Welfare Team certainly had first-hand experience of knowing how many vulnerable, disenfranchised and ignored people were out there in our society and fortunately, also had the experience and the knowledge to help them.

As for the show itself, I'm not naive to the fact that many viewers probably tuned in at 9.25 am most mornings just to watch a conflict story because, like many, some people can't look away when a disagreement is taking place. There seems to be an endless appetite for watching the full unfolding drama of a public disagreement or argument. Some find it entertaining as they observe facial expressions, behaviours and dramatic gestures while listening to challenging ripostes, humour, and accusations. Once it's over, they are then able to engage in the popular pastime of gossiping and judging with friends, family and even strangers.

It's much like those rubberneckers who can't look away as they pass by an incident in the street or on the road, and often even slow down to take in the full unfolding drama of what's happening. Others become part of the paparazzi, recording every detail of their experience, and then sharing it with friends or on social media for others to have an opinion.

There just seems to be an endless appetite for observing drama.

Some may say this behaviour is just human instinct dating back millennia, others that it's merely a public display of the very worst side of human nature. Whatever your view, there is clearly an appetite for it and if the viewing figures for the Depp v. Heard trial are anything to go by, it's not going away anytime soon.

This six-week trial with its elements of drama, mudslinging, argument, and conflict was watched and devoured by millions. As the real lives of these two celebrities slowly unfolded before the camera, gossip, judgement and opinion ran rampant on social media. The attendant mocking memes and sensational clickbait must have filled the coffers of many commercial interests handsomely.

With the minute details of the fallout surrounding the infamous Will Smith slap at the Oscars, the Rooney v. Vardy trial and the ongoing drama between Harry, Megan and the Royal family also being lapped up by millions, it's probably best if we're not in denial about the human appetite for observing conflict.

Disagreement and argument were certainly part and parcel of the 'JK Show', and from my observations, it did feel like a shouting match on stage somedays. Physical aggression, however, was never tolerated and every guest was made fully aware by production that the show would never condone any attempt to physically intimidate anyone, whether it be another guest or a member of the 'JK' team.

At the slightest sign of aggression, 'Big Steve' and 'Our Dan' from security would always be at the ready.

Filming was delayed one day, however, when we were recording at Media City as Dan and Steve had suddenly gone AWOL, (Absent Without Leave), and we couldn't start filming without them. They were soon located in the BBC Philharmonic studio directly next door sorting out a physical altercation. I initially thought it might be a dispute between the string and woodwind sections and, anticipating such, I quickly made my way to their studio. Alas, I didn't arrive to members of the orchestra manhandling each other but there was certainly a row going on between members of the audience.

I'm not sure what the dispute was all about, but calm was eventually restored when the vociferous audience members were removed from the studio, while still expressing their dislike for each other at full volume - and littered with profanities. It came as somewhat of a surprise to me as the people involved seemed well-heeled and culturally not conditioned to being loud. I expect they were normally ever watchful of their behaviour in public and probably looked down on those who they felt didn't conform to their standards. To be fair, it was probably about the same volume used on some of the stories on 'The JK Show' but probably less than in the House of Commons during a typical Prime Minister's Questions Time.

Though Dan, Steve and their colleague, Jimmy, were an integral part of 'The JK Show' team, the show's content was much more than just conflict resolution, rather a comprehensive mix of life realities.

Those selective in their viewing who chose to focus only on the conflict episodes perhaps missed the shows about family reunions and celebrating inspirational children, or the episodes that challenged Homophobia, Transphobia, Racism, and Inequality, or those that raised public awareness of Grief, Domestic Violence, Bullying, Homelessness, Abuse, Poverty, Knife Crime and Addiction etc. Those shows were definitely recorded and broadcast but I suspect many of the show's detractors missed that type of content.

I got a sense of that one evening as I sat in the Foreign Office at an awards event, for which *'The Jeremy Kyle Show'* had been nominated for a 'Pink News Award' to recognise its commitment to LGBT issues. As our nomination was read out, certain people sat around me clearly didn't approve and sat sniggering, whispering with an open hand covering their mouths. But I certainly wasn't going to lose any sleep about being judged by sanctimonious snobs who, after all, seem conditioned to speak disparagingly and be judgmental behind people's backs - privately of course and with like-minded people, all the while at a safe distance.

I assume that's their version of politeness - or maybe they're just being sensible for fear of being challenged by the people they are judging harshly and being disparaging about. It's quite the opposite to the way I was raised, when if you had something to say about anyone then you just said it directly and honestly to their face so that the concerning issue could be sorted, albeit with raised voices at times.

It was an interesting evening to say the least and from the outset I had my suspicions of being judged as one of the 'Great Unwashed.' No one actually approached me or said anything to that effect, but rather they just stared, or should I say sneered, in my direction. Occasionally, I'd get the half smile as I attempted to engage others in conversation, but it was just a sardonic smile before they disengaged quite quickly and without even speaking.

I did ponder why I was experiencing such hostility in a room primarily full of mediocrity and found the whole experience quite amusing. I finally concluded that *'The JK Show'* must have been the guilty secret of several people in the room because how else would they recognise me. They probably just didn't want anyone else to know of their secret viewing habit. Maybe they just couldn't cope with the fear of being judged and therefore lied about watching the allegedly unpopular show. Oh, and they didn't want me to eat with them either.

When someone finally wanted to engage me in conversation, it was only to ask if I would like to uninvite myself from dinner. Apparently there were too many people and not enough dining places. Of course I fully understood the real reason why I, one of the 'Great Unwashed,' was one of the chosen ones to give up their place. To be honest, I was quite happy and content on my train journey home as I tucked into my *'Upper Crust'* baguette.

As I engaged in friendly conversation with my neighbouring passenger - it's a Northern thing and no apologies for that - we were entertained throughout the journey by several well-heeled inebriated city workers. Apparently they had loads of money and their houses were worth a fortune – facts that I established from the endlessly loud public discourse between them. I wasn't overly impressed by their talk of endless wealth or, for that matter, their shameless behaviour and chat littered with profanities. Not least because their audience in the carriage included children and young adults. I'm also not sure how the guy wearing the posh suit - worth more than all his mates' suits put together - felt the following morning as he observed his urine-stained trousers. I was truly back in the real world.

Incidentally, Victoria Derbyshire was a worthy award winner that evening but the behaviour of some people in the room spoke volumes to me. I suspect their disapproval was not just about the show's content, but also the participants. I can just imagine their conversations, "Who are those people on that show and where do they come from - and who decided they could be visible and talking about their lives so publicly? We need to get them off TV immediately." Such comments I heard often when approached by critics of the show.

I'm sure many critics of *'The JK Show'* might have disapproved, struggled, and felt uncomfortable and offended with the openness and honesty of some participants, many of whom were willing to talk, or sometimes yell, about their lived reality. I bet though that those same critics never took into consideration the stark truth that the UK is full of different people, raised in disparate conditions and in diverse cultural settings.

Certain commentators described some of the *'JK'* participants as being feral or underclass, whereas I prefer to see many of them as the 'ignored class,' if not the ignored working class; that is, ignored by successive governments and social policies. After all, the working class never fully recovered from the mass rapid deindustrialisation of the 1980's -1990's, when millions of proud working people lost their jobs and were forced to accept long-term unemployment and claim welfare benefits indefinitely.

Some people might describe this positively as a period of great economic and social change for our country, others as an unmitigated disaster. What can't be denied is that the sinister upheaval that mass unemployment had on many working class families was catastrophic. Firstly, they were robbed of an important part of their culture based on work, and secondly, they experienced at first hand the far-reaching consequences that long-term unemployment has on families and communities.

Thousands upon thousands of lives came to a grinding halt on the day they collected their final pay packets and boarded the train of lost generational wealth and social mobility, its ultimate destination being a station called despair. They were effectively a condemned workforce forced into a future of hardship and declining living standards, staggering from one financial crisis to another. An abandoned unemployed workforce of millions -what could possibly go wrong?

Overnight, lives became blighted by disadvantage as the ladder of opportunity and social mobility simply disappeared. It must have felt as if their lives did not matter as their once-important labour and industrial and manufacturing skills were deemed surplus to requirement and of no further value. In essence, they became a forgotten people, left to survive on benefits and stripped of their work identity, ambition, self-esteem, confidence, good health and well-being, slaves to welfare dependency and debt.
This huge social shift had a devastating impact on many families and communities and, while their suffering was obvious to so many, to the 'Powers that be' they were more or less invisible. It was a supreme act of social negligence which decimated many people's lives and pushed many strong, collaborative working class communities and their families to the margins. Many families and communities have struggled ever since from this legacy. The dispirited mindset of being abandoned has been passed down through the generations, even though the stigma and shame associated with welfare dependency has now long gone.

Perhaps 'judging eyes' should consider and acknowledge this when they condemn and look down on others, or perhaps reserve their distaste for those who facilitated this absolute catastrophe on the working class. Their lives, it would appear, were an acceptable loss in the name of progress.

Many, I suspect, would experience the '5 stages of Grief' (Kubler - Ross Model) in their attempt to adapt to their overwhelming loss. Experiencing shut down in Denial and ruminating on the 'what if's' in the Bargaining Phase. Some despairing and depressed at the hopelessness of their newfound situations and their anger profound at such injustice and unfairness. Certainly many would struggle to accept the unacceptable loss of work, income and erosion of their working class cultural identity.

While many chapters in the story of the 'left behind' continue to be written by both academics and politicians, their numbers continue to grow exponentially, as do areas of social deprivation. I take issue with the new political buzz phrase of 'Levelling Up' the Left Behind People/Places because it implies people didn't keep pace with social changes and/or failed to catch up. That's not the case; they were not left behind, they were purposely and cynically ignored and left to survive on welfare without the prospect of future employment. For many their lost jobs were not replaced.

Perhaps some of 'The JK Show's' detractors might have been less condemning had the show been set to music and recorded on a colourful Greek island, with a few ABBA hits thrown into the mix and all participants affluent, middle class and well-dressed. After all, the celebrated stage and film production 'Mama Mia' was a huge success, but yet it was not a million miles away from a 'JKS' DNA story. It's a simple tale about a Mother, (Donna), who slept with three men around the same time, but consequently didn't know who her daughter's biological Father was. Her daughter, however, desperately needed to know and therefore gathered together her trio of potential Fathers on a Greek island to establish paternity. It is a beautiful location, with wonderful music, and affluent Donna and the three affluent potential Fathers are celebrated, not judged. But then - it's also not real. Had Donna been a *'JKS'* participant from a poor economic background with nothing to sing about, then I'm sure she and the three potential Dads would have been judged much more harshly.

All things come to an end, though, and the show was finally cancelled after a 14-year run, following the tragic death of a man who had appeared on it just days earlier. News of his death was both devastating and distressing for his family and friends and it also impacted the mental health of many JK employees. He died as a result of a suspected suicide and so, several days later, ITV announced:

> "Given the gravity of recent events, we have decided to end production of *'The Jeremy Kyle Show.'*"

However, the broadcaster was clear to point out that *'The JK Show'* wasn't being pulled because it had done anything that infringed regulations. On the contrary, the Production Team had closely followed processes and procedures and had strictly adhered to all the key guidelines for a conflict resolution show, with the detailed Duty of Care processes in place for contributors pre-, during- and post- show, which had evolved meticulously over the show's 14-year tenure.

The subsequent inquiry to determine the facts surrounding the man's tragic death would take approximately four years to conclude and as I write it is still ongoing. In the meantime, the after-effects of this tragedy reverberated all around and had far-reaching effects on many people's lives. Many words and pages were typed and written, and there was even a documentary produced about the demise of the show.

It seemed everyone had an opinion; some were disappointed, others rejoiced. Then I noticed something interesting was happening. While the debate between detractors and supporters continued unabated, another hateful bunch got involved in the debate - the moral grandstanders. They knew little or, in many cases, nothing about the show or its content, but were clearly very angry and offended on everyone else's behalf. Particularly on behalf of 20,000 'JK' participants, whom many perceived as being unintelligent and unable to make informed choices of their own.

Some 'JK' participants may not have had the same education as some of those who allegedly spoke on their behalf, but that does not make them unintelligent. There is a difference between education and intelligence, although I accept that education gives people greater opportunities in life.
However, I have also met many so-called educated people who distinctly lack any semblance of intelligence or common sense. The consensus I got from guests following the demise of the show indicated strongly, that in their opinion, the grandstanders should mind their own business, rather than demeaning and insulting them by

labelling them unintelligent in order to raise their own self-esteem and level of virtue.

I recently read a survey which concluded that some Southerners judge Northerners to be unintelligent because of their regional accents. 'Accentism' it would appear is alive and well! In my mind it's a pretty insulting supposition to judge people as unintelligent based on how they pronounce their vowels, but apparently it does still exist. Word to the wise, however, I wouldn't recommend anyone challenge the intelligence of Northerners.
Although that was exactly what those who allegedly knew better did following the Brexit result. "Northerners were uninformed and knew not what they did, they didn't think about the consequences of leaving the EU." They did actually! Simply put, many were not swayed by the remain debate. The Northern Brexiteers through critical thinking weighed up both sides of the argument and then swayed the vote in favour of leave.
However, 3 years later, the Brexiteers must also be wondering why they're not seeing the promised rewards of leaving the EU, or for that matter, benefitting from the alleged weekly saving of £350million once exiting.

Over many months, the grandstanders piled in and ramped up their attacks, but despite their claims of being caring and virtuous, they showed little concern about the impact their behaviours were having on those they publicly abused. It was far beyond simple criticism and it would appear that once again social media had triggered harmful anti social behaviours that impacted adversely on the mental health of others. Their condemnation and negative narrative became relentless. Collectively, they cared not one bit about the mental health or welfare of those they attacked.

All of the staff on '*The JK Show*' were provided with counselling and support during this very difficult time. However, 9 months later we needed each others help and support in abundance when our beautiful friend and colleague died. - She ended her life by suicide.

'*The JK Show*' was the first job in TV for many members of its team and often they came from working-class backgrounds. Some had university degrees, others had dropped out of university, while others only had the qualifications they'd obtained at school.
Without exception, though, all of them were prepared to work hard. They worked the longest hours and while I worked remotely from the Production Office on most days, I know this to be a fact.

Despite this they still remained dedicated, hardworking, and diligent and at times worked under relentless pressure to achieve. Without a doubt, they were a talented mix of people from a diverse range of cultural backgrounds who bonded together seamlessly as work colleagues, friends and, for some, even as flat mates. All of them shared the same enthusiasm for work and everyone celebrated the diversity within '*The JK Show*' team with pride.

On studio days, the show even brought young adults into the team who, through no fault of their own, had struggled for many years to find work due to mental health problems. The uniqueness of individuals was fully recognised by everyone and nobody was judged because of their race, ethnicity, gender, sexual orientation, physical abilities, political or religious beliefs, nor their socio-economic status.

They were certainly ambitious and eager to learn too and, over 14 years, I had the immense pleasure of watching them as they pursued their dream jobs and goals. Many started their careers as runners on the show but eventually ended up with their dream jobs. They became Directors, Camera Operatives, Sound Engineers, Editors, Producers/Assistant Producers, Production Managers/ Coordinators, Makeup Artists Wardrobe Supervisors etc

In all cases, my joy at their achievements was boundless and, while it wasn't my job to get involved in their careers,I constantly pushed many towards their career path, but what they achieved was down to their own hard work and effort.

CHAPTER TWENTY FOUR

'The 'other' Show'

Interestingly, 'The JK Show' was likened on several
occasions - and even by MPs themselves - to their own
'House of Commons Show.' It is easy to see similarities
in content, especially conflict stories.

Some viewers were shocked by some of the stories on 'The
JK Show' but I'm not sure why, as they paled into
insignificance when compared to the goings-on in the
other show broadcast daily from the House of Commons.
Some of its participants have entertained us for decades
with stories far more shocking. Their track record over the
years certainly leaves a lot to be desired.

Criminal convictions for harassment, sexual harassment,
theft, perjury, fraud, physical and sexual assault seem
disproportionate within this group and their colourful
private lives (family feuds, infidelity, cheating, paternity
disputes, drug and alcohol misuse, allegations of bullying,
lying, brawling in public) is well documented.
Unlike the 20,000 'The JK Show' participants, however,
who appeared voluntarily and without payment,
participants in the HOC show earn substantial incomes for
their appearances.
Some even have second jobs to supplement their wages of
£84,000, plus substantial allowances and expenses.
One wonders where they can find the time to do all this,
but they do and I can only assume they are permanently
exhausted.

Some days, the behaviour on display during the HOC Show
is spectacularly bad. Other days, the performance can be
quite boring, usually when participants read from their

well-prepared scripts, parroting the words others have meticulously prepared for them. Nevertheless, many find their conflict shows entertaining as they shout, scream and hurl abuse and insults at each other across the stage - sorry, I mean the House - only to be admonished by the Presenter, aka the Speaker, who steps in to act as referee when the chaotic exchanges and attempts to talk over each other reach fever pitch.

Of course, this behaviour is rightly considered unparliamentary and unacceptable, as is their occasional use of profanities. Yet it still happens and, apparently, it is because our MPs are passionate about issues. Sometimes other MPs sitting in the stalls - let's call them the audience - get tired of the theatrical political performances and decide to flex their vocal chords by heckling, jeering and booing like contributors in a pantomime. The main difference is that these show participants run our country.

Yet, from what I've seen, the HOC Show actors seem to perceive their performances as acceptable, emotional, and energised, and in no way comparable to 'The Jeremy Kyle Show.' For my part, I strongly disagree.

The good news for anyone still missing the animated discourse that sometimes occurred on 'The JK Show,' they can still tune into the HOC Show, which continues to be televised daily as it should be, because these people definitely need keeping an eye on.
Especially those caught watching porn on their mobiles in the HOC. One MP subsequently resigned for this and should be congratulated, as it makes a change from the usual, "There will be an inquiry into the allegations and we should all await the outcome." Then again, perhaps he resigned rather than join the lengthy queue of his colleagues already awaiting an interview with the

Independent Complaints and Grievance Scheme (ICGS) for allegations of bullying and sexual misconduct, ranging from sexual harassment to more serious wrongdoings.

My Dad and his mates often described them as being the sort of people who "Talk a load of flannel, piss in the same pot and line each other's pockets." They encouraged us as children never to believe a word that comes out of their collective mouths, and they just might have had a valid point.

I advise anyone not to take too seriously anything that happens on the 'HOC Show' stage, as in my view it's mostly just a talking shop. MPs harp on about what they plan to do, yet never seem to follow through on their pre-election promises, such promises often turning out to be undeliverable or getting filed away in boxes marked 'Too difficult to handle,' or 'Will cost a lot of money.' Not that those same promises won't be retrieved whenever suits, which is usually just prior to the next election.

To be fair, I'm certain most of the actors on the 'HOC Show' stage don't perceive the daily goings-on as a talking shop, but rather a democratic display of skilled debate. They like the debate game because, if nothing else, it's an opportunity to satisfy their desperate need for political grandstanding and attention. Most seem to enjoy honing their debating and public speaking skills - practised at university and polished up when they become MPs - in front of a rapt audience of their peers, more often than not using carefully prepared scripts littered with jargon that most of us don't even understand. The declared winners then leave the stage in mock triumph, feeling proud and powerful that their opponents have been put in their place by their intellectual prowess. In a nutshell, our 'honourable' parliamentary representatives all want to be top of the bill. However, the real losers are us, the public, sat at home who are paying for all this political posturing with little or no reward. It's perhaps time for some MPs to remind themselves they are Members of Parliament not members of a Debating Society.

As for me, I'm not an actual fan of the show because some days it makes me feel as if I'm back at school in my Physics class, but with the roles reversed; myself and the general public being the educators desperately trying to teach the pupils - our MPs - about the actual lived reality, struggles and experiences of people living in the UK. Unfortunately though, in this classroom, the struggling pupils seem not to grasp the complexity of the subjects being taught i.e.poverty, education, unemployment, housing, crime, public services, cutbacks, current cost of living crisis etc
No wonder the general public feel frustrated at their lack of effort and resolve in these matters. It's not enough that their report cards – (like mine in Physics) - state 'Could do better,' "Must try harder," and "Needs to pay more attention in class." It's just not good enough.
No wonder so many people now believe that politics and politicians are becoming irrelevant, dysfunctional, and self-serving.

Many of those appearing in the 'HOC Show' are also master patronisers, dispensing advice to us minions in their superior way. They seem to be quite comfortable telling us just how we should lead our lives and which rules we must follow, while frequently absenting themselves from them. The breaches by some MPs during the Covid-19 lockdowns are a prime example.
Genuine compassion and concern for people is what government should really be about, with an emphasis on improving the lives of the thousands upon thousands of

people facing enormous difficulties on a daily basis. Many MPs appear to have little understanding of those challenges and even if they do, they are either forced or choose to adhere strictly to the tired old script provided for them.

Sadly, nothing is likely to change until the collective members of our government are truly representative of the diverse society in which we all live. Certainly social and economic class needs to be recognised within that diversity, because it is not just about race, religion, sexuality, disability and gender. Classism existed when I was a child and it still exists today. The UK's working class and its ignored working class need much greater representation, not least because they truly live the reality of their lives every single day, which unfortunately, is not the same reality perceived by many academics and careerist politicians. There needs to be less talk and more action and our elected representatives need more than ever to do the job for which they are employed. More importantly, some MPs need to put compassion before party politics and find their lapsed moral compass. A great start would be to find more real long-term solutions for people's real life problems.

******

CHAPTER TWENTY FIVE

'Some gather more than they need'
'Other get less than they deserve'

For 15 years, I was fortunate to meet thousands of participants and non participants on *'The JK Show'* and it was a privilege, enabling me to learn directly about the realities of living in socially deprived and marginalised areas in the UK. This didn't apply to everyone who appeared but, for those it did, it was refreshing to hear from their view, rather than the skewed views of academics, politicians and others who allegedly speak on their behalf. Their raw honesty was enlightening as they spoke from personal experience and with a deep understanding of the history and culture of the communities in which they lived. I was fortunate enough to hear thousands of backstories which, though at times didn't make for easy listening, at the very least it educated me first-hand about their needs and suffering. During our conversations they were always kind, articulate, friendly and sociable and despite the many challenges they had to deal with, I was constantly amazed by their coping skills and sense of humour. Maybe humour was the best line of defence when trying to cope with unrelenting daily stressors.

Some described childhoods spent in unsafe and unstable homes, others of being raised in a Care system - often a far from positive experience for them - feeling unloved, abandoned and, in some cases, separated from their siblings. They are not alone because I read recently that there are currently 80,000 children in the Care system (*Source: Independent Review of Children's Social Care 2022*). It's a number that is steadily rising and experts are voicing their concerns that our Care system is at crisis point and in need of urgent attention. After listening to these backstories, I would argue this system has been in crisis for a very long time. I listened to stories of children who had lived with parents addicted to alcohol, drugs, and prescription medication and some who had witnessed domestic violence at a very young age. Others spoke of chaotic childhoods while living in environments not conducive to good early childhood development.

Many of them made reference to the harsh realities of family lives lived on low incomes, dominated by the tyranny of poverty and the immense impact this had on family break down, their developing lives and educational achievements. I heard stories of parents struggling to cope financially and emotionally, often unemployed, in debt and unable to pay utility bills.
Some were in poor mental and physical health and others were struggling to care for children in substandard accommodation, sometimes under threat of eviction.
In some cases, raised in temporary accommodation, which when translated means a whole family living in one room and without hope of moving to secure permanent accommodation.

Some had experienced periods of homelessness, but when you consider that there are 274,000 homeless people in England, of which 126,000 are children, (*Source: Shelter 2021*), it's not surprising that I would meet some of these people. Few, however, spoke of adequate support systems being in place during their times of immense need, but rather their feelings of abandonment, being unable to cope and struggling to find solutions.

The stress that these children, now adults, had lived under was immense. Some had started using alcohol and drugs at an early age - some even as young as twelve - to temporarily cope with the many social stressors they faced. In some cases alcohol and drugs had become their most trusted friends during a crisis but, sadly, it also became the enemy which took them to their darkest times. Many carried their unhealed childhood traumas into their young adult lives, these early childhood experiences shaping the adults they became and the parents they would later become.

I spoke with young adults with few or no qualifications, and some who had been excluded from school for making bad decisions.
Others had voluntarily excluded themselves from school - or dropped out - because they either lacked interest or motivation, struggled to learn in the classroom, or saw no future in education. As a result, many were unemployed and believed that they would never achieve their full potential. They spoke only of a bleak future without employment and many had reached a point where they didn't even apply for jobs because they lacked education or employment skills - so why bother.

Some of those I interviewed were homeless and completely detached from their families. They felt alone, isolated and abandoned and had little confidence or knowledge about how to move their lives forward positively. Consequently, many were struggling to cope with the existing realities of their young adult lives. In some cases, all support systems had collapsed entirely. They were truly alone in the world and barely surviving.

They didn't see a glass half-full or half-empty, just an empty glass devoid of any optimism. I sensed their despair and feeling of hopelessness and injustice which, at times, was palpable and for some, deeply ingrained. Not just with them, but with their friends, family and sometimes within whole communities. They felt they had been written off at an early age and perceived the same bleak future for themselves as had been experienced by several generations of their own family before them.

They believed their adverse childhood experiences would blight their lives forever and, consequently, felt resentful when going about their lives bereft of any future progress. They felt they had no stake in society and that political promises and public services were not for them. I lost count of the amount of times I heard the phrase, What's the point, Graham?" because some felt so crushed they believed that any attempt to change their life was futile and that the odds would always be stacked heavily against them. Sadly, and this breaks me, I spoke to many young adults who had already submitted to a fate of long-term unemployment and living in survival mode. They didn't focus on future goals only the struggles of the day - Trying to get through it and instinctively surviving the ever present stressors that awaited them most days.

There is no doubt that some adults I spoke to had made poor life choices and would continue to make them, largely shaped by their past and present realities and often at times of great hardship and stress. However, the choices they were making were not resolving their problems. rather, if anything, making them worse. They were just surviving and, while I'm not trying to justify their poor decisions, surely the impact of their early childhood years is worthy of consideration before making judgement on them?

In contrast, I also met young adults who could only be described as positive and engaged. Some were working voluntarily to gain work experience, others in a myriad of short-term, low paid jobs and more of them still engaged in employment training programmes.

Equally, I lost count of the times I heard someone say, "I wish I had done better at school, Graham." This group had not been defeated by their childhood experiences.

On one level I empathised with their life experiences but, to be honest, my childhood paled when listening to theirs. There simply was no comparison between the environments in which we were raised. Yes, both of our childhood experiences had provided us with a sense of who we are and our value to society, but I would choose mine any day of the week.

At the very least I could reflect on how lucky I had been, growing up on a council estate and within a supportive and collaborative community. My childhood experiences afforded me stability, safety, security, love, and I was definitely cared for and was able to avoid the care system. It also afforded me the opportunity to learn, explore, take risks free from fear and install a belief in myself and my abilities.

My community were my extended family. They were the ones who set the rules and boundaries from which I and everyone else benefitted. We were dependent on each other for our survival and rarely did we fail to support each other in times of need or crisis. We did not have food banks, clothing banks or charity shops - Just the help and support of each other in times of hardship.

Every family on my estate was on constant standby to help each other out practically, financially, and emotionally and we always had each other's backs.

We were also lucky because work was plentiful for our parents and, although poor, we were not living in poverty. Our parents instilled a strong work ethic in us for when we eventually left school but, before that happened, the focus was solely on education. Our parents were dogmatic in their approach to learning and our full attendance at school was insisted upon. If our school reports did not reflect any educational progress or near-perfect attendance, then questions were asked and solutions quickly found. No child on my estate ever wanted the truancy officer knocking on their door, because if that ever happened, there would be serious consequences.

In simple terms, our parents wanted us to do better than they had, hence the emphasis on educational achievements. Fortunately for us, on leaving school, work was plentiful. Maybe not the jobs we wanted but work nonetheless and this brought security and a sense of independence that we could build upon. We of course faced the bigotry of low expectations and discrimination due to our lack of formal qualifications, but nobody could say that my peers and I weren't well educated, both academically and socially.

While the availability of apprenticeships, vocational training and job opportunities facilitated any future successes we had, importantly we still needed to believe that we were good enough.
Our parents constantly supported and motivated us to believe we could achieve anything; all we needed were the right opportunities. This, our beneficial early childhood emotional and social development, and their focus on our education, enabled us to have better lives, even though we may have struggled with doubt at times.

From the many discussions I had with some young adults I certainly gained an understanding of their self-perceived lack of value. Put simply, many just didn't believe they were good enough to achieve their full potential and had little belief in themselves or their abilities. Much of how they viewed themselves had been learned in childhood and within the environment in which they were raised. This had impacted their self-esteem enormously, with the result being that they were trapped in an unhealthy belief system of not feeling good enough.

Of course, they did not want their lives to be this way. At the same time, they just couldn't see a way out. They were desperate to feel connected to society, to contribute and not be excluded and ignored. It was obvious to me how their desperation increased as their hopes and dreams decreased in equal measure. The reality of their lives was soul destroying and the pressure under which they lived relentless. Many I spoke to felt that they were abandoned, ignored, and written off at an early age - and they had a point.

They have been served a grave injustice in life and so it is understandable if they continue to feel resentful and angry. It's not rocket science to realise their exclusion, rather than inclusion, creates a 'them and us' society and communicates a message that their lives don't matter. They are also fully aware of the bigotry of low expectation, which is often directed towards them, often accompanied by taunts to, "Get a job!"
But, in order to land a worthwhile job, they will also need an excellent school education because that is also a reasonable expectation of employers. Sadly, recent research suggests that doesn't bode well.

It highlighted that, in 2018, almost 100,000 children in England had left education, aged 18, without the proper qualifications to enable them to enter the workplace. These children would have spent 15 years in compulsory education, often having more than £100,000 of public money spent on them and yet they still exited the
education system without basic benchmark qualifications. Accordingly, many of them will not be able to begin an apprenticeship, start technical courses or enter some workplaces simply because they cannot meet basic entry requirements. A significant number of them will be from disadvantaged backgrounds and will be drawn from a
diverse demographic, because living in a disadvantaged community does not discriminate against skin colour, religious beliefs, sexuality or gender.

It is also massively concerning to learn that in 2022 a quarter of a million children a year are entering secondary school education without basic Maths and English
In essence they are leaving primary education without the right level of skill in reading, writing and maths.
The basic foundational skills that we all need to flourish. This unbelievable reality might partly explain why some pupils struggle to learn in secondary school, lack
motivation and interest, or in some cases, exclude themselves from school before gaining an adequate education and formal qualifications.

On a lesser scale I'm familiar with that journey of leaving school without the necessary formal qualifications
expected by employers in order to pursue a career of my choice; I know the feeling of having low expectations being placed upon me because I was working class; I know the frustration and anger I felt when doors of opportunity closed rather than opened; I know that feeling of being excluded and being denied the chance to progress my life. I still remember the times I stood on the edge of

the precipice of despair, choosing the path to nowhere whilst laying on the couch at home instead of going to work. I was lucky because I got the rude awakening I needed from my Father by being frog-marched to another job once caught. He never gave up on me or wrote me off, even though there were times I did that to myself. Believe me when I say there is a very fine line between motivating oneself to move forward positively and giving up entirely.

Sadly, I spoke to young adults who failed to make the transition from school to work and, no doubt, they will continue to feel let down. Their dreams, opportunities and ambition were stolen from them in childhood and the cycle of disadvantage which, for some, starts at birth, remains largely unbroken. I constantly ask myself the same questions: 50 years after I left school, why are so many children still being let down and leaving school without an adequate school education? How is it even possible in the 21st century for Education Ministers still to be talking openly about improving literacy and numeracy skills for primary and secondary pupils? These children have been failed and this is not 50 years of educational progress.

On the subject of children being failed, I will be forever reminded of a comment I read from one of the girls in the 'Rochdale Grooming Scandal.' - "Police weren't arsed with us really. They weren't bothered ....when you're from a shit home. They don't give a fuck when you're not from a wealthy background". This scandal, which was perpetrated in my hometown of Rochdale, was a scandal of epic proportions and involved vulnerable white girls as young as 12, many in care and from working class backgrounds. They were groomed, repeatedly raped, and abused by gangs of predominantly British Pakistani men, but despite this happening in plain sight nothing was done by the very people who were supposed to protect them.

At the time they were not considered child victims of sexual exploitation or abuse, but rather they were judged, blamed, ignored, disbelieved, and discriminated against. In some cases labeled 'bad,' and by others, they were accused of making their own choices and consenting to sex. To say these children were failed by people employed within public institutions to protect them would be putting it mildly. They were betrayed on a massive scale. I can only imagine how this horrendous abuse impacted so cruelly on their childhood and future lives. Once again no doubt we will hear that 'Lessons must be learned from this.' It should not have happened at all and the sad thing is - the really dreadful thing is - I think we all know the answer as to why these young girls were ignored and not believed when they initially reported their abusers to the authorities.

In the same year I read about the avoidable death of a two year old boy in Rochdale. He died as a result of a severe respiratory condition caused by exposure to black mould in his home environment.
Over three years his parents raised concerns with the landlord (Rochdale Borough Housing) regarding their uninhabitable living conditions, but their voices went unheard and concerns ignored. Surely the question to be asked is why their voices were not heard ?.
Sadly, there are still many more children and adults living in houses that are similarly not fit for human habitation and who's voices are not being heard.

We're currently living in a society that broadcasts loudly and often the progressive liberal view of inclusion within society – and long may this continue. However, we seem to fall silent when it comes to the ignored working class.

Despite this social group encompassing all the protected characteristics of the equality act in terms of gender, race, ethnicity, sexuality, disability, and religion, it still appears there is no invite for them to join the all-inclusive workplace or to be part of a fair and just society.

I ask myself why this discrimination towards millions of people in this country continues? Who is representing the oppressed children from poorer backgrounds who are being left behind in early childhood and at school? Who is raising awareness of their equality and inclusion struggle, or for that matter, the major issues affecting their communities?

The ignored working class still remain invisible to many and they will continue to be exploited because of the sheer fact they are powerless to enact significant change without the right representation, support, and investment to move their lives forward. Certainly there are individuals and organisations who valiantly represent the ignored in this country but their voices also need to be heard by those with the power to facilitate change.

At a time when we are rightly addressing the all-important issues of diversity, equality, and inclusion in this country, surely it's also time to address the oppression of children from poorer backgrounds who are being left behind both in early childhood and at school. Every child in the UK should be afforded the best possible start in life irrespective of their social class.

'It is easier to build strong children than to repair broken men.'Frederick Douglass.

I firmly believe that people can change, even when the odds are stacked against them. But meaningful change will only come about through a comprehensive social improvement programme, not by throwing more money at broken systems. We need to create the conditions that enable people to have better lives through focus on good early childhood development, better education, job opportunities and a massive investment in under-resourced communities. This is achievable and if Politicians want to do it, they can.

In the meantime I would start by investing in 'Centres of Advancement' in all disadvantaged communities around the UK. Centres that are staffed by Social Workers, Mentors, Role models, Therapists, Counsellors, Youth workers and Educators. All with experience in life coaching and social work. Teams that truly understand the colossal challenges many people face in disadvantaged communities and who could work alongside them to facilitate change and improve wellbeing.

Centres that provide face to face services and are staffed by those who could proactively identify and solve the myriad of social and personal problems that many people face. A place where individuals could have meaningful conversations about their real lived experiences. Support for parents, and provision of a comprehensive counselling services for those most in need and motivational counselling for those who need to cultivate a belief that change is possible.

In short we need a holistic approach to improving lives, because for some, lacking motivation will always be a major obstacle to change. They need help, support, solutions, hope, encouragement, optimism, self esteem, confidence and opportunities. Ignoring their actual lived experiences is not the answer and one size does not fit all when it comes to finding solutions.

This is what they deserve and I'm pretty sure the British taxpayer would have preferred the eye watering £10 billion spent on lost, unusable, or over-priced PPE during the Covid pandemic to have been spent on something like this. Instead this money was just wasted and written off.

Until these causes are addressed, the odds will continue to be stacked against those living in socially deprived areas. We will continue to live in an unrepresentative, unfair, and unjust society and we will continue the devastating impact on those children who already begin their life way behind the start line in the equal opportunities race.

Those politicians who represent us in the House of Commons, and whose salaries we pay, need to feel a measured amount of healthy guilt about how the failed are continually being ignored. If politics doesn't strive to improve people's lives then, in my opinion, it's pointless. Improving the lives of many within this country takes purpose and hard work and it needs to start from the bottom up.

"Not every child has an equal talent or an equal ability or equal motivation, but they should have the equal right to develop their talent and their ability and their motivation, to make something of themselves"

John F Kennedy

CHAPTER TWENTY SIX

'Aftercare Service'

I implemented 'The JK Show' Aftercare Service during my first month in the role and, over the 14 years that followed, it became an integral part of the show and my life. We were possibly the very first show to include a comprehensive Aftercare Service and it made complete sense to me. Simply put, people were bringing a problem or an issue to the show, seeking a resolution and we were there to assist, support, guide and facilitate access to services they might need going forward.

It was the perfect job for me and I loved every minute of it. Helping people and providing them with opportunities was, and still is, massively rewarding for me. Sometimes the solutions were easy to find, sometimes they were a bit more complex, especially if the problem being highlighted was merely a symptom of a much deeper underlying issue.

I didn't keep close tabs on my department budget, nor did I count how much we were spending. To be honest, I didn't even know what my total allowance was, because I'm a terrible accountant. I just spent ITV's money as needed and, when it ran out, I went cap in hand looking for more. Most of the time I got it and if I didn't, then I begged for help from generous individuals and organisations.

My biggest budget expenditure was on counselling and not just for the few diagnosed with a mental health condition or those looking for solutions to difficult life events, but also for the many who just wanted to feel better about themselves. Counselling provided them with an opportunity to gain insight into how their feelings were affecting their everyday lives, particularly their relationships with family and friends. They learned how to handle their emotions and situations differently and how to develop a greater understanding of the connection between their thoughts, moods, and behaviours. It also provided the opportunity to identify and change behaviours learned in childhood, sometimes during times of trauma and bad experiences, but nevertheless, behaviours that were not working for them in their current adult life. In some cases it allowed them the opportunity to identify their self imposed limiting beliefs. How else could they learn to feel better about themselves and potentially progress with their lives.

Arranging counselling/therapy appointments could be tricky at times, however. You'd be amazed at the number of times we called practitioners who were initially happy and enthusiastic about taking a referral from a TV company, but then suddenly had no appointments when they became aware their potential client was a referral from *'The JK Show.'*

Suspicious I know, but maybe they carried out a spontaneous self-assessment and acknowledged their inability to overcome the wide cultural gap which existed between themselves and the referred client. Therefore, and thankfully, they politely declined.
After all, Psychotherapy is predominantly a middle class profession and if practitioners are raised and only socialise in middle class culture then they might struggle with cultural competency - 'cultural blindness.'

Only a true and empathic understanding of a clients personal cultural values, lived experience, beliefs and background will facilitate effective therapy. I need to check my cultural competency often since my clients come from all socio economic groups, but in my clinic, everyone is treated the same. They are all afforded the opportunity to share problems and emotional distress, be self centred, talk, shout, cry or even be angry. - I'm never afraid of the volume levels or words they might use. Just grateful that they trust me to listen without judgement.

However listening to some childhood backstories and learning about emotional injuries can be difficult at times. In some cases those injuries will be dictating their present and future lives, and whilst they are not to blame, they are still charged with the responsibility of healing from them - This takes enormous courage on their part and they have my respect.

On my part I just want them to overcome their problems and emotional difficulties and develop sustainable coping mechanisms for the future. I want them to leave therapy happier, healthier and with the ability to move their lives forward independently of me, and preferably, with a good support network in place.

Nevertheless despite the lack of available appointments some weeks, we managed and were able to use the services of some amazing Counsellors and Therapists up and down the country. All of those private counselling sessions and services were provided at no cost to the participant and most were arranged within 48 to 72 hours of their appearance on the show. Or in some cases their non appearance on the show as it was not unknown for us to fund counselling sessions for those who chaperoned guests to the studios. Usually this would happen if a guest specifically requested help and support for them and didn't require any aftercare themselves.

Many individuals we arranged sessions for had previously been left sitting on endlessly long NHS waiting lists, during which time their conditions had worsened perceptibly.

We provided countless life-changing opportunities over the years, sometimes sending people to take part in residential weight loss programmes, where they not only achieved that main goal of losing weight but also had their self-confidence and self-esteem boosted. Others went on to residential rehab programmes for drug, alcohol, prescription drug and gambling addictions. We provided hundreds of rehab places to addicts over the years, often when they were at their lowest point in life and desperately in need of help.

Some of the addicts I saw had given up all hope of ever recovering from addiction and often had disengaged from community-based treatment services altogether. As a result they were also suffering financial, health and social consequences. Some were homeless, others had a history of overdosing and many were living in the poorest communities in the country. Every addict I interviewed had a story and a reason as to how they had got to where they were and, without a doubt, many had hit rock bottom.

While those with addictions would sometimes contact the show themselves, in the majority of cases, it would be a concerned family member who got in touch, having exhausted all other avenues available to them. Often it was because they could no longer watch their loved one suffer or, even worse, die. Addict or not, their life mattered to them as it mattered to me and together we provided the best possible chance of their recovery. All we needed in return was a high level of commitment and motivation from them. Every addict I interviewed who gave true accounts of their life provided a heart-breaking history of when it all went wrong for them. I say true

accounts because, for some, their past was still
too painful to address. Stories of homelessness, trauma,
domestic violence, childhood abuse, neglect,
mental health problems and poverty were common, as
were the narratives about their repeated, failed attempts
to stop.

During the recording of these addiction stories, viewers
would observe compassion, frustration, resistance, denial
and even anger in a shared exchange between the addict,
their family, and the Presenter but there was also hope of
a new beginning.
One thing I will always remember during these shows is
the moment when an addict acknowledged - maybe for
the first time - that they had alienated their loved ones
and had traded them and other supportive relationships
for addiction. For me, those were moments of elation and
new beginnings and the joy everyone felt when an addict
sat in the car and went to rehab was palpable, not just
from family and friends but from all the crew in the
studio. Addicts were being offered the opportunity for
a three-month stay in a Residential Rehabilitation Unit,
free from temptation and other influences, in order
to help them focus solely on their recovery.

I can honestly say that most of them embraced this
opportunity of a lifetime. It was a chance to medically
detox, engage with treatments, educate themselves about
addiction and hopefully work through and resolve the
traumatic experiences that had either led to their
addiction or resulted from it.
Importantly, it provided them with an opportunity to make
some significant changes to their lives. Hundreds of
participants on 'The JK Show' were offered that chance,
but thousands of people benefited from it because, when
an addict is in recovery, it not only improves their life but

also the lives of their family, friends, the people in their community and even society itself.

In the early days, however, there were occasions when admitting addicts into rehab didn't go quite as smoothly as I would have wished. While the individuals were motivated to change their life, some also had the fear factor holding them back as they contemplated a future without the substances they'd been using for years to help them cope. Sometimes the fear got the better of them and they ran for the hills at the point of admission.

Maybe that was my fault for not giving them enough reassurance prior to rehab, or maybe they didn't ask the right questions to solicit that reassurance. In any event, on more than one occasion I would find myself looking at an empty chair in rehab facility's reception which had previously been occupied by the addict.
Accompanied by security staff, I would then head off in hot pursuit, running down the road while being directed by anyone and everyone in our quest to find them. We often found them in parks, shops and even on one occasion hiding in a locked café toilet - frequented by ladies who wear hats - steadfastly refusing to come out. On that occasion, the ladies formed an orderly queue while I negotiated with the addict to leave the cubicle. I thanked them as we left because it took quite a while.

Sometimes, but not often enough for me, we also filmed recovering addicts once they'd graduated from their treatment programme. On those days, we brought them back to studios and the audience couldn't applaud loudly enough. It was such a great feeling to see the recovering individual looking so well and basking in their well-deserved acclaim because it validated all the hard work and effort that they'd put into their recovery process.

Importantly, we were also getting a very strong message out about addiction, primarily that it is treatable.

Hopefully it inspired others to get clean, whatever their addiction; alcohol, drugs, prescription drugs, tobacco, sex, gambling, shopping, eating etc. The beds were free of charge to the addict and a lifesaver for many. Sadly though, when the show ended, so did that service. I will be forever haunted by the fact that, on the day the show ended, I still had six empty beds to fill.

I remind myself of that often because I know only too well that by not filling those beds, six addicts could possibly die, either from the medical consequences of substance abuse, suicide, or drug overdose, or through continuing their spiral downwards into an abyss of despair and hopelessness. I knew that was the harsh reality the day I read a newspaper article about a vulnerable woman who had penned a letter to *'The JK Show'* begging for help because her life was spiralling into drug addiction. She, like many other addicts who contacted the show, was clearly of the opinion that we might be able to help by providing the right resources to support her recovery. Sadly, she never posted the letter and it was only discovered following her death. She had been murdered by someone who was targeting vulnerable women, leaving behind a devastated family and three young children.

We worked tirelessly over the years trying to secure beds, but none of the work we did would have been possible without the kindness and generosity of the Residential Rehabilitation Treatment Centres and their amazing staff. They were generous to a fault. Over the years, however, we never had enough beds to meet the demand.

That said, we did on occasion find beds for addicts who never appeared on the show because they'd made it very clear they couldn't endure their misery any longer and had every intention to end their life - and believe me they were serious - so we provided the bed. On these occasions I simply went cap in hand to beg a service providers for a free rehab. Thankfully, and in all cases, they did, and once again I could breathe normally and look forward to a restful sleep.

I know that the show made a difference and changed the lives of many addicts and those of their families for the better. To this day, I'm still reminded of the great work we did and I am filled with joy when I read amazing success stories on my social media account, like this one:

> *"This time three years ago was when the JK team came to my flat in Walsall to do a recording. I was so frightened. I didn't know what to expect. I had hit rock bottom. My flat windows were smashed through and it looked like a crack den. My drug use was so out of control. I had given up on life. I just wanted to die. I didn't want to live anymore. I couldn't live the life I was living anymore. I knew everyone would see my show and I didn't care. I'm so blessed that my beautiful princess emailed the show."*

When I read the post I remembered it like it was yesterday and I loved the subsequent update:

> *"I'm living life today. I couldn't be any happier with what I have in my life. Having my family back. I'm a Mom, Sister, Daughter, Auntie, Cousin and it's all thanks to me finding a solution."*

I wish she'd never had the problem in the first place but I'm so glad we were able to help. She wasn't actually living in a crack den but I certainly know what a crack den looks like. I visited several during my time on the show.

343

But it never phased me. It didn't faze our security guard Steve either but he would worry if I went missing in action. That was always Steve's main concern when we arrived at filming locations to surprise someone with an offer of a residential rehab. He knew from past experience that I could vanish without trace when searching for an addict who was not at the planned location. He would always find me though. When he did, he was sometimes calm, other times breathless from running around, but always worried, stressing time and again to make sure I stayed where he could see me and not just walk off without telling him.

Those treatment programmes certainly saved lives, but sadly there are still many more addicts out there in need of intensive treatment programmes who are not currently receiving any support. For those individuals, the future remains bleak because the funding for addiction treatment services is forever diminishing.

When we didn't have beds available, our only option would be to refer people to local community drug and alcohol services but, sadly, those services are constantly under tremendous pressure, often under-resourced and struggling to cope with the demand. For many addicts, these services are like a revolving door.

During my time working with those with addiction, the one thing I learned was that they have an absolute need for an intense and comprehensive treatment and support programme to facilitate their recovery.
What they definitely don't need is to be demonised, punished, or criminalised, because this neither works for them nor society itself.

Addicts are so often the unheard, doubted and ignored within our society and to help them get noticed, I became a prolific letter writer on their behalf. In some cases they didn't even have GPs and before we could even start to engage or re-engage them with services, we first needed to sort that problem out. I wrote letters regarding drug and alcohol issues, physical and mental health conditions, and letters to Social Services for many varied reasons. Some weeks, the letters were endless and when I wasn't directly involved in writing them, the Production and Aftercare Teams would be beavering away providing information and advice to people either in person or on the 'phone, often sign posting them to much needed services for them and their families. As well as the show participants, we provided this valuable help and support to non-participants too, as many viewed 'The JK Show' as their helpline.

Over the years we must have been responsible for a steep rise in self-referrals to local Citizens Advice Bureaus because they were often our go-to option, especially when people had money issues as a result of their benefits being sanctioned or capped, or because of rule changes when universal credit was introduced. Sometimes they were in debt, sometimes they were destitute and, sadly, often threatened with homelessness because they were unable to pay their rent.

In some cases - and when we were made aware of their hardship - we also provided care packages of food, baby formula and children's clothing to tide them over until their benefits had been sorted out. It was not unknown for us to even put credit on their electricity and gas keys. Of course, we were not supposed to do that but we did anyway because we cared. It's what we all did because in life you don't turn your back on someone in need. That's the way I and many others on the show were raised. I even wrote letters for people who I learned were homeless to support their desperate need for emergency housing.

I remember writing a letter to Social Services about a young man who felt unsafe living in an area in which he had been placed after leaving Care. He had no family or friends locally and had been a victim, several times, of physical assaults and had been threatened repeatedly with a knife. Understandably, he feared for his life and worried constantly about the perpetrators making good on their threats to stab him to death. Despite several meetings with a Leaving Care worker, his request to move to a safer area had been denied and he faced three options: staying in his current accommodation; homelessness; or going to the Police. He decided to stay put because he felt going to the Police would only exacerbate the situation and further endanger his life. Homelessness wasn't an option.

Consequently, he also carried a knife for protection and intended to use it should anyone pull a knife on him again. He was living in total despair and had developed an anxiety condition, but no one was listening to his concerns or taking his fears seriously.

I appreciate that Social Services don't have the resources to cope with the sheer number of people and problems they are faced with, but when someone is at high risk of losing their life, then surely they cannot be ignored. My letter got him noticed. I have to say too that Social Services were faultless the day that I referred two children with unexplained bruising and injuries on their bodies. Abuse and neglect can occur in all social classes and this was an isolated incident but, fortunately, the vigilance and professionalism of *'The JK Show'* Creche Staff paid off that day. The children were clearly in danger and, following a full investigation by the Police and Social Services, the children were placed in long-term foster care.

Many months later, as I sat in my office sifting through my mail, I opened an envelope addressed to me and marked confidential. Inside were three photographs and a note. Before reading it, I looked at the photos and peering back at me were two happy, healthy children laughing and playing together in a park. I recognised them immediately as being the two children we had referred to Social Services. The note just said: 'Thank you. Xxx.' I still have those photos in my desk drawer and some days I look at them and smile, happy that we all did a good job that day. We did a good job most days, it's just that some days are more rewarding than others.

There were many memorable moments and I always look forward to the updates and progress reports about the people we had provided opportunities and services for, or those we had helped and supported during difficult times. I still vividly remember the day I interviewed a man because of concerns about his 'happy relationship' as he described it, although his family and friends certainly did not concur. Instead, they suspected he could be a victim of domestic violence and voiced their concerns during Production and Guest Welfare background checks. These were standard procedures on the show and were carried out to validate stories and obtain additional information from family and friends as part of the overall risk assessment process.

Sadly, during his face-to-face interview - and once he had been provided with the opportunity to speak privately and without any external influences - the concerns voiced by his friends and family were slowly confirmed. He was a meek and mild mannered individual, very polite, well-dressed and with no signs of any physical abuse. But certain things started cropping up during his interview; his self-criticism and fear about upsetting his partner, his isolation from family and friends, his lack of confidence and self-esteem. As we continued asking questions and listened to his responses, slowly building a rapport with him, he disclosed his fears - and his wounds.

He described in detail the physical and emotional abuse he had sustained over many years from his partner. As recently as the previous week, he had been assaulted while asleep. The wounds on his body had not been treated and his pain was obvious as he removed his clothing to reveal injuries that would require medical care. He left the relationship that same day and was immediately taken to hospital for treatment, ensuring beforehand that he had a future safety plan, ongoing support in place and a safe place to stay. Criminal charges were subsequently brought against his former partner, the perpetrator and he didn't appear on the show.

I also met several women over the years on 'The JK Show' who lived in fear of their partners. Some had been physically harmed, others were isolated from family and friends, many enduring threats of harm, destruction of their property, humiliation, intimidation, harassment, and all of them worn down. We were always vigilant in such matters; these women were never ignored and when we became aware, they didn't appear on the show. But we still provided them with a safe plan and information about support organisations that could help them. Survivors of domestic violence also appeared on 'The JK Show' and raised awareness of the issue. We also provided the opportunity for others to speak about their traumatic life experiences, including ex-servicemen suffering from PTSD. They were survivors and providing a platform and in some cases counselling for these individuals was an honour and a privilege.

Some participants on *'The JK Show'* spoke openly and movingly about losing their childhood to the horrors of physical and sexual abuse. Others spoke of unimaginable grief, bereavement, trauma and others of their struggles with eating disorders and distressing physical health problems, such as Infertility.

The stories they told informed and educated the viewer but, more importantly, they also celebrated the strength and courage of the survivors as they spoke bravely and honestly, giving hope and courage to those in similar situations who might be suffering in silence. Their stories were painful to hear but by telling them, they were reaching out to others who might have been through - or were going through - a similar experience.

Providing them with a platform also mattered to me and I will be forever grateful for their contribution because I know they did not only change lives but made a difference.

I received this message years later from a male survivor of sexual abuse who appeared on the show "The best thing was also sharing it with you on *'The JK Show.'*"

'There is no greater agony than bearing an untold story inside you.' **Maya Angelou**

The show received many grateful messages from participants both directly and indirectly such as, "If I hadn't gone on *'The JK Show'* I'd probably have been dead within a few months because of my weight. It was a lifeline." The gratitude of guests didn't always need to be spoken either. As was the case with a guest who's tears of joy and happiness spoke for themselves. Post show she had been abused and vilified by trolls on social media because of her misshapen front teeth which had been damaged in an accident when she was 6 years old. Once aware of the abuse I visited her at home to surprise her with an offer of free private dental work to correct her damaged teeth. Her now beautiful smile is smiling back at the trolls.

It also mattered to *'The JK Show'* Producers and their teams to provide a platform for many inspirational children coping with serious illness. As well as rewarding their extraordinary courage and bravery, it was a way of putting the spotlight on their parents, friends, families, and carers for their selfless acts in caring for others.

We took many children diagnosed with life-limiting or life-threatening medical conditions on holiday, and those times were truly memorable. The fun and laughter they experienced with their parents and siblings were immeasurable and it was always a joy watching them as they built amazing memories together that they could treasure forever. For many, it was the break and respite that they all needed.

Family reunions on the show were also memorable. Often it was a child, now an adult, seeking an absent parent or relative and only through diligent research by the Production Teams was this possible. They were able to reunite hundreds, if not thousands, of people over the years. Sometimes it was siblings separated during childhood and, occasionally, we even found further siblings that they were previously unaware of.

As I well knew, the reasons for someone's absence could be long and colourful and therefore every reunion was unique. In most cases, everyone was prepared to forgive and forge ahead with new relationships but despite that, careful planning had to go into every reunion prior to, during and after the show. All possible implications and expectations had to be considered and participants needed to be emotionally prepared and supported prior to being reunited. Family mediation was also always on offer because, occasionally, not everyone's hopes and expectations will be met.

During my time working on the show, I also met many Fathers who spoke about being airbrushed out of their children's lives. Some were callously excluded and denied access to their children and many were firmly of the belief they would never get to see their children again. In a few cases it was Mothers who found themselves in this position, but predominantly it was Fathers.

Their hurt, pain and suffering was real as they spoke of being marginalised and pushed out of their children's lives forever, but the love they felt for their children was also very real and palpable. They often spoke of having to defend themselves against a myriad of false allegations being made by an ex-partner, whose sole aim was to permanently exclude them from their child's life.

They spoke about the breakdown of their relationship and the process of their bitter separation. Some even spoke of losing everything, including their homes, and becoming dependent on family and friends to accommodate their 'sofa surfing.' All they asked of the show was to help them see their child. They hoped beyond hope that we could facilitate access for them because every effort on their part had been blocked and denied. Most of them felt that they'd been let down by the Justice System and Social Services, whom they believed should have been doing more to help them.

I was speaking to men at their lowest ebb who were becoming increasingly desperate, not least because they felt all hope of seeing their children had been lost. They felt helpless and often perceived their custody battle as being futile; many found little comfort in the idea that someday their child might come looking for them. Some absentee Fathers admitted they had not done enough to maintain contact or provide support for their children and many took ownership of this fact. They accepted it was entirely their fault, deeply regretted their actions and wished to make amends.

In the majority of cases, there seemed little or no reason to exclude a Father from their child's life but it was also abundantly clear that both parties had communication issues, especially following an acrimonious split.Dads were not the only ones suffering; Mums were too and as these situations escalated, the real victims of course were the children who often felt under real pressure to choose between their Mum and Dad. In the war between their feuding parents, there was a real danger that the children could be left emotionally harmed.

While on stage, it wouldn't be long before the underlying problems revealed themselves. Sometimes Mothers felt vulnerable and scared to provide access; some were still angry at their ex, whom they perceived as being wholly responsible for the breakdown of their relationship. Some had just moved on and were being influenced unduly by their new partner, family, and friends. A few of the Fathers were expecting far too much, too soon and were being unreasonable in their demands, once again being unduly influenced by new partners and family members. It was an emotional minefield sometimes and I could only imagine the pain the Father, Mother and children were all going through as they tried to resolve their issues, although many of them did.
Following the show, these couples were able to build bridges, resolve their dispute and reach a mutually acceptable compromise that would allow an excluded parent to regain access to their children.

However, there were also many times when parents were unwilling to meet with each other. When that was the outcome, we could really only provide much-needed support and guidance, but with a healthy portion of encouragement to take part in mediation.

We arranged countless of these sessions to resolve family conflict and, encouragingly, many attended and were able to focus on making the decisions that would be in the best interests of their children.

More difficult cases arose when paternity was disputed, whether by the Mother, Father, family, friends or even neighbours. In many instances, the paternity disputes were unfounded and were little more than malicious gossip but, in others, there was some evidence to support the claims. In all those cases, once the seed of doubt had been sown it didn't go away and the enormous emotional impact it had on people's lives was clear. DNA testing was never a simple process because, although it would establish paternity and provide a child with their biological origin, it could also have devastating and life-changing consequences both for those being tested and for their families.

Because of that, all guests had to be spoken to prior to the procedure and all the potential ramifications considered. They needed to think through their options carefully, proceed with caution and have a complete understanding of how the test results could affect them and their family before deciding to proceed. In most cases, however, they were selfless and the decision was to go ahead with the test because they wanted to end the doubt and ultimately believed it was in the best interest of the child.

Many expressed concerns about the damaging emotional impact paternal uncertainty might have on the child growing up. Others wanted the truth and to put an end to neighbourhood gossip. Sometimes they just wanted to save an existing relationship or even end a previous relationship more amicably. They all agreed, however, that the child was the innocent party.

Despite everyone being prepared for both the worst case and best case scenarios, revealing the results was always an emotional experience; whether a biological link was proved or not, there was always shock and surprise at the outcome. The real challenge was how they were going to move forward once the results were known. Despite being offered private individual and/or relationship counselling and mediation, many simply carried on with their lives surrounded by the love and support of their family. In certain cases though, it was necessary for us to refer some anxious new parents to parenting classes because some had never learned the skills necessary for bringing up children. How I wished for the perfect world where parents were - and are - prepared financially, emotionally, and physically for parenthood, but far too often that is not the case.

Guests also contacted the show for adult DNA tests in an effort to either confirm or disprove a belief, held for years, that they were biologically related to each other. Often they had hit a brick wall trying to prove or disprove their suspicions and didn't know where else to turn. If they were searching for a missing Father whose identity was unknown to them and their Mother, numerous tests had to be carried out and without any guarantees that we would find a match.

Many participants benefited from the Aftercare Service provided by the show. It had a positive impact on many people's lives, no matter how small. For some it was the kick-start that they needed to move their lives forward in a positive way. For others, it was just resolving a problem which alleviated stressors that had been holding them back. Some even learned that in order to move our lives forward, we also need to let go of something in the past.

On a personal level, I miss that feeling of knowing the work we did in Aftercare mattered - and it definitely did improve some people's quality of life. To those who ask the question "Why would some people contact a TV programme for help, support, guidance, practical support, counselling, and in some cases life-saving treatment services." Perhaps they might want to consider it's because of their actual lived experience when trying to access underfunded and over-burdened Health and Social Care services, or in some cases, services not fit for purpose.

Perhaps our parliamentarians might choose to do more and ease the burden on these difficult-to-access services. In addition they might also address some of the wider causes of poor physical and mental health. How about poverty and low income for starters, which intersect with other social determinants such as education, poor housing, unemployment, and poor community conditions.

Words do very little to address the wider issues that lock many into a downward spiral of ill health and despair, the effects of which can, and do, last a lifetime. What these people need are real solutions to real problems and not just spoken or typed words, debate and yet more platitudes.

On a personal note, helping others is inextricably linked to my whole self-esteem and I will be forever grateful that I was given the opportunity to provide whatever help I could. I devoted 14 years of my life to the Aftercare Service on *'The Jeremy Kyle Show'* and it was an absolute pleasure. I accepted decades ago who I was within myself and I'm happy being me and I won't be changing any time soon.

> '*You may be 38-years-old, as I happen to be. And one day, some great opportunity stands before you and calls you to stand up for some great principle, some great issue, some great cause. And you refuse to do it   because you are afraid …… You refuse to do it because you want to live longer…. You are afraid that you will lose your job, or you are afraid that you will be criticised or that you will lose your popularity, or you're afraid that somebody will stab you, or shoot you or bomb your house; so you refuse to take the stand. Well, you may go on and live until you are 90, but you're just as dead at 38 as you would be at 90. And the cessation of breathing in your life is but the belated announcement of an earlier death of the spirit.'*

> ## Martin Luther King Jnr

I've held this quote in my heart and mind since visiting MLK's birthplace at 501 Auburn Avenue, Atlanta, Georgia, USA more than 25 years ago. During my visit I experienced many emotions as I visited his birth home, neighbourhood and the national historical park. He was a great and wonderful man and sought equality and human rights for African Americans, the economically disadvantaged and all victims of injustice.

In 2022 I once again went on a MLK pilgrimage to discover more about this great leader, his life, legacy and teachings. This time to Montgomery, Alabama, USA to celebrate MLK day. I visited the Dexter Baptist Church, Legacy Museum and the National Memorial for Peace and

Justice. On this occasion I discovered a lesser known MLK quote but one I will truly remember.

"True compassion is more than flinging a coin to a beggar. It comes to see that an edifice which produces beggars needs restructuring". -

Martin Luther King Jnr

******

CHAPTER TWENTY SEVEN

'Secrets revealed after death'

Over the years, people often asked which stories I remembered most and what show content I preferred and it was always a difficult question to answer. On a personal level, reunions were always high on my list. Those shows always triggered emotional memories for me and caused me to reflect on my own reunion with my Mother, brother and meeting my two biological half-brothers for the first time. All of that had happened prior to me working on 'The JK Show' and I recalled how special it had been for me and how important those first meetings are.

I just wanted the reunions to go well and ensure that any unreasonable expectations were kept in check. Importantly, I didn't want participants to be seeking revenge or retribution, but to establish connections and opportunities to get answers to their numerous questions. I wanted them to be healing experiences. Some participants knew exactly why they wanted to find someone; usually to fill a void in their life which had been present for many years. Others couldn't quite put their finger on why - they just felt the need.

No matter the circumstances of the case, my words of warning were always the same: build the relationship slowly; establish boundaries and have a support network available; keep expectations in check and remember that while reunions should be a healing experience, they can also be very emotional and unpredictable.

On a personal level I was just curious and interested to meet my Biological Mother and learn about my maternal ancestry. I wanted to know about my life before she left me, her life and, of course, I needed answers to the hundreds of questions I had - and she was the only person who could give me those answers. But the real revelation was discovering that we looked like each other and I cannot tell you how much meaning that gave to me. I have never regretted setting out to find my Mother and I celebrate the fact that I didn't leave it until it was all too late.

Shows which featured absent parents would also trigger strong emotional memories for me. Some days, I would reflect upon my Mother's absence in my life during my childhood. Other days, I would reflect on the constant presence of my Father and how he provided my brother and I with a very safe and secure life. The idea of his love and kindness being absent from my life was unthinkable and on some days when the show content was about Dad's being denied access to their children, it hurt.

There were days when stories and show content resonated profoundly with my own life and I could feel my emotions being nudged along as the narratives unfolded. In the same vein, there were days when I needed to contain my emotions in order to stay objective. I definitely needed to stay open-minded once my Mother's life started to unfold for the second time and, even though I consider myself a functional adult and in control of my emotional wellbeing, that second phase proved to be very difficult.

"Oh, what a tangled web we weave, when first we practice to deceive." What cleverly constructed words Sir Walter Scott gave us, which encapsulate perfectly just how complicated life can become once people are not

359

authentic. My Mothers words, "I have told you everything and there are no more skeletons in my closet," came back to haunt me while I was working on the show.

It had been a long run of filming on *'The JK Show'* and I was looking forward to some much needed downtime over the Christmas break. Little did I know at that time that I was in for another surprise. I received my customary call from Warran on Christmas Day and the background noise suggested that his house was in full festive celebration mode. Our next conversation was scheduled to happen with my customary return 'phone call to him on New Year's Eve, but this particular year the routine was
disrupted when he rang me again on Boxing Day. However, he wasn't making much sense when he spoke and it was left to his wife, Jean, to explain his consternation. "A woman has been on the phone and she's claiming to be his Sister!" No wonder they had both been left in a state of shock.

After several minutes of nothing making sense to any of us, Warran, who had by now composed himself, came back on the line. He confirmed that a woman had indeed called him out of the blue claiming that she was his sibling. On the one hand, he suspected that it could be a prank call by one of his mates, but he also thought that what she was saying just might be true. Either way, he was very clear about one thing, I would have to sort it out.
Fortunately he'd obtained a 'phone number from the woman before ending his call with her. By the end of our conversation, I was of the opinion that it was indeed a prank call, albeit in poor taste, from one of his mates. I never gave it much thought for the remainder of Boxing Day, but the following day - and only because the woman's phone number was staring up at me from a piece of paper - I decided to call.

I genuinely never expected anyone to answer, but she did and the woman immediately confirmed the details she'd given to Warran and her claim that she was our sister. She explained that she had proof via a document she had in her possession. There followed several minutes of confused conversation between us until eventually I was able to establish that she was not alleging that my Dad was her Father but that my Mum, Dorothy, was her Birth Mother. I was both shocked and relieved at the same time as she clarified she was not my Father's child.

With my mind racing ten to the dozen and thoughts ricocheting everywhere, she read verbatim from a heavily redacted Social Services document relating to her adoption.

I slowly processed everything as she disclosed more and more details and concluded there was a distinct possibility it could be true. Even more surprising was the fact that she was living just a couple of miles away from my brother in Rochdale and she had been able to find him through a process of elimination using the local telephone directory. Our call ended amicably and with her agreeing not to contact anybody else, particularly my other brothers, until I'd had the opportunity to see her paperwork, which she agreed to forward on to me.

For the next couple of days, my mind was preoccupied with the situation but I was determined not to contact any of my other brothers until the document arrived. On the one hand, I was mindful that this information could easily derail the existing relationship between the five brothers, who were getting along fine, on the other, if what she was saying was true then she just might be our sister and as such, entitled to know about her Mother and her extended family. Days passed by and finally the paperwork arrived.

As soon as I opened the envelope, I could see immediately that, without a doubt, she most definitely was my Mother's daughter.

I called Warran and Geoff to give them the news that we had a sister, named Christine, and that Dorothy was indeed her Mother. They were shocked initially but accepted it as fact. Once again, Warran took this as being an opportunity to remind me about the can of worms I'd opened, but Geoff agreed to accompany me on my visit to meet her. That evening, I called her and arranged for us to meet up with her the following weekend. In the meantime, I was living in the hope that Geoff would be able to recall some early memories of his time with our Mother.

It was clear from the documentation that our sister had been born after my Mother's divorce from my Father, but before her second marriage. The burning question remained, however, who was her Father? The one thing I did know was that it certainly wasn't the man she'd left my Father for, because she was pregnant with Geoff at the time and that relationship ended before he was born. Unfortunately Geoff's memories of his time with our Mother, and before he went into care at the age of four, were at best vague and neither one of us was any the wiser to Dorothy giving birth to a Daughter.

We arrived at Christine's house in the late morning, gave her a huge hug when she answered the door, then all settled down in her living room with a cup of tea. She explained that she'd been adopted at the age of two but, prior to that, had been placed in Care and raised by a loving family. However, from an early age she had always known that she was adopted and had longed to meet her Birth Mother. Sadly, at that point, Geoff had to inform her that our Mother had died the previous year. The room fell silent for several minutes. She was tearful on hearing the news but seemed unsurprised and said she'd anticipated that it may possibly be the case. Moments later her own daughter arrived, and Christine gave her the news that her Grandmother was not alive. There was clear disappointment on both of their faces and, once again, the room fell silent.

I felt immense sadness at the whole situation and had no idea how we were going to move matters forward, or indeed how my sister was genuinely feeling. The best I could do at the time was to inform her that she was indeed Dorothy's daughter but she was also our sister and therefore part of our family. I reassured her that my brothers would welcome her into the family with open arms but first I would need to inform my two younger brothers about her existence. It would be as huge a shock to them as it had been for us because we were all of the opinion that my Mother had only given birth to five boys.

Christine understood the complexity of the situation and accepted that it had to be handled carefully. As best we could, we gave her a potted history of her Mother's life, including her two marriages and five sons, but the one thing we couldn't provide was any information about why she'd been adopted or who her Birth Father could be. That information, it transpired, would follow only weeks later. Meanwhile, Christine, was awaiting yet more paperwork from Social Services, which would enlighten us all further about our Mother, as well as Christine's heritage.
After several hours together and countless cups of tea later, we said our goodbyes, leaving her with contact numbers for her other three brothers.

It wasn't an easy call to make but, when my youngest brother answered the phone, all my careful rehearsing flew straight through the window. I just blurted out, "We've got a Sister!" followed by several minutes of trying, incoherently, to explain the situation. He was as shocked as I had been on hearing the news and equally as clueless about how and when our Mother had given birth to a daughter. However, he accepted it as fact, gave his permission for us to share his number with Christine and then assumed responsibility for informing his brother.

Over the next few days, our sister obtained contact with all five brothers and, slowly but surely, we all started to connect with her. She later met up with Aunt Hazel and Uncle Barry and within weeks she'd visited Dorothy's grave and was gently and successfully integrating into the family. Aunt Hazel was able to provide her, and us, with a more detailed account of our maternal ancestry but, once again, she was at best vague about our Mother's early years, having been adopted herself and not in contact with her blood siblings for many years.

A few further weeks later, Christine received more Social Services reports and, at that point, we were all a little more enlightened about the circumstances of her birth, her potential Father and our Mother's past, even though it was still sketchy. We'd all assumed there was just a short period of time between my Mother's divorce from my Father and her second marriage. In fact, it had been five years and, during that time, our Mother had caused a great amount of chaos for many. As we'd all heard at her funeral, she had deducted five years off her actual age and I'm guessing that's because it was a time of her life she would much rather have forgotten. It certainly wasn't done out of vanity, because my Dorothy was not a vain woman.

So what else had my Mother been up to that none of her children were aware of? I painstakingly started to search through her life history, focusing on those missing five years between the marriages to my Dad and my younger brother's Father. Using the library, reports from Social Services and spending time with my now fifth sibling, Aunts and Uncles and family and friends, I finally got the answers I was seeking. Patience is most definitely a virtue and I needed bucket loads of it while researching my Mother's activities during those missing five years. From my research, I would discover that Dorothy had three more children, all of whom had been adopted, a secret marriage and, sadly, that she and Geoff were also victims of the most horrific domestic violence.

******

CHAPTER TWENTY EIGHT

'The missing five years'

Slowly but surely my Mother's past started to reveal itself and it was clear that for five years, her life could only be described as chaotic. I learned that she lived for a brief period of time as a single mum raising Geoff, but it was only for a short time because, within a year, she'd secretly married and fallen pregnant. Nobody seemed to be aware of that fact, but it was true because I had read the official paperwork confirming it. Her second marriage, therefore, was not to the Father of my younger brothers, but to a man named Peter.

Certificates confirmed both the marriage and the birth of her daughter, which I assumed finally solved the mystery of the identity of Christine's Father. The problem was that there appeared to be a discrepancy within the paperwork. The newborn's name was Carol Ann, not Christine as expected. It would be easy to conclude that her name had been changed at a later date by her adoptive parents, but then the birth date presented another anomaly. Scrolling through all the paperwork, including documents from Social Services, the obvious answer was staring me right in the face: I had *another* sister.
I couldn't even begin to describe my feelings when I discovered that I had a second sister and sadness overwhelmed me when I learned that she had been placed in care and later adopted.

Once again, my Mother had felt unsettled in her secret marriage to Peter, just as she had been in her marriage to my Father and so when Carol Ann was only two months old, she decided to leave the marital home with my brother, Geoff.

For some time afterwards, her whereabouts became a mystery to everyone and for weeks she was nowhere to be found, that is until Social Services finally caught up with her. She and Geoff were found living with her new boyfriend, Colin, and when asked how she intended to care for her newborn daughter, Carol Ann, she refused point-blank to get involved and suggested that her husband, Peter, could do that. It was history repeating itself.

Sadly her husband, unlike my Father, was also unable to care for Carol Ann and so at the age of just three months she was placed into Care, where she remained for two years until being adopted at the age of two. She was the first of my siblings to be adopted and, as my research continued, I would learn a great deal more about Carol Ann's life. It was a painful read and one which left me drowning in an emotional whirlpool.

I would learn that Carol Ann was placed in a loving and supportive adopted family and had achieved all the important childhood milestones during her young life. Unfortunately, all that changed in adolescence when she became increasingly rebellious. She'd known from an early age that she had been adopted and grew up feeling angry because she wanted to know where she came from. When she was old enough, she started to search for her Birth Mother and, after years of fruitless searching, she contacted Social Services to see if they could help. They confirmed they could and were able to contact my Mother on Carol Ann's behalf.

Several attempts were made to facilitate a meeting between Mother and daughter but, sadly, this did not happen. Dorothy did, however, agree to provide a written statement confirming that, in her opinion, she'd made the right decision to have her daughter adopted.

Further research revealed that, tragically, at the tender age of 25, my sister, Carol Ann, died leaving behind her own baby daughter. Her passing was documented in the local press and to this day I wonder whether my Mother was ever made aware that her daughter had passed away.

The local papers reported it as 'A sudden death with no suspicious circumstances.' On the fateful night of her death, she, and her boyfriend — and Father of her baby — had gone out drinking before returning to a friend's house where they both fell asleep. When her boyfriend woke up the following morning, he found Carol Ann in a sleeping position by the side of a chair but, on closer inspection, he discovered that she was no longer breathing.

Woman (25) choked to death after drinking

The death of a 25-year old Rochdale woman was an example of the dangers of 'over consumption' of drink, a Rochdale Coroner said on Monday. "I trust this will be a lesson to other people." Recording a verdict of 'Accidental Death,' the Coroner said that by no stretch of the imagination could she have been described as sober. It is an example of the dangers of not lying in the correct recovery position to void the stomach contents safely.

I'd lost a sister I had never met, or even known, and yet she meant so much to me and I voiced my emotions loudly but privately. My only comfort was knowing she had been raised by her adoptive parents in a loving, stable home.

It would be weeks before I could continue what I had started, so the search for my Mother's missing five years went on hold. Finally, after about a month, I again reopened the 'can of worms' as I was still very curious about my Mother's new boyfriend and had insufficient evidence to prove who Christine's Father was.

It would appear that my Mother was blissfully happy with her new boyfriend, Colin, whom she described as being the real love of her life and, together, along with Geoff, they were living as a family unit. However, her happiness was very short-lived as their relationship soon faltered. Dorothy had been seduced by her new beau's charm and good looks, but within months of setting up home together he had become an abuser and perpetrator of domestic violence - and once again she had fallen pregnant.

On this occasion, it was very obvious why she was becoming unsettled in her new relationship. Colin was constantly meting out verbal and physical abuse to both her and Geoff, particularly when he came home drunk. Sadly, they both suffered at his hands and fists for almost a year before she finally took Geoff and fled back to her husband, Peter.

It appears he was agreeable to a reconciliation and forgave her adultery but made it very clear that he was not prepared to raise her boyfriend's then unborn child. Dorothy agreed to this condition, her relationship with Peter resumed and on Christmas Day that same year she gave birth to another boy. He was named Christopher and was immediately put up for adoption, the second of my siblings to be adopted.

One secret marriage, two adopted siblings - one of whom had died - and an abusive relationship. I was learning so much about my Mother's missing five years but still had no concrete evidence as to the identity of Christine's Father. I also had to face up to the painful and uncomfortable truth that my Mother's pattern of impulsive behaviour continued for a further several years.

Three months after Christopher's birth, her unsettledness within marriage returned once again and she left her forgiving husband, Peter, returning to live with the abusive Colin. I'm guessing at that point that he was charming my Mother into believing that he loved her, if not adored her, and was a changed man.
Clearly that wasn't the case because the physical abuse towards her and Geoff soon started all over again. It's something of an understatement to say that Colin was not a pleasant character and within three months of her being reunited with him, he was finally charged and found guilty of cruelty to my brother. Such was the level of his cruelty that he was imprisoned.

As a result, Geoff was officially removed from her care and placed into the care of Social Services on a 'Place of Safety Order.' At that point, it meant my Mother no longer had any of her five children in her care.

Dorothy was waiting with open arms for Colin when he left prison, and she also had some news for him. She was pregnant once again with his child. Their chaotic relationship continued and in January the following year, Christine was born. As I was already aware, this child would also be placed up for adoption - the third sibling to have been so. Christine's Father was now known, but the circumstances surrounding her adoption made for heavy reading.

A telephone call was received by the NSPCC (National Society for the Prevention of Cruelty to Children) from Colin informing them that my Mother had left Christine (then aged two months) at home and that he didn't think she would be returning. He was requesting, therefore, that the child be placed into Care. At midnight, the NSPCC officers arrived at their address to find Christine laid on the sofa dressed and wrapped in a shawl, looking clean, happy, and contented. Colin, however, was far from happy and started shouting at the officers, who had the distinct impression that he'd been drinking. He bore a strong grudge against the Attending Inspector because he was the officer who had been responsible for the prosecution which had led to his imprisonment for cruelty to Geoff.

When he was asked what had happened that evening, Colin would only say that there had been a row between him and Dorothy and that he didn't think she was ever coming back. Further information elicited by the NSPCC officers revealed that Colin was not working and at that time was on National Assistance. In addition, it transpired that Christine's birth had not been officially registered. Subsequently, it was agreed by all parties that, in the absence of her Mother, Christine would be taken into Care that night and that there were no grounds for pursuing a prosecution against Dorothy for abandoning her child. The NSPCC officer further commented that they were fully aware of both Colin and my Mother as they now had three of her children in their care; Geoff was on a 'Place of Safety' order, Carol Ann was awaiting adoption and now Christine, aged just two months old, was being taken into Care. Christopher was not in their care as his adoption had been immediate.

Once more I had to pause my research because it felt as if my emotional whirlpool had ceased revolving and was now dry. I felt drained and would spend days pondering the questions that, rather than decreasing, had instead accumulated throughout my fact-finding. I would eventually find answers to those questions and that's when I really boarded the emotional roller coaster. I would learn the finite details of the savage beatings my Mother had endured at the hands of Colin; how he terrorised, brutalised, and controlled her at a time when she had few, if any, family and friends around her. I suspect no child wants to read about their Mother being a victim of domestic violence.

The following is an abridged version of Dorothy's interview with Social Services, the day after my Sister, Christine, was taken into care:

My Mother arrived at the Social Services office to explain what had happened between her and Colin the previous day. She had some nasty looking bruises on her face around her left eye and also on the bridge of her nose. She then went on to show far worse bruises, with deep discolouration at the top of her chest where the neck joins the trunk — extensive bruises caused by what looked like punches. She told them that her boyfriend, Colin, had also broken her arm near the wrist by giving her a good kicking about a month earlier and that she'd gone to hospital to have her injuries treated. Her arm was subsequently put in a plaster cast which went beyond her elbow but, because she couldn't manage at home, washing nappies and feeding the baby and so forth, she had eventually removed it. Her arm was visibly still badly swollen and she was unable to lift anything with it. She then went on to say that she'd been kicked in specific parts of her body, including between her legs, and had recently been kicked in the groin by Colin while he was wearing his heavy work boots.

At that point, my Mother began to cry. She said that she'd suffered so much from Colin during the past four weeks or so that she just couldn't take any more and had to run away. She said that he hadn't worked for three weeks and that he'd spent most of his National Assistance money on drink. He would then come home, kick her about and brutalise her.

My Mother looked like a woman who was nearly all in and it was strongly suggested to her that, in her own interest, she should go to the Police Station, make a formal complaint, and leave it for the police to deal with. This she did but after some time. The female Police Sergeant who interviewed her said that Dorothy had run out of the Police Station mid-interview, which was taken to indicate that she was not proceeding any further with her complaint.

My Mother then returned to the Social Services office and said that she was afraid of what Colin would do to her and that was why she felt she couldn't go on. It was pointed out to her that as long as Colin continued to act the way he did, without let or hindrance, he would obviously believe that he could do what he liked with her and so it was in her interest to stick by her complaint to the Police. She couldn't, however, be persuaded to press charges. The Police concluded the interview by informing my Mother that they couldn't agree to keeping Christine separated from her and that, after she'd had a couple of days to recover from her present situation, she should go and see them in the Social Services office so that they could make plans accordingly.

Unfortunately, she didn't return but instead moved back in with Colin - and all within three days of his savage beating of her. No doubt he once again apologised, told her that it wouldn't happen again and how much he loved her.

Social Services paid another visit to my Mother and Colin at their home as they wanted to let them know that they were not prepared to keep Christine in Care indefinitely, not least because she had a Mother to look after her and a man who admitted he was her Father and who was living with her Mother. The interview rapidly spiralled downwards as Colin quickly worked himself up into a passion, blaming the Childcare Inspector for everything. He still harboured a deep resentment for his imprisonment for cruelty to my brother, Geoff. The meeting concluded that day with Colin saying that he didn't want Christine back in the house. My Mother agreed that it was for the best if Christine stayed in Care.

Several months later, at the Rochdale Adult Court, action was taken against Dorothy and Colin; in the first instance, for a 'Bastardy Order' against the latter. My Mother, however, brought the proceedings to a standstill at the commencement of the case by denying that Colin was Christine's Father. He would not, therefore, be responsible for making any maintenance payments to my Mother for Christine. Such was his control over her and her level of fear of him.

Partly in view of her attitude that day, the Magistrates then dealt with my Mother and told her that it was up to her to obtain Maintenance Orders against the Fathers concerned.

Later that day, Dorothy once again stood in the dock but this time at the Juvenile Court, regarding the abandonment of Geoff. It was well-reported in the local press:

You're a disgrace to motherhood, says JP

A Mother who refused at Rochdale Borough Juvenile Court today to take her four-year-old son back home was told by the chairman, Mr. H.W. Winstanley: "I consider you a disgrace to the name of Mother. I only wish we could do something about you but we can't."

The child had been brought before the court as in need of care and protection because an offence had been committed against him by the man with whom his Mother had been living. Mr. Keith Hudson said the man had been sent to prison for ill-treating the child, which was not his own son. The Mother said she could not take the boy back just now because the house she lived in belonged to the man she lived with. - Colin.

Indifferent

"You can't expect him to take the boy back when he has been convicted for something he has not done. I will take him back when I am ready."

When asked why she shouldn't get alternative accommodation, the Mother said: "Because I'm not doing." Said Mr. Winstanley: "We can't have that attitude adopted towards children — absolute indifference and throwing them on to the authorities to deal with." The child was placed in the care of the local authority.

Several weeks after her court appearance my Mother was once again brutalised to within an inch of her life, but this time, she finally found the courage to leave and never return and I was later to learn how her arm had been broken. Her abuser had placed it on a kerb and jumped on it whilst wearing his work boots.

I was also to learn that My Mother had been planning to escape her abuser for some time and prior to her court appearances and last savage beatings. Sadly, her escape plan had been delayed because she was unable find a safe place to stay. She eventually found safety and refuge with a Sister-in Law. I will be forever in debt to my Aunt Betty for this life saving act of kindness to my Mother.

******

CHAPTER TWENTY NINE

'Social Reports on Dorothy'

The details of my Mother's missing five years were now known to all of her children. However, there is always a story behind every person and reasons why they act the way they do - and so my research continued. I finally discovered another redacted document of an interview Dorothy had given to Social Services.

Social Services report on my Mother, Dorothy.

Dorothy is relatively small in height, of medium build and has auburn hair. Her face, which looks younger than her years, is pleasant and neither outstandingly attractive nor unattractive. She has hazel eyes which are more oval than round, broad full cheek bones, and a relatively round face. She is on the short side and has short squat fingers with well-bitten nails.

Dorothy told how her mother had died in childbirth when she herself was very young (age 9). Her Father, who later remarried, could not cope with her and her brothers. He placed her privately with friends who brought her up. Her brothers were placed separately in other families. She was reared by more than one such family, partly because she became very temperamental and to use her own words, bad and disturbed. "I had a chip on my shoulder about not having a Mother of my own." She felt unwanted. Whenever things didn't go the way she wished, whenever she felt jealous of things which the family she was living with did for their own children, she would have an outburst of temper.

She remembers that the tempers were very bad, that she sometimes screamed and even scratched herself and banged her head. Sometimes she would run away from the people she was living with, usually to her Father. He generally talked to her kindly, but always firmly and took her back to the people she had run from.

She felt she had no security and no real love and this was because her Mother died. At the age of 15, she left what had been home. Between then and the end of her teens, she had what she described as a horrible time - she would not like to go through any of it again. She hurried into her first chance to marry and subsequently had three children. This did not last long; she was unsettled and left home and she eventually married again - to Carol Ann's father Peter. There followed a brief period with another unsettled youth who was decidedly aggressive and whom she was scared to leave.

She talked as if her life only really began to be happy when she reached her 30s, when her temper died down and when she found her present stable husband. She only wished she hadn't had to go through all the suffering beforehand.

Additional Report

She (Dorothy) commented that she could never forget her adopted children and often lay awake at night wondering what they were like and how they were. Her biggest fear was that her two daughters might hold the same big chip on their shoulders about their Mother. She was sure at the time her

decision to let the children be adopted was the right one, even though it hurt her to do this. At that stage in her life she was so unhappy and disturbed that it would have been a terribly unsettled time for any child to be with her and she didn't know whether, or how long, it would be before she grew out of it. She hoped her daughters would understand this and would not go through the same as she had. She would not like anyone to go through the same unsettledness. She has wondered whether the children might ever try to find her and whether it would be a good thing to find each other. She knew, however, the importance of this not happening until the child is an adult and a settled one.
Nor would she like to undo the relationships the children had with the proper parents.

Her interview with Social Services provided me with a much needed insight into her childhood and, although once again it made for difficult reading, it was an important milestone in my research because it genuinely helped me make sense of some of her behaviours in those missing five years.

I struggled to imagine what it must have been like for her losing her own Mother when she was just nine years old. She was, after all, just a vulnerable young child and no doubt would have struggled to cope with a whole range of difficult emotions. It would have been a very challenging time for her, during which she would have needed a great deal of support and guidance from her family.
Unfortunately, that did not happen. Instead she grieved alone as, within the same year, she was separated from her Father and siblings. I just cannot imagine a more devastating scenario for a grieving child than to be separated from their family and support system at a time when they most need it. The very people she was

emotionally connected to, loved and was dependent on were no longer available to her. She would have to grieve alone and, additionally, experience the profound heart-rending pain of abandonment.

I can only but imagine her distress but, when I do, I picture her feeling unloved, sad, fearful, angry, and confused at being uprooted from her loving, safe, and secure environment at a time when she needed it most. She must have felt like the world had turned its back on her and any trust she had previously placed in loving relationships would have been damaged immeasurably. What went through her young impressionable mind during this time of painful abandonment only she will know but I suspect she would have been continually questioning why this was happening to her.

Although she was placed permanently with friends of her Father, in reality, they were strangers to her and the distress and anguish she was experiencing at being separated from her family must have been clear and obvious for all to see. She screamed, cried, self-harmed and railed against the injustice of her abandonment but sadly her pain was ignored and anger became her only way of coping. How loud did she have to scream in pain before someone actually noticed her distress? In the event, no matter the volume or pitch, it was all to no avail because all her acting out fell on deaf ears.

Understandably, her anger was loud and explosive, the 'bad and disturbed' period as she herself described it, and that label was reinforced each time she protested about her enforced abandonment.I sometimes wonder if she ever stopped screaming and, if she did, whether she believed she was deserving of being abandoned and unloved because of her difficult behaviour.

It pains me to think she was so deeply unhappy, powerless, and feeling punished, when in actuality she was an innocent blameless child craving the love, attention, and happiness she once knew when she lived at home with her parents and siblings. On the many occasions she ran away from her assigned carers, she headed straight to the person she hoped would rescue her, her Father. Sadly, he never did and no doubt she was kicking and screaming each time she was returned to her assigned carers.

She must have learned a great deal from these early childhood experiences and I can't help but think she may have believed something was wrong with her, that she was either unlovable or not worthy of love and commitment.

There is no logical explanation as to why she was separated from her Father and siblings during a time when she was grieving the loss of her Mother, other than her Father — my Grandfather — couldn't cope and wanted to move forward with his life.
Conversely, the impact of my Mothers' abandonment and her negative early childhood experiences would mean her adult life would be held back for many years.

From the age of 15 and throughout her early adult life, I sense Dorothy was constantly searching to fill the void of love and happiness which was absent during some of her childhood. There were times when her searching was fruitful and she found herself in loving relationships, had children and settled down. However, at the same time, she would also feel 'unsettled and unhappy,' with the result that she would then quickly end the relationship and abandon her children, leaving a trail of destruction in her wake.
I suspect that she never did fully invest in these early relationships, but then I have to consider that maybe she was also afraid of commitment. Perhaps, sadly, she just

didn't recognise happiness and healthy love anymore or even didn't feel worthy or deserving of love and happiness.

Whatever the reason, she engaged in some very unhealthy and reckless behaviours which, though I don't condone them, at the same time I do recognise that her early childhood and experiences of abandonment did not provide her with the right skills for coping with her adult life.
In her pursuit of love and happiness, Dorothy walked away from several healthy and loving relationships into the arms of a man she believed was the love of her life, but who in fact turned out to be a violent bully. I imagine that this was her rock bottom and a time when her self-worth was at its lowest point. When she finally found the courage to leave him - and believe me, it did take courage - she had to face the reality of being alone, with no permanent place to stay, no material possessions and encumbered with the baggage of her emotional and physical wounds of the past.

With all my heart I want to believe the day she left her abuser was the moment she finally realised she had the power to change her life for the better. It may also have been the time when she realised that healthy love was not supposed to be scary, painful, hurtful or make you feel unsafe.

She did eventually invest and settle in a relationship with the Father of my two youngest brothers and, from my observations, she felt both safe and secure within what was a very loving family unit. She was certainly happy and able to receive and give love and, without a doubt, she adored her boys. Although this brings me great comfort, I

don't think she did ever escape the pain, guilt, and shame of the missing five years, or forgive herself
for them. These painful wounds, though invisible to us, were something I believe she carried all her life and her only way of coping with the unresolved pain of the past was to remain silent and bury everything deep within herself. Even today, there are many men and women like Dorothy with unresolved emotional injuries and trauma from their childhood, and which, profoundly impact their adult lives.

All of my Mother's children were now accounted for, with the exception of our brother, Christopher, who'd been adopted immediately after his birth. Though we had to consider that perhaps he didn't want finding, Christine was as tenacious as I was in her quest for finding her family and recruited the services of an Adoption Agency specialising in tracing someone after adoption.

It didn't take long for Christopher to be found and informed by the Agency that someone called Christine had personal information to share with him. He discussed it with his wife, Barbara, and daughter, Lisa, and they all concluded that it was possibly something relating to his adoption. He was encouraged by them to attend a meeting at the Agency's offices in Manchester. Christopher, however, didn't fancy the journey into Manchester on a busy weekday and instead arranged for a home visit to take place. The meeting duly took place, during which Christopher was given the news that he was one of eight children.

Christopher had no reservations about meeting Christine and such was his eagerness to get together, he telephoned her the very next day and arranged to meet at her home address. Just as Geoff and I had done a year earlier, they sat together in her living room sharing their stories. Christopher had already worked out who I was because he'd asked the Agency representative about his siblings' names and occupations.

He was told that he had a brother, called Graham, who worked in TV and my niece, Lisa, picked up on that straight away. At 9.25 am the following morning, they all tuned into the '*The Jeremy Kyle Show*' and Lisa pointed me out and exclaimed, "It's him - he's your brother, I know it!"

Two days after their first face-to-face meeting,
Christopher and Christine met up again in Manchester and that's when she called me to say she'd found Christopher and put him on the phone to me. We were finally whole but, oh, what I would have given for my sister, Carol Ann, to have been at our first all siblings get together.

"She (Dorothy) has wondered whether the children might ever try to find her and whether it would be a good thing to find each other – *(extract from Social Services report)*

Well, we certainly did find each other, Mother, and it *was* a good thing - and they all attended my wedding!

****

A brief trip down memory lane.

Turner Brothers Asbestos Children's Xmas Party (No doubt my brother Warran (Right) had Dad's words ringing in his ears) - "Stick fast to his hand Warran and don't let him out of your sight!"

'Dressed to the Nines' for a wedding.
Me, Warran and sister Barbara

Double Trouble in
Blackpool

My Brother Warran (Right) and I

I was not aware of this photo of my Father until after his death. He never spoke about his time working on the Artic convoys which delivered essential supplies to the Soviet Union during World War 2. I only learned of it and his near death experience, (almost drowning in the below freezing temperature of the Barents sea) from his youngest brother John.

An organised community social event. Held either
before or after the pub closed. I suspect it might have been a
Dads and Lads football match or a Peggy game.

Left to Right -

Bill Benson (Landlord of the Black Dog), Mark Pilling, Harry
Hallsworth, Frank Dewhurst, Jimmy Waring, Billy Hines,
Harry Howarth, Jim Fetch, Keith Fetch,Ernie Stanier, Frank
Wynne, Ronnie Hines, Graham (Ear Flap hat), Linda Forden.

At no point could my Father be described as a Master Brewer. However, he made gallons of home brew, alcoholic and non alcoholic. Some good, some bad, and some that could only be described as being 'bottled explosives.' My Father is pictured far left.

My Mother, Dorothy Green, (far left),
and her workmates taking a break from the factory.

My Maternal Grandfather - Harry Green
(front row centre) and his 'Lads.'

Certificate and £25 awarded to employees of Turner Brothers
Asbestos after 25 years' service and the
celebration party in the canteen afterwards.

We surprised our Art Teacher, (Dorothy Smith), on her
wedding day. She was the best listener, always
approachable, empathic and patience was truly her virtue.

On the town with David Pearce (Sunshine - Right) at age 15. Adolescence was cut short once I started work and adult social behaviours kicked in very quickly.

Nursing school photo - three stripes on our sleeves - and wide belts for the girls. We had finished our 3 year training programme and the moment of truth had arrived. Our final hospital and state exams awaited.

Hendy and I settling into our home in Holland.

JK and myself at the orphanage in Mombassa, Kenya.

I've returned to Barbados many times over the last 40 years and I'm able to sit outside on the veranda chatting and reminiscing with Coleen (Hendy's sister) and Andy Man.

My Mother had wondered if her children would ever find each other - We did and we celebrated my wedding together.

Back Row Christine, Dean, Paul, Christopher
Front Row Warran, Graham, Geoff.

Wedding photo- - Mainly my 1st Cousins and their partners from my Fathers side of the family.

One of my greatest achievements

Printed in Great Britain
by Amazon